Y0-AFJ-666

Black Teachers in Urban Schools

Catherine Bodard Silver
foreword by
Sam D. Sieber

The Praeger Special Studies program—utilizing the most modern and efficient book production techniques and a selective worldwide distribution network—makes available to the academic, government, and business communities significant, timely research in U.S. and international economic, social, and political development.

Black Teachers in Urban Schools

The Case of Washington, D.C.

PRAEGER SPECIAL STUDIES IN U.S. ECONOMIC, SOCIAL, AND POLITICAL ISSUES

Praeger Publishers New York Washington London

Library of Congress Cataloging in Publication Data

Silver, Catherine Bodard.
Black teachers in urban schools.

(Praeger special studies in U. S. economic, social, and political issues)
Based on a 1967 questionnaire survey of Washington, D. C., elementary school teachers.
Bibliography: p.
1. Negro teachers—Washington, D. C.
2. Washington, D. C. —Public schools. I. Title.
LC2803. W3S54 371. 1'04 72-92467

PRAEGER PUBLISHERS
111 Fourth Avenue, New York, N.Y. 10003, U.S.A.
5, Cromwell Place, London SW7 2JL, England

Published in the United States of America in 1973
by Praeger Publishers, Inc.

Printed in the United States of America

ACKNOWLEDGMENTS

This research was made possible by a grant from the Urban Center of Columbia University, which provided for support and research costs during 1969-70. The data were drawn from a study of the Washington, D.C., school system, directed by Professor Herbert Passow of Teachers College; almost all of the analysis is based on questionnaire data from the Passow report's study of District public-school teachers, carried out by Drs. Anna Lee Hopson and David Wilder, then of the Bureau of Applied Social Research.

My attention was first drawn to these data and their potential interest by Dr. David Caplovitz, to whom I am indebted for much help in the initial phases of the research. I am also much indebted to Dr. Sam Sieber for his intensive and critical reading of drafts; and to Dr. Robert Dentler, of the Center for Urban Education, for fundamental and comprehensive guidance.

It is a pleasure also to acknowledge the timely help of Patricia Lander, colleague and friend extraordinary, of Charlotte Fischer whose typing and associated skills are so exceptional and of Allan Silver.

CONTENTS

APPENDIXES

LIST OF TABLES

Table		Page

Table		Page

Table		Page
7. 6	Satisfaction with Students' Work and Track	135
7. 7	Job Satisfaction, School SES, and Track Among Very Satisfied Teachers	136
7. 8	Teachers' Relations with Peers and School SES	137
7. 9	Teachers' Relations with Principal and School SES	138
7.10	Teachers' Autonomy and School SES	140
7.11	Job Satisfaction, Relations with Students, and School SES	141
7.12	Job Satisfaction, Perception That Students Liked School, and Track	142
7.13	Job Satisfaction, Satisfaction with School Work, and School SES	143
7.14	Job Satisfaction, Satisfaction with Students' Work, and Track	144
7.15	Job Satisfaction, Peer Relations, and School SES	147
7.16	Proportion of Washington-born Faculty and Peer Relations	148
7.17	Average Years Teaching in System	149
7.18	Job Satisfaction, Relations with Principals, and School SES	149
7.19	Job Satisfaction, Perceived Autonomy, and School SES	150
7.20	Job Satisfaction, Participation, and School SES	151
8. 1	Black Teachers' Perception That Standards Were Maintained for the Able	155
8. 2	Black Teachers' Perception That Curriculum Satisfied Deprived Children's Needs	156

Table		Page

FOREWORD
Sam D. Sieber

The substantive merits of the research reported in Dr. Bodard Silver's book will be recognized by the reader without the help of a preface. Her findings and interpretations concerning the powerful impact of teachers' subcultures in shaping their professional lives are of deep significance. Rather than dwelling on substantive points, I would like to draw a few lessons from her research that need to be implanted in our sociological imaginations.

The first lesson is how terribly dilatory sociologists have been in appreciating and intensively examining the internal social dynamics of schools. Willard Waller's observations on the "culture of the school" have been published for some 40 years, and yet the number of empirical studies focusing on teachers' subcultures in particular can probably be counted on the fingers of one hand. I recently shared with David Wilder the chore of compiling a book of readings in the sociology of education, and our efforts to find a single piece of outstanding research on the multiple functions of teachers' subcultures met with failure. (Dr. Bodard Silver's monograph was the only work on the subject that merited consideration, but its length prohibited inclusion in a book of readings.) The present study testifies conclusively, I believe, for the importance of turning our immediate attention to the conduct of sociological research on the cultural and social systems of discrete school settings.

To give one example: It is astounding to contemplate the possibility that peer relations might be of greater motivational significance to teachers than daily experiences with their own students. What other surprises await us behind the school walls? And Dr. Bodard Silver's discussion of "defensive subcultures," "collective generalizations," and the "dual society" of the school demonstrates the enormous potentialities of viewing schools as relatively self-contained societies.

Lesson number two is related to the first but bears more directly on methodology. There may well be some reluctance to accept Dr. Bodard Silver's findings as definitive inasmuch as they are based not only on survey research but also on "secondary analysis" of survey data collected as part of a broad evaluation of the Washington, D.C.,

---

Sam D. Sieber is on the Bureau of Applied Social Research, Columbia University.

school system by Professor Herbert Passow and his colleagues. Dr. Bodard Silver did not enter the picture until after the survey had been conducted. She was therefore faced with the not uncommon problem of having data in search of hypotheses rather than, as is classically recommended, hypotheses in search of data. In this sense, her conclusions are ex post facto. Precisely because she recognized the pitfalls of this type of analysis, she resorted to earlier research and theory on occupational subcultures to lend her study a comparative perspective and placed her analysis of survey data within the historical and contemporary context of the Washington, D.C., black community. Thus, her survey work was buttressed and tested by broad sociological theory, census data, historical writings, and earlier field observations of American schools. In short, she resorted to a multiple strategy to counter the weaknesses of secondary analysis. The value of this procedure is amply demonstrated in her study; and in view of the masses of survey data now accessible for secondary analysis, it would be a fine thing if one day our research methods courses presented this strategy in a formal way. Many examples for such a course could be drawn from this single volume.

A biographical footnote seems in order at this point. Before coming to Columbia University, Dr. Bodard Silver was trained in historical and theoretical sociology at the Sorbonne. This European training was perhaps largely responsible for her insistence on examining her survey data within the context of historical trends and general theory, a procedure not as common as it should be in survey research. This convergence of the two traditions of European and American social research is most fortunate for the sociology of education.

The third lesson is a logical extension of the preceding one. As invariably happens, survey data collection and analysis are so time consuming that follow-up field work for the purpose of verification is foregone. This was the case with Dr. Bodard Silver's study. Deadlines often do not permit us to pursue a research question to the limits of our scientific abilities within a single "project." Sometimes, we present our researches as finished products and, in the process, even manage to persuade ourselves that such is the case.

In the present instance, it would be a shame if the leads provided by Dr. Bodard Silver's analysis were not followed up by more intensive investigation. If the teacher subculture is as powerful a social mechanism as she suggests, then both social scientists and policy-makers will have to revise many assumptions about the functioning of American education. Interventions will have to be designed that harness this powerful force, and the narrow focus on teacher-student relationships, rampant in educational research, will have to be broadened to include the influence of peers. (Perhaps it is our assumption that schoolteachers are not professionals, in the sense that college teachers are, that has diverted our attention from the influence on schoolteachers of their colleagues. Many efforts have been made to examine the orientations of college faculties, but very few have sought to do the same for elementary and secondary teachers.) Nor is the task ahead of us simply a matter of improving peer relationships; for, as Dr. Bodard Silver suggests, greater cohesion may actually interfere with better teaching or greater commitment to students—a conclusion that is in full accord with research on industrial work groups where "productivity" is the desired outcome. Nor can a full comprehension of the scientific and policy-oriented implications of her study be achieved by debating its substantive and methodological merits, but rather by confirming, elaborating, and refining its interpretations through a series of investigations. And indeed there are so many ideas on the subject scattered throughout her book that an entire program of sequential studies could be planned on their basis alone.

The research reported in this volume will not soon go out of date; indeed, it will become increasingly timely as the cities become more ghettoized and as the pervasive inadequacies of public education become more evident. With the help of studies such as this, however, there may be time to develop strategies to counter both decay and mediocrity.

Black Teachers in Urban Schools

CHAPTER

1

INTRODUCTION

American Schools have been a center of controversy for at least 15 years. The discussion has had two foci: (1) the needs and problems of low-income groups, especially blacks, who have formed mounting proportions of the public school systems in non-southern cities and (2) the general adequacy of the schools to educate, apart from racial and class strains. This book deals with aspects of a special case in the crisis of urban education, in which blacks are central both as teachers and students; but it also attempts to consider aspects of the more general issues as well.

It reports research on the behavior and attitudes of black elementary-school teachers in Washington, D.C. That city's system is in some ways distinctive, owing to the special history and status of the District of Columbia and to distinctive attributes of its black population. But its rapid transformation since the mid-1950s into a system very largely black in student population and its many difficulties render it comparable in many ways to other urban school systems. At the same time, the book focuses on sources and character of teacher adaptation in such a setting—adaptations that are found widely in American schools. Studying black teachers in an urban school system who are dealing with a massively black student population, we have been able to focus on problems of teacher functioning that cannot be attributed to racial differences. In this introductory essay, it is suggested that the behavior of these teachers, although perhaps more accentuated because of the setting of the District of Columbia schools, also reflects more general characteristics of American schools that have implications for the schools' over-all performance.

It is striking that in spite of the difficulties that urban public schools have faced in providing adequate educational services and in spite of teachers' widespread complaints about students and school administration, four-fifths of the black elementary-school teachers in the Washington elementary schools reported being satisfied with their jobs, with their colleagues, and with their students. In studying attitudes among professional and service workers in inner-city areas of 15 American cities, Rossi et al. found that 82 percent of the teache reported themselves as satisfied with their jobs, 85.8 percent with their colleagues, and 79.8 percent with their students.[1] How can such a surprising observation be explained?

The research presented in this book suggests the existence of a defensive subculture among teachers that helps them to adapt to personally and professionally difficult situations in the schools. The creation and maintenance of this subculture is shown to have negative effects on students, while positively affecting teachers' level of job satisfaction. Thus, teachers' job satisfaction may be achieved at the expense of the students through adaptive mechanisms used by teachers in the classroom and in the school to insulate themselves from the students. Recent research done for the Fleischmann commission of New York State on 15 high schools, 5 of them in New York City, shows the existence of such mechanisms of insulation.[2] The report asserts that teachers are usually unaware of their students' feelings, that students do not enjoy relating to teachers, and that students feel their teachers are not understanding and helpful. Even more striking, teachers seem to be unaware of their students' negative attitudes and deny the existence of the students' feelings about them; their assessment of what students feel about them and about the school is grossly inaccurate.

This situation appears to be the result of structural rather than value considerations. In large measure, students and teachers, though of varying racial and ethnic backgrounds, showed considerable agreement on values. For example, both students and teachers espoused th importance of self-understanding and of working for change in current social institutions. We may expect value differences between students and teachers to be more pronounced in schools with large lower-class student populations and yet be reluctant to ascribe causal significance to this circumstance. Indeed, the Fleischmann commission report argues that the insulation of students and teachers from each other is a consequence of the large size, monolithic structure, and hierarchical organization of the schools.

The importance of structural factors in affecting teachers' perceptions of students and their level of occupational job satisfaction is further suggested by the fact that teachers' background characteristics and professional attributes—with the exception of age and length of time spent teaching—are weakly related to teachers' level of occupational job satisfaction. These findings have been reported by several researchers in very different school contexts.[3] In addition, in the present study, social class differences between teachers and students did not significantly affect teachers' level of occupational job satisfaction. Since background variables did not account for variations in the level of teachers' job satisfaction, we examined factors operating within the school. We found that the organizational structure of the school is in some measure responsible for the emergence of a defensive subculture among teachers.

Research on education has been characterized either by the analysis of the relationship of the educational system with other subsystems in the larger society or by the study of teacher-student interaction in the classroom. Very little research and only a minimum of literature deals with the school as a social organization. The school as a "people-changing" institution has been less studied than the mental hospital or correctional institution, despite the growing concern about the ability of schools to provide adequate educational services, especially among the poor. This is all the more striking since, unlike mental hospitals and correctional institutions every native-born American spends, in principle, 8 to 12 years as a "client" of primary and secondary educational institutions. Indeed, there is little systematic information about what actually happens in the schools.[4] In the past few years, a few case studies about schools have yielded some insights into the authority structure of the school, the use by teachers and principals of formal and informal mechanisms of control, and the role of peer relations among teachers. Concern over improving educational outcomes has led to an emphasis on teacher-student relationships in the classroom over structural and organizational analyses of the school as a unit, since structural characteristics of the school were thought not to have direct impact on the learning process. Rather, the structure of the school was seen as a "neutral" element in the educational process. The introduction into educational research of organizational considerations seems a shift in emphasis from the behavior of individual teachers to the school as a whole and an acknowledgment that studying the school as a total institution is important in understanding educational outcomes. In approaching these matters, this book focuses on the role of the teachers' occupational subculture as one consequence of organizational structure and as a force affecting educational outcomes.

We have already referred to some evidence for processes of insulation on the part of teachers. An evaluation of the More Effective Schools program in New York City gives further evidence of such processes and points to their structural basis.[5] Changes that were introduced into school by this program had a positive effect on the overall school climate, staff attitudes, and level of job satisfaction but no significant impact on the academic level of the pupils. Thus, changes seemed to affect the teachers independently from the students. The lack of a statistically significant relationship does not mean, however, that the structure of the school does not affect students. The insulation of teachers from students, encouraged by the structure of schools, means that teachers define situations by social processes occurring among themselves. Under such conditions, students' needs cannot be continuously and sensitively taken into account. The structure of the school is not only not neutral; it affects educational outcomes negatively. This book suggests that teachers' rather high level of occupational satisfaction may be achieved at the expense of students' needs.[6]

How can we explain that changes that improve school climate and, in turn, improve the level of teachers' occupational satisfaction do not appear to increase students' level of educational achievement? The answer, in part, lies in the structural characteristics of schools. Let us approach this question by briefly comparing aspects of school structure with the structures of some other organizations in which professionals deal with people.

In schools, interpersonal relations among teachers have little or no formal or informal function in coping with work-related problems central to the achievement of organized goals. In welfare agencies or hospitals, peer relations do have such functions. Among nurses in hospitals, the peer group is used to carry out instrumental tasks of importance. All nurses are located in groups in which activities are coordinated and responsibilities shared. Thus, peer relations are central to the performance of work activities, and the peer group is formally used by the organization.[7] In welfare agencies, it has been shown that interpersonal relations are important in helping individual workers cope with problems stemming from the work situation and are directly related to aspects of client-professional relationships. Although the peer group is not used formally by the organization, peer relations are instrumental in carrying out the goal of the organization, service to clients. Peer relations in such context are important, since they directly, if informally, work to cope with professional problems.[8] Under such conditions, peer relations can give rise to collective solutions among the staff to problems stemming from professional-client relations. In this case, as in that of nurses, there is a mutually facilitating interplay between organizational structure and interpersonal staff relations in carrying out the goals of the organization.

In industry, the human relations approach uses peer relations to change work attitudes and work satisfaction and at the same time to affect level of productivity and quality of the goods produced.[9] In the case of organizations dealing with people, changes in the level of staff morale have led to an increase in job satisfaction, which in turn has improved the quality of service to the clients. Peer relations were thus important as modes of adaptation, affecting levels of occupational satisfaction and service to the clients.

However, in the case of schools, changes in morale climate do not seem to affect educational outcomes. One observer commented:

> Happy relations among members of the staff do not necessarily make it possible for the organization to fulfill its goals. Thus in some "happy schools" where relations among the staff members are pleasant and where good human relations techniques are used, . . . the children still do not learn and educational goals of the institutions are not met.[10]

An analysis of the organizational setting of peer relations among schoolteachers may help account for the lack of positive relationship between occupational satisfaction and educational outcomes.

We must seek to understand the distinctive aspects of schools as social and professional structures. What little has been done in this area has built upon the classic analysis by Willard Waller, published 40 years ago.[11] Schools are characterized by structural looseness, low level of bureaucratization and bureaucratic control, low level of professionalization of staff, vulnerability to outside pressures, and the compulsory nature of the student population. All these features are important in describing the school as an organization; however, for present purposes, I will focus on two key and summary features—the isolation of the teacher and the duality of the school structure.

Teachers' isolation has several dimensions. First, it refers to the physical isolation of the teacher in the classroom; the teacher has to deal alone with a group of children. Second it refers to teachers' isolation in the classroom from the control of peers and the principal. Third, it enhances insulation from outside influences and from pressures for change.[12]

Several authors have studied teachers' isolation from the authority structure of the school and from professional communities both inside and outside the school. Dan Lortie has analyzed the consequences for school functioning of the low level of bureaucratic control and discusses the prevalence of informal controls in their place.[13] Other studies have shown that principals exercise little direction over teachers; or, rather, control over young teachers may be quite strict, while older teachers are quite independent. This can be considered a kind of "trade-off" between the principal and the older teachers.[14] Isolation from bureaucratic authority and control would be a sign of teachers' strength if there were strong professional communities of teachers both inside and outside the school.

Teachers are also professionally isolated from their peers in the sense that there is little possibility of professional control and evaluation of them by fellow teachers. This aspect of isolation limits the opportunity to communicate on professional matters, to learn from one's own mistakes or from others' experiences, and to promote professional growth and evolve professional solutions to recurrent problems. Thus, teachers have peers—but not colleagues.

Teachers' isolation in the classroom does not mean that they enjoy professional autonomy, though they may like to think so. Autonomy from bureaucratic control, state control, or public pressures neither prevents nor guarantees professional control. Professional autonomy only makes sense in a context in which professional behavior can be promoted, encouraged, and evaluated. But, in reality, teachers' isolation in the classroom means that there is little possibility for professional evaluation and for change based on the accumulation of shared experiences among the staff. The situation has been well characterized by Morris Janowitz:

> . . . in its current organization teaching is a solo practice profession, in contrast to many other professions which emphasize group practice or at least close colleague relations. In the typical slum school, teachers do not have close personal and social contacts with their colleagues. Direct supervision and the opportunity for staff conferences is limited. The result is not overprofessionalization in the actual performance of the job, but rather professional isolation and excessive vulnerability to the impact of the social and administrative environment of the slum school.[15]

Furthermore, teachers are not professionally accountable for the quality or nature of educational outcomes—if only because the school is unable sufficiently to control the "intake" and "production" of students. In this sense, the school may be more appropriately described as a "people-processing" rather than a "people-changing" institution. The school faces a stubborn dilemma; its official goal is to change people, but it has little control over the quality of the "product." Dealing with a large number of "clients" and confronted continually by new cohorts of "clients," it has no alternative but to make room for them by processing older cohorts.

The isolation of the teacher in the classroom has implications for understanding the nature of teachers' occupational satisfaction.

Teachers describe interaction with the students in the classroom as a source of job satisfaction. However, because the isolation of the teacher undermines the professionalism of teaching, occupational satisfaction secured from interaction with the students may reflect teachers' own definition of the classroom situation independently from students' needs. This book shows that teachers' perceptions about students' liking school and students' quality of work was weakly related to students' background characteristics and level of achievement. It laso shows that teachers' satisfaction in the classroom is more a function of students' conformity to teachers' own definition of the situation than a reflection of teachers' perceptions about students' achievements.[16]

Similar findings were reported in the Fleischmann commission study of New York State high schools. Teachers' job satisfaction seems to reflect their own definitions of the situation independent from the realities of the classroom and their perception that students conform to such definitions. The same mechanism has been described by various authors. For example, Marian Wasserman comments that teachers do not perceive that the children they teach are watchful and suspicious.[17] Gertrude McPherson, in a study of a middle-class school, describes the social mechanism through which teachers' job satisfaction reflects their conviction that students conform to their own expectations.[18] No wonder that teachers report classroom teaching as the most important, intrinsically rewarding part of their work. Such rewards, however, do not seem to reflect professional considerations. The isolation of the teacher in the classroom may mean that teaching as a source of job satisfaction is based on rewards that have little to do with students' achievements and needs.

In a recent study conducted at the Stanford University School of Education, John Meyer and Elizabeth Cohen compared two types of school structures.[19] One was the traditional structure in which teaching is a solo practice and where the teacher is isolated in the classroom. The other was the open school system, in which the teacher works as part of a group and the children move freely in a large room where several teachers are located. The study shows that, in the second type, there were marked increases in the levels of interaction among teachers and in the level of their occupational satisfaction. They valued the continual feedback and stimulation from other teachers. The need for cooperation, coordination, and planning that emerges from such a structure leads to the collective evaluation of teachers' behavior and thus was not resented by individual teachers. Furthermore, in the open school structure as compared with the traditional, teachers' sense of professional autonomy is increased, and they are more likely to view their colleague group as having influence in the school; they are also more likely to be satisfied with their jobs and to be committed to teaching as a profession. The differences we have described between the traditional school and the open school suggests that teachers' isolation has far-reaching consequences for teachers' relationship with the authority structure of the school and for teachers' level of autonomy and professional commitment.

Although the study did not focus on the effects of open classroom on students' level of achievement, the report indicates that students' needs and wants are more likely to be taken into consideration. Other studies on team teaching have also reported that teachers become more responsive to students and tend to behave less routinely and more responsively.[20] The isolation of the teacher in the classroom, by minimizing work-related interaction among teachers and not allowing shared work experiences, creates a situation in which teachers' job satisfaction may be personal and emotional but not thereby professionally based.

The second key aspect of school structure, for our purposes, is duality. This refers to the sharply distinguished, separate worlds of students and teachers, to the existence of two distinct and separate social systems with different sets of norms, codes of behavior, and values. For Willard Waller, these two systems are intrinsically incompatible, grounded in structured antagonism.[21] Duality of the school structure fundamentally affects the nature and function of peer relations among both teachers and students. Both students and teachers tend to see each other as members of groups, rather than as individuals cooperating together. This has been reported by the Fleischmann commission study and applies to schools of all sorts, not only those in "slum" settings.[22]

Teachers as a group are in a position of dominance and authority over the students as a group. Since the "definition of the situation,"* to use Waller's words, reflects teachers' ideas to the exclusion of those of the students, one consequence will be the necessity to impose such definition on the students. A large part of the teachers' task is to implement such collective definitions. How do teachers' peer relations function in this setting? Waller insightfully remarked that teachers' interaction takes the form of competition in the enforcement of the existing social order. It takes the form of acts visible to their peers—"on-stage behavior"—the meaning of which is shared by the peer groups. "On-stage behavior" is thus very important in enlisting other teachers' support and approval and in

---

*The "definition of the situation" is the collective product of the interaction of several overlapping generations, defining behavior that is acceptable under given conditions.

strengthening the teachers' collective position vis-à-vis the students. Thus duality as an organizational setting contributes to a form of peer-group behavior among teachers in which behavior is produced and evaluated primarily with respect to issues of power and authority, not professional considerations.

The teachers' position of dominance in the school is in turn enhanced by their collective support of the school's organizational structure and administrative order; peer relations play an important role in this process, since schools often use teacher peer groups to implement administrative decisions: Teachers' meetings and discussions often revolve around administrative or extracurricular matters, not professional ones. A good example of the way peer relations implement an administrative order is the use of discipline in the school. Teachers' interaction on professional matters being quite limited, emphasis on discipline is a way not only of enhancing teachers' authority but also of reinforcing and continually asserting teachers' position vis-à-vis the students.

In open classrooms, the duality of school structure is minimized, since the prevailing definition of the situation is no longer that of teachers alone but results from the combination of both students' and teachers' interests. In this situation, teachers are no longer preoccupied with maintaining a preexisting order but are concerned with the continuous solution of professional problems.

The duality of the school structure has a further impact on the role of peer relations in school. All teachers are faced with similar problems revolving around the inability to carry out one's professional role. All teachers are under similar pressures from students; they all experience some threats to their professional status. Drawing upon Albert Cohen's analysis of the conditions under which a subculture emerges and is maintained—continuous interaction and the existence of status threat—we can easily see that such conditions exist in school.[23] However, what needs to be explained is the subculture's defensive nature.

A subculture among semiprofessionals or professionals may help define professional norms of behavior or may help define what the subculture considers to be professionally acceptable. For example, among policemen there is a strong subculture that helps them to cope with their relationships with clients by defining codes of police behavior. It has been observed that police working in lower-class and poor neighborhoods tend to behave less professionally than in middle-class neighborhoods and that the occupational subculture will tolerate deviations from professional behavior in order to maintain subcultural standards. In other words, nonprofessional behavior may be accepted as necessary for the achievement of professional goals.

This comparison helps us understand the nature of teachers' subculture. Teachers in all schools are widely concerned about defending or protecting their professional status. Furthermore, teachers may find it very difficult to achieve their professional role in the classroom. However, teachers as a group have to define their situation so that they will collectively perceive their role as successful. This has been described by E. Levy in a participant observation of a ghetto school:

> Everyone is reminding everyone else that we are doing the same thing. The suspension of moral judgment and the swapped stories enable the teachers to consider their experience in the school as a collective reality where responsibility for what happens is not personalized or individualized but attributed to the nature of the school itself.[24]

Because teachers are isolated, it is difficult for them to assess professionally their work. In such a situation, peer relations create collective meanings and standards to interpret teachers' behavior. The duality of the school structure, combined with the solo aspect of teaching practice, means that peer relations in schools are relatively unconstricted in defining the situation. Since peer relations among teachers are not anchored in professional considerations, professional roles and status can be valued independently of educational outcomes.

Many teachers have said, when confronted with students' low level of learnings, "If students do not learn, it is not our fault." In this research it is possible to show that teachers collectively redefine and rationalize the situation so that professional failure can no longer be perceived as such.[25] Their perception of students' needs is less a reflection of the students' characteristics than of their own interpersonally grounded definition of the situation. This mechanism is a way by which teachers insulate themselves from the students' needs.

Even though the conditions that give rise to a defensive subculture in the school are mostly structural—a result of the isolation and duality of the school structure—there are differences in the degree to which the subculture works to insulate teachers from the students. In this research I was able to compare schools with students from different levels of socioeconomic status (SES). The lower the school SES, the more often teachers reported difficulties in their teaching and the less likely they were to be satisfied with their peer relations. However, the striking fact is that even though peer relations were less satisfying in low SES schools, they played a more important role in the creation of a defensive subculture. The lower the school SES, the more likely was discipline to be a salient aspect of teachers' subculture and the more likely was satisfaction with peer relations to influence teachers' definition of the situation. The lower the school SES, the more likely were satisfactory peer relations to influence teachers' perceptions of the quality of educational outcomes and to influence positively teachers' decisions to continue teaching, even in "ghetto" schools. Thus, it is in the lowest SES schools—where students' needs are most pressing and the professional strains on teachers the greatest—that teachers' peer relations, even though less gratifying than elsewhere, operate most strongly to sustain a defensive subculture: insulating teachers, defining the situation in terms of teachers' perceptions, and serving as sources of teacher satisfaction independently of educational outcomes.

Since teachers' peer relations in schools are not in general professionally grounded, they may become a source of gratification in themselves—operating to optimize consummatory rather than professional goals. Indeed, the world of adults in the dual school structure is a crucially important source of gratification for teachers. Teachers cannot fulfill their emotional, and psychic, not to speak of intellectual, needs, by dealing continuously with groups of children or adolescents on a solo basis without the support of adult colleagues. Here, both duality and isolation, as aspects of a school organization, heighten the rewarding significance of what Waller called "the society of teachers." However, as I have observed, teachers' peer relations are not, in fact, those of colleagues—not professionally structured. They are thus freer to serve not only adjustive functions but also consummatory ones; owing to the strains of teaching, both outcomes contribute to a "defensive" occupational culture.

These speculations may help to explain why teachers report such high levels of occupational satisfaction even under professionally stressful circumstances. That peer relations are indeed an important component of teachers' level of occupational job satisfaction is shown in this book. But the duality of the school structure and the solo practice of teaching are reflected in the nature and sources of occupational job satisfaction.

Teachers have two main sources of job satisfaction, one rooted in the day-to-day interaction with the students and one in the interaction with peers and other adults in the school. However, peer relations are more important as a source of satisfaction; and, moreover, each source of satisfaction contributes independently to an aggregate measure of job satisfaction. No wonder that changes in the occupational climate may affect the level of job satisfaction independently of educational outcomes. Sources of job satisfaction not grounded in professional matters may be more important than educational outcomes for teachers. Thus, the structure of the school seems to contribute heavily to the creation in schools of a defensive subculture among teachers. If this is so, then all schools with a traditional structure, not only "ghetto" or "inner-city" schools, will generate a defensive subculture among teachers at a significant level. This conclusion seems to be supported by the results of a study of a middle-class integrated school.[26] Also, in schools where the traditional school structure has been broken down, it is possible to see the existence of a subculture of a different nature. Indeed, in the open school, teachers' work-related interaction has allowed for the emergence of a professional community.[27]

As Morris Janowitz has suggested, segmental and partial changes in school structure cannot alone bring meaningful changes in educational outcomes. It is necessary to introduce changes in the authority structures of the school and in the structure of rewards. Then it might be possible for teachers to generate peer relations that are linked to professional goals and positively affect educational outcomes, rather than create mechanisms of insulation from the students. Only if peer relations play a professional role in the daily work process can a link be created between occupational job satisfaction and educational outcomes.

In the traditional school, there are few possibilities of creating a professional community among teachers. On the contrary, its structure creates what I have analyzed in this book as a defensive subculture among teachers. That schools are characterized, in Charles Bidwell's terms, by a large and undifferentiated teaching cadre might, as he argues, be seen as a resource for the creation of professional work communities among teachers.[29] However, structural changes of the sort analyzed in this research will need to be made if this potential is to be fulfilled.

Research in education has given considerable attention to problems of racial and social segregation between schools but has not sufficiently studied another and pervasive form of segregation within the schools themselves—that between teachers and students. That these issues emerge so clearly in this case study of black teachers in the highly segregated Washington, D.C., school system suggests how pervasive is this issue for the entire range of American public schools.

NOTES

1. Peter Rossi et al., "Between White and Black: the Faces of American Institutions in the Ghetto," Supplemental Studies for the National Advisory Commission on Civil Disorders (Washington, D.C.: Government Printing Office, 1968), p. 134.

2. Alan E. Guskin, High Schools in Crisis (Ann Arbor, Mich.: Community Resources, 1971).

3. John Meyer and Elizabeth Cohen, The Impact of the Open-Space School upon Teacher Influence and Autonomy: The Effects of an Organization Innovation (Stanford, Cal.: Stanford University, Center for Research and Development in Teaching, November 1970); James Fennessey, The Faculty Peers (Baltimore: The Center for Study of Social Organization of Schools, The Johns Hopkins University, November 1968); J. D. Mann, "Dimensions of Teachers in Schools" (unpublished Ph.D. dissertation in social psychology, University of Michigan, 1970).

4. Seymour Sarason, The Culture of the School and the Problem of Change (Boston: Allyn & Bacon, 1971), p. 166.

5. David J. Fox, Expansion of the More Effective School Program: Evaluation of New York City Title I Educational Projects, 1966-67 (New York: The Center for Urban Education, 1967).

6. Our results support an observation by Gerald Levy, in Ghetto School: Class Warfare in an Elementary School (New York: Pegasus, 1970), p. 68: "The question, 'Are you satisfied with your job?' may mean for the teachers successful adaptation, irrespective of educational achievement from the students."

7. Charles Perrow, "Hospitals: Technology, Structure and Goals," in James March and A. Simon, eds., Handbook of Organizations (Chicago: Rand McNally, 1965), pp. 910-66.

8. Peter Blau, "Orientation Toward Clients in a Public Welfare Agency," Administrative Science Quarterly, 1960, pp. 341-61.

9. F. S. Roethlisberger and William J. Dickson, Management and the Worker (Cambridge: Harvard University Press, 1939).

10. Estelle Fuchs, Teachers Talk: Views from Inside City Schools (New York: Anchor Books, 1969), p. 85.

11. Willard Waller, The Sociology of Teaching (New York: Wiley, 1932).

12. Meyer and Cohen, Impact of Open-Space School.

13. Dan C. Lortie, "The Balance of Control and Autonomy in Elementary School Teaching," in Amitai Etzioni, ed., The Semi-Professions and Their Organization (New York: The Free Press, 1969), pp. 1-53.

14. Robert Dreeben, The Nature of Teaching (New York: William R. Scott, 1970), pp. 51-54.

15. Morris Janowitz, Institution Building in Urban Education (New York: The Russell Sage Foundation, 1969), p. 30.

16. See Chapter 7, below.

17. Marian Wasserman, The School Fix (New York: Outerbridge and Dienstfrey, 1970), p. 29.

18. Gertrude McPherson, Small Town Teacher (New York: Cambridge University Press, 1972).

19. Meyer and Cohen, Impact of Open-Space School.

20. They are reviewed in Mary Jo Bone, "Five Books on Open Education," Harvard Educational Review, Vol. 42, 1972, pp. 173-81.

21. Waller, Sociology of Teaching.

22. Guskin, High Schools in Crisis.

23. Albert J. Cohen, Delinquent Boys: The Culture of the Gang (Glencoe, Ill.: The Free Press, 1956).

24. Levy, Ghetto School.

25. See Chapter 8, below.

26. McPherson, Small Town Teacher.

27. Meyer and Cohen, Impact of Open-Space School.

28. Janowitz, Institution Building in Urban Education, p. 6. Changes necessary in the Washington, D.C., schools are elaborated in Kenneth Clark, A Possible Reality (New York: Emerson Hall, 1972).

29. This is the view of Charles Bidwell, in "The School as a Formal Organization," in March and Simon, eds., Handbook of Organizations, pp. 1003-9. Bidwell writes,

> The formally undifferentiated character of the teaching cadre increases the likelihood of the development of the school faculty as a more or less cohesive, well-integrated colleague's group. If this occurs, the social controls of a small professional community within the school and the strength of professional norms may increase the probability of responsible and similar performances by the teacher.

CHAPTER

2

HISTORICAL OVERVIEW AND DESCRIPTION OF THE CURRENT SYSTEM

This chapter is intended to provide a historical background for the study of black teachers in a ghetto school system. The encounter between black middle-class teachers and black lower-class students, the sources of job satisfaction under ghetto conditions, and the individual and collective modes of adaptation of teachers to problems of functioning can be best understood in the light of forces that have influenced the Washington, D.C., system and its teachers in the past.

The historical analysis to be presented here is neither exhaustive nor thorough. There has been no effort to analyze all the forces that have affected the school system. The intention is simply to suggest some themes that are, in our opinion, important to an understanding of the present educational crisis and of the values and attitudes of black teachers in Washington, D.C. Among such themes are the relations among various groups within the black community, the attitudes of these groups toward education and the dual school system, the role of the black middle class in promoting a specifically black institution, disagreement over educational philosophy (classical versus professional education), and the role of a black institution in the black community. At a time when problems of community control and black power are entering the educational arena, the Washington school system provides an opportunity to study an all-black school system dealing with a primarily lower-class clientele, a system that has been for a long time an important black institution controlled and administered by blacks.

Our historical sketch reveals some of the continuities in the problems, as well as in the values, of black teachers, who are generally representative of the black middle class, in an urban setting.

It has two parts, a chronological account of the themes mentioned (such a presentation seems most appropriate in view of the complex interrelations among the various themes) and a description of the Washington, D.C., elementary school system as it is today. In the latter part we also introduce the measures applied to the schools in later analysis.

A HISTORICAL OVERVIEW

In 1960 Washington, D.C., became the first major city in the United States to have a black majority in its population, the unsurprising result of converging social, economic, demographic, and political forces over 160 years.

Shortly after the site for the nation's capital was chosen in 1791, the Negro population of the new city began to grow rapidly. The town quickly became one of the nation's main centers of the slave trade, and it also served as a temporary stopover for slaves in transit. The extraordinary manpower demands created by the construction of capital buildings brought slaves and free blacks from Virginia, Maryland, and as far away as Philadelphia. In addition, Washington's growing white population employed large numbers of slaves as house servants. The mulatto offspring of liaisons between masters and house slaves were often freed and educated, and these mulattoes swelled the free black population of the city. As a result, before the Civil War, Washington, D.C., had the largest population of free black men in the nation.

Starting in 1862, with the declaration of emancipation in the District of Columbia, large numbers of blacks began to migrate to Washington from the southern states; in 1870, one-third of the population in the capital was black.

The increase in the black population continued even after the Civil War. Although southern Negroes continued to come, the major source of the increase before World War I was the high birth rate of Washington's native black population.

Although both white and black populations have increased in the District since 1880, the growth rate for blacks has been much higher than that for whites. Table 2.1 includes figures for the entire District of Columbia (Washington, Georgetown, and Washington County), but it does not show the gradual steady decrease of the white population in Washington proper and the corresponding increase of whites in the wealthy suburb of Georgetown. In 1880, for example, more than half the white population of the District had been born in Washington itself. But by 1960 only a quarter of the white population had been born there. The exodus of the white middle class to the suburbs has been continuous in Washington since 1880.[1] (See Table 2.2.)

TABLE 2.1

Population in District of Columbia, 1800-70

	1800	1810	1820	1830	1840	1850	1860	1870
Total	3,210	8,208	13,117	18,826	23,364	40,001	61,122	109,199
Whites	2,464	5,904	9,376	13,367	16,843	29,730	50,139	73,731
Blacks								
free men	123	867	1,796	3,129	4,808	8,158	9,209	35,392
blacks							5,831	
mulattoes							3,378	
slaves	623	1,437	1,945	2,330	1,173	2,113	1,774	

Source: Constance McLaughlin Green, The Secret City: A History of Race Relations in the Nation's Capital (Princeton, N.J.: Princeton University Press, 1967), p. 63.

Washington's black middle class has similarly fled the slums and in the last decade has established itself in two newly developed suburbs of the city. As a result, Washington can be easily partitioned on the basis of race and income. In 1960 the inner city was 90 percent black and characterized by poor social and economic conditions. The north and southeast sections were the strongholds of the black middle class, and in the center of the city a small enclave of poor whites endured. Whites with higher socioeconomic status (SES) occupied the northwest section of the city.[2]

The ghetto slums of Washington, D.C., are among the poorest in the country. In 1965 Green reported Negro families who were striving to live on budgets of 40 cents per person per day for food, clothing, medicine, entertainment, and sales tax. In an area near the Capitol 41 percent of the families earned less than $3,000 a year, and 9 percent earned less than $1,000 a year.[3]

Washington, like many large American cities, has been undergoing rapid change through urban renewal, new construction, expansion of suburbs, and demolition of old neighborhoods. The capital must be distinguished from other cities, however, because of the unique influences to which it has been subject. For example, the great social and industrial changes that surged through the rest of the nation in the mid-1800s had only a slight effect on Washington. During the nineteenth century the United States received successive waves of immigrants, and its social history was marked by violent conflicts between capital and labor, concentration of industrial wealth, the growth of cities in a predominantly rural nation, and emergence of the nation as a world power. But few immigrants came to Washington, and, as the city has never been the site of great industrial activity, it escaped labor battles. Washington was very much subject to political influences from the southern states, which had great power in Congress and thus controlled the law and the educational system.[4]

The city possessed a large, stratified, and stable black community. Before the Civil War, except for the upper-class Negro, for whom there was the possibility, however small, of securing a salaried government job, the free black men were generally employed as carpenters, bricklayers, hairdressers, cooks, and the like. The survival and importance of the black mulatto aristocracy were based on their ability to control and assimilate the influx of blacks from the South. Both free blacks and slaves from the South were quickly put into contact with organizations like churches and charitable agencies from which they could obtain some education and skills. Before the Civil War and the emancipation of the slaves, the black community of Washington had thus organized itself to educate and train its own members. Education was the most important goal after freedom. As early as 1807 three blacks and a white Englishman

TABLE 2.2

Population in District of Columbia, 1880-1960

	White	Black
1880	118,006	59,596
1890	143,695	75,572
1900	191,532	86,702
1910	236,860	94,446
1920	326,860	102,966
1930	352,914	132,068
1940	474,326	187,066
1950	517,865	280,803
1960	345,103	411,737

Source: Constance McLaughlin Green, The Secret City: A History of Race Relations in the Nation's Capitol (Princeton, N.J.: Princeton University Press, 1967), p. 200.

established schools for black children. The desire to control entry into the black community of Washington led to the creation of the Columbia Institute by John Prout; later, in 1934, it was renamed the Union Seminary. Blacks also began to organize their own churches around 1814. The role of missionaries and churches in organizing schools and adult education classes should not be underestimated. Indeed, the role of southern black Christian churches in the diffusion of values like industry and thrift is very important to an understanding of the prevalent severity and puritanism in black schools.[5]

In 1857 the U.S. Supreme Court decided, in the Dred Scott case, that persons of African descent were not and could never be American citizens. Nevertheless, the drive for black education continued. At that time more than 50 percent of the free Negro population was literate and 1,000 black children were attending private schools, many with whites. Miss Myrtilla Miner, a white woman from New York State, opened a "high school for colored girls" in 1851. The quality of education there was apparently higher than what was available for white children.[6]

Education was always important in the black community, running parallel to the issues of abolitionism and later of desegregation. Before the Civil War it provided the main basis for stratification and control within the black community. The high percentage of well-educated blacks permitted the community to entertain good relations with whites. Furthermore, the blacks tended to adopt white codes of behavior, thus reinforcing the importance of the black aristocracy, whose manners were most like those of the whites. Education was and remained for some time the privilege of those who had some white ancestry or were protected by white masters. Washington was in that sense exceptional. In most southern states, teaching slaves to read and write was officially a crime.

Emancipation of the 3,100 slaves in the District of Columbia was enacted by Congress in April 1862. The position of established black Washingtonians was now threatened, for they could no longer control and direct gradual assimilation of new arrivals into the black community. In addition, the mutual esteem and good relations between the black and white communities were threatened by the very fact that whites would now judge the entire black community by the behavior and manners of the newcomers: It was no longer possible to indoctrinate all blacks about the obligations of the city's self-respecting and self-protecting Negro group.[7] The mass arrival of "black field hands" from the South thus created difficulties and threatened the status of the black community. The black upper stratum therefore organized itself to preserve its position in society. For example, one group organized the Lotus Club, to which only leading Negroes could belong.

The organization of black education in the District must also be understood in the context of these cleavages within the black community and of opposition between the black and white populations. In 1862 a law requiring Washington to establish public schools for black children settled the question of Negro education. Ten percent of the taxes on black property in the District was to be used in financing black schools under the supervision of a board of trustees to be appointed by the Secretary of the Interior.[8] That is, local money was used to finance the schools, but control and supervision were left to the federal authorities. Private education for blacks meanwhile was supported by northern white philanthropists. After 1862, education in Washington was thus not a local responsibility.[9]

The white population was not altogether against educating the blacks. It saw education as a means of control and training of manpower for industrialization. An educated population seemed less dangerous to society as a whole. White preoccupation with education for the freed slaves led to the creation by Congress in 1865 of the "Bureau for Freemen, refugees, and abandoned lands," designed to establish a system of public education. To support it the first universal school taxes in the District were levied. The emancipated slaves sought education as a mark of their new status.[10] The need for black teachers to take on the educational task led to the establishment of higher education for blacks. Frazier reports that three years after the abolition of slavery there were 14 institutions nationwide providing teacher training, among them Howard University.[11]

The appropriateness and usefulness of black education was, however, already being questioned by both whites and blacks for economic reasons. The black aristocracy,* consisting mainly of mulattoes, was very much in favor of an integrated school system as part of its striving to achieve "whiteness" in all possible ways. It refused to send its children to segregated schools and had them tutored at home or sent them to some northern integrated institutions. Another part of the black population, the middle class, was achieving new status within the black community. It was composed of the increasing numbers of blacks who held clerical positions in federal government agencies, black shopkeepers, and teachers in the black school system (mostly trained at Howard University). Most members of the black middle class did not strongly favor an integrated school system. The main reasons for their preference for segregated schools were, first, that black children might find competing with white children too stressful; second, that an integrated school system would deny opportunity to black teachers (whom Howard University in Washington was training), whose prestige in the black community was higher than their income alone would have given them; and, third, that it seemed important to prove to the white community that blacks were able to organize and maintain a high-quality educational system that could be compared with that of whites. An act passed in 1878 defined the District of Columbia as "a Colony," providing for no local voice in District matters in exchange for financial support from the federal government.[12] The consequences of this decision seem to have been far-reaching over the next 90 years. Indeed it has been pointed out that this legislation ended political association between whites and blacks, who had previously had contact in dealing with community affairs, and encouraged estrangement of the two groups. And it became increasingly apparent that financial support of the black school system was being neglected. Washington became the "voteless city." The absence of local say in public affairs may have had an impact on the relationship between the communities and the schools. Teachers may have been affected inasmuch as no decisions about schools could ever be a result of local control.[13]

The black community in Washington was far from united during the 1890s. The aristocrats of predominantly white blood drew further away from the darker-skinned middle-class families, and the gulf

---

*The aristocrats were described as follows: light-colored, the qualification of antiquity of family, money, education, and honorable occupation. The Washington Negroes "four hundred."

separating both groups from the former black field hands grew wider. The black community seemed to adhere to the common social pattern of the South: conflict and tension within the caste, and acceptance and concealed hostility toward the white group outside.[14]

The famous case of Plessy-Ferguson in 1896 produced official approval of the doctrine of "separate but equal." The issue was a Louisiana statute requiring separation of blacks and whites on trains traveling within the state. Plessy, a man of one-eighth black ancestry asked the court to invalidate the Louisiana law because it violated his personal rights under the Thirteenth and Fourteenth Amendments to the Constitution. The court refused:

> Laws permitting and even requiring separation of the races in places where they are liable to be brought into contact do not necessarily imply the inferiority of either race to the other and have been generally if not universally recognized as within the competency of the State Legislature in the exercise of their police power. The most common instance of this is connected with the establishment of separate schools for White and for colored children, which has been held a valid exercise of legislative power even by Courts and States where the political rights of the colored race have been longest and most earnestly enforced.[15]

The black aristocracy saw the fight for an integrated school system as the first and essential step toward combating discrimination in obtaining social recognition through civil rights. Among the middle class, the group that was most vulnerable economically, interest in maintaining a separate school system grew stronger with the expansion of the system to employ an increasing number of black teachers. Green has quoted from the Star, a black newspaper, to show how the issue of school integration was dealt with in the District:

> There is a small sprinkling of colored children in the White schools, but for the most part the colored people prefer to have their separate schools, with a superintendent, with teachers of their own race, just as they prefer to maintain their own benevolent associations. The colored schools get their full share of the school money, and in proportion to numbers are supplied with better school commodities than the White schools. For various reasons colored children get on better in schools of their own. One is that they are spared the disadvantageous competition with White children of their own age who have greater opportunities at home and elsewhere for

> advancement in their studies. Again were the schools to be merged it would necessarily throw 165 colored teachers out of employment as it could not be expected that the White school population of the District, outnumbering the Negroes about two to one, should give up their teachers to make room for colored teachers. . . . Better let well enough alone.[16]

The black community was divided not only on the issue of a separate school system but also on the content of the education to be offered in black schools. The controversy over professional education reflected the opposition among various black groups. In the 1800s Booker T. Washington formulated the demand for vocational and industrial training. Of the adult black population in 1880, 60 percent were unable to write, and Washington's supporters argued that such training would be a wiser goal than would a more literary education for most Negroes. The central theme of Washington's philosophy was thrift, industry, and Christian character as the road to eventual attainment of constitutional rights for blacks.[17] He believed it proper that blacks would have to measure up to broader American standards of morality and material prosperity if they were to succeed in achieving equality. He also believed that, as economic and moral development permitted blacks to assimilate broader American middle-class standards, prejudice would diminish and the barriers of discrimination would crumble. His philosophy was not equally appealing to all groups in the black community, however. The old upper class opposed it.[18] Not only did they want their children to receive a liberal arts education and a certain set of attitudes, but also they saw Washington's philosophy as a surrender in the fight for equality, an acquiescence in their own inferior status for decades to come.

Washington's program stressing moral values and the acquisition of definite vocational skills was supported mainly by the rising middle class. The emphasis on struggle and self-help in achieving success also appealed to racial pride and solidarity among these "self-made" blacks. Washington's program also appealed to the white population, for it promised a source of semiskilled labor while satisfying the prevailing public moral sense.[19]

Washington established Tuskegee Institute to further his philosophy; it is still one of the main institutions for training black teachers. Although vocational education is no longer primary, Booker Washington's fundamental principles—like the importance of practical rather than academic training, self-help as a means to success, and "moral standards" combined with Christian values—may well still be the main sources of educational philosophy and general value orientation among black teachers. In this study we shall examine these principles, especially the scope of their acceptance among the District's black teachers and their congruence with the values and interests of the rising black middle class as a whole.*

Another school of thought originated with W. E. B. Du Bois. Whereas Washington, a member of the middle class, gave more importance to economic factors in promoting the black cause and the ultimate integration of the blacks into white America, Du Bois, an "upper class" mulatto, stressed the importance of political rights for blacks. Without political rights, he believed, blacks, primarily a working-class group, could not achieve economic opportunity. Besides championing liberal education and leadership by a college-educated elite, Du Bois embraced socialism and interracial working-class solidarity. Du Bois had comparatively few contemporary followers, however, and these were primarily black and white intellectuals and members of the old black aristocracy.[20]

It seems appropriate to say a few words about these two black leaders, in view of their different backgrounds, educational philosophies, and political ideologies—and their varying impacts on groups within the black community. Although both educational philosophies have evolved, awareness of how they might influence teachers, especially in their orientations toward students, seems necessary if we are to understand today's educational and political problems in the ghettos.

By the 1890s the black school system of Washington, D.C., had succeeded in establishing standards nearly comparable to those of the white schools, although facilities and teachers' salaries in the black schools were at lower levels.

At the turn of the century educational institutions became the focus of an intensifying black struggle for acceptance in American society, with resulting "politicization" of the issues around integration. At the same time racism among whites was mounting, and economic opportunities were diminishing. The latter changes did

---

*It may be of some interest that during approximately the same period whites were rejecting formalism in the classroom; indeed, in 1876 a "progressive" educational philosophy took shape. The main goal of the progressive-education movement was to work with each child's whole personality, in order to promote creative self-expression; the teacher was expected to build upon students' needs and interests. This movement, which originally had a genuine intellectual basis in philosophy of child development eventually lost its vitality, so that by 1940 it was regarded as an anti-intellectual trend in education. It seems to us that one of the new tendencies in black education today is to adapt the forms of progressive education to content and values derived from Booker T. Washington's philosophy.

not greatly affect the mass of the black population but struck the middle and upper classes very hard; these groups had more to lose in terms of status than did lower-class blacks. Black enterprises made little progress; the first black savings bank in Washington failed. The black upper and middle classes reacted by turning their efforts toward the defense of blacks against discrimination. They played an important role in the organization in 1912 of the local branch of the National Association for the Advancement of Colored People (NAACP), founded in 1909. The black community of Washington after decades of internal dissension had gained a new cohesion and solidarity.

World War I opened new jobs and other opportunities to blacks in Washington, but it also adversely affected both the white and black middle classes, who suffered from rising costs of living while their salaries remained relatively fixed. Among them the teachers were especially hard hit, and this aspect increased their sense of social decline. The discrepancies between levels of middle-class skill and education, on one hand, and available economic opportunities, on the other, decreased. The new wave of migrations from the South added to the difficulties.

The riots in Washington, D.C., in 1919 signaled a new militancy among blacks. The upper classes became more deeply involved in the struggle for equality when the U.S. Supreme Court upheld, in 1926, the legality of voluntary restrictive covenants—aimed at preventing blacks from purchasing or occupying houses in white neighborhoods. The depression of the 1930s worsened economic conditions in the black community.

Despite growing militancy, however, most blacks still preferred the dual school system to an integrated one. The Washington system was the best black school system in the country, though more funds and facilities were needed to improve upon what had already been accomplished. But, as the years passed and these needs were ignored, conditions deteriorated, and it became increasingly clear that the black school system was no longer even approximately equal to the white system.[21] Blacks were given old school buildings in neighborhoods deserted by whites, and new schools were constructed for whites in the suburbs. The District also experienced a strong influx of rural families after World War II.

In order to assess the quality of black education, Superintendent Garnet Wilkinson asked for a study of its output, and in 1943 Howard Long presented a report on the achievements of black children. This report was never made public by Wilkinson because of the embarrassing findings. Long reported no discernible decline in average intelligence ratings between 1935 and 1943 but did note a downward trend in the achievements of pupils in all grades. Among the causes for this decline he cited ineffectual instruction and especially the socioeconomic status of the students. This report led to reexamination of the idea of a separate school system. The division of educational funds between whites and blacks had become increasingly unequal as enrollment in white schools had dropped steadily and that in black schools had risen continuously. This inequality put blacks at a disadvantage in competing with whites for jobs. Although many blacks wanted to send their children to the half-empty white schools, very few challenged the segregated system in the courts, possibly because in 1910 federal district judges had ruled that a child with one-sixteenth-part black blood could not attend a white school (which suggests how strongly threatened by blacks whites had come to feel).

In 1947 the father of Marguerite Carr sued the superintendent of schools for denying her a transfer from an overcrowded school to a sparsely attended white school nearby.[22] The attack was based on the inequality of accommodation. The Carr v. Corning case led to the opening of school buildings for black children, and the plaintiff's plea was satisfied.[23] Protest was thus directed not against the dual system per se but against inequality in buildings, facilities, and number of teachers. Other protests were also directed against conditions of accommodations rather than against the dual system itself. In 1948 the congressional Subcommittee on Appropriations requested a team of experts headed by George Strayer of Columbia University to undertake a survey of conditions in the public schools of the District of Columbia. The report brought to the attention of whites the downward trend in achievements among black children and the educational difficulties created by the southern migrations. Strayer's data also verified the central thesis of the National Committee on Segregation that segregated schools underlay the city's entire social structure.

The effects of World War II upon blacks were very important. It provided for many blacks their first experience of prolonged close contact with whites. And then the transformation of a war economy into a peace economy always implies a period of reconversion and increased unemployment and that following World War II was no exception. Segregationists at that time headed most congressional committees. Increased racism after a war fought against Nazism, coupled with the creation of the United Nations and issue of the Declaration of Human Rights, stimulated greater attention to the position and role of blacks in the United States. Gradually the attention of the black community shifted from denouncing unequal accommodations to concern with the inequalities of a segregated school system in itself.

Attacks had first to be centered on the unconstitutionality of the laws requiring segregated schools. Despite the strong desire among the District's black community to keep the separate school system, for reasons already mentioned, there was simultaneously a continuing struggle, in Washington and elsewhere, for nondiscrimination in restaurants and travel facilities. As the courts had argued, in various suits, that if the separate-but-equal doctrine was accepted in the schools it must then be applied in other spheres of life, in order to break the general barriers of racism in all spheres of life, it was necessary first to show that the separate-but-equal doctrine was detrimental to the minority group.

Many groups, both black and white, organized and exerted pressure on Congress to consider the problem. White liberals seem to have played an important role in encouraging and pushing many blacks who were afraid of competition in the only field in which they had ever achieved control. Indeed, though the educational system was under the nominal control of blacks, we must not forget that their reliance on private money and federal financing did very much reduce their range of free action.

In May 1954 the Supreme Court ruled, in Brown v. Board of Education, that separate educational facilities are inherently unequal.

> We come then to the question presented: Does segregation of children in public schools solely on the basis of race, even though the physical facilities and other "tangible" factors may be equal, deprive the children of the minority group of equal educational opportunities? . . . To separate children in grade and high schools from others of similar age and qualifications solely because of their race generates a feeling of inferiority as to their status in the community that may affect their hearts and minds in a way unlikely ever to be undone.[24]

This court ruling resting on the Fourteenth Amendment's equal protection clause held that "in the field of public education the doctrine of 'separate but equal' has no place." By that time, however, Washington, D.C., had become a huge urban ghetto, what Frazier has called "the city of destruction." The educational system was in such poor condition that it contributed to the flight of whites from Washington to the suburbs; this flight was further stimulated by the desegregation decisions.

A retrospective look at the history of the Washington, D.C., school system suggests the importance of the long-prevalent theme of resistance, both individual and social, to desegregation. The black school system was for many years the best of its kind in the country, the only public school system entirely organized and mainly (although not financially) controlled by blacks. It had become an institution of vital importance in preserving the economic and ethnic integrity of the black community. The role of the middle class in preserving this dual school system had been extremely important, reflecting the ambivalence of this group toward both upper- and lower-class blacks as well as its fear of competition with white teachers. The middle class also disseminated its conservative values through the schools.

For black Washingtonians, the dual system not only provided economic opportunities for blacks free of competition with whites but also protected black children from white racism.[25] For a long time, it furnished the black community with a source of pride, demonstrating that blacks, given the means, could provide as good an education as whites. The great achievements of school desegregation and legal acknowledgment of equal rights for blacks were thus made at the cost of a school system that had both concrete and symbolic value for the blacks of Washington.

This historical outline emphasizes the special character of both Washington, D.C., and its black population; it also reminds us of problems now characteristic of every large urban center. Indeed the relationship between the black middle and lower classes is not peculiar to Washington, nor is the controversy over educational philosophy, which still centers on academic versus professional training for a lower-class clientele. Furthermore, the study of Washington's former dual system and its all-black component may throw some light on the general issue of community control.

THE WASHINGTON, D.C., ELEMENTARY SCHOOL SYSTEM TODAY

In this section we shall describe the current status of the Washington, D.C., public elementary school system. In some respects it is similar to that of any large city. The same broad trends and population shifts affect it, especially the increased concentration of blacks in the inner city and the rapid migration of whites to the suburbs.

The increased concentration of the black population in the inner city, the frantic migration of the whites to the suburbs, are characteristic of large urban centers and affect directly the school systems of these cities. They are among the many factors, described by the U.S. Commission on Civil Rights, that lead to racial isolation:

> Racial isolation in city schools is caused by many factors. Isolation is rooted in racial discrimination that has been sanctioned and even encouraged by government at all levels. It is perpetuated by the effects of past segregation; reinforced by demographic, fiscal, and educational

changes taking place in urban areas; and it is compounded by the policies and practices of urban school systems.[26]

The consequences have also been made clear by the commission. Negro children suffer serious harm when their education takes place in racially segregated schools.

Havighurst has studied the changes in the social-class composition of urban centers and their effects upon public schools.[27] Migration to large cities is associated with the creation of slums in central districts where rents and building costs are high. The rural poor are becoming the urban poor as most urban blacks live in such densely populated, racially homogeneous areas that the available schools are entirely segregated.

Colin Greer has pointed to differences in the role of the public school for immigrants and urban blacks.[28] He maintains that comparison between the urbanized immigrants at the turn of the century and newly urbanized blacks is misleading. The schools were more effective in the case of immigrants because the communal structures of the ethnic group could provide economic support. The expanded requirements for social functioning and stable family life since that period mean that the schools encounter lower-class urban blacks who have fewer collective resources and who, given the structure of the schools, are widely seen as "ineducable."

Foster has analyzed the relations of slum schools to the neighborhoods where they are located, showing that the latter are characterized by high degrees of family disorganization and illegitimacy, and explaining the consequences for the school children. Many urban blacks are immigrants from the South, and they have brought with them the social and educational characteristics engendered by their rural background, which handicap them in urban life. Unemployment, like delinquency and the use of drugs and alcohol, is very high; these factors influence the quality and usefulness of education in the ghettos. Social, economic, and political roots of riots in the ghettos have been analyzed in the well-known Kerner commission report of 1968.[29] All these factors exist in Washington. In addition, it seems that Washington and its school system may foreshadow many future trends in other American cities.

How do teachers in such schools respond to these conditions? What are their attitudes toward the students? How strong is their commitment to teaching in slum schools? Before answering these questions, we shall describe more specifically the circumstances in which they teach in the all-black Washington elementary school system, circumstances resulting from both de facto segregation based on patterns of residential segregation and residual segregation from the old dual system. The demographic characteristics of the District of

Columbia have been thoroughly studied by George Carey, who used data from the 1960 Census.[30] The city can be divided into five sectors, as suggested by Carey, according to the race and social class of its inhabitants. The northwest sector is inhabited mainly by whites of high socioeconomic status. There are two black middle-class residential areas: one in the north, which is the settlement of the old bourgeoisie and is integrated, the other in the southeast, which attracts a newer black middle class. The center of the city consists of black slum areas, with a small enclave of older poor-white residents.

This area is near the federal buildings. Passow has described the city of Washington this way:

> The District is a City of great contrasts. The dignity of the national and international capital adjoins some of the worst slums in the country. As the Nation's first predominantly Negro city, it houses an affluent segment of Negroes which has resided in the District for generations; a newer group of well educated, salaried middle class Negroes and a hard core of impoverished families. The population is three-fifths Negro, but its school system is more than nine-tenths Negro.[31]

Washington, because of its demographic characteristics, and the racial, social, and economic isolation of its residential groups, furnishes a unique opportunity to study an all-black school system and to differentiate between schools serving black slum children and those serving black middle-class children.

De facto segregation in the schools is among the most striking characteristics of the system. It can be gauged from the residential distribution of both the students and staff, for the elementary school system not only reflects but even exaggerates the general racial and economic imbalances of Washington. In 1966 there were 91,994 elementary-school children in the public schools; 91 percent were black, and 9 percent were white. Of the black students, 90 percent attend schools that are 90 to 100 percent black, 99 percent attend schools where blacks are in the majority.[32] The trend toward an entirely black school system over four decades can be seen in Table 2.3. Although the white population as a whole kept increasing, the absolute number of white children attending public schools diminished. The effect of the Supreme Court desegregation ruling was drastic. In 1950 there were still 46,736 white children in the public schools. Between 1950 and 1955 there was a decrease of 18.3 percent. Between 1955 and 1960 the decrease was 34.5 percent; the desegregation of the Washington school system thus seems to have accelerated the

TABLE 2.3

School Enrollments, Washington, D.C., 1920-60

	1920	1931	1935	1937	1941	1944	1948	1950	1954	1955	1960
Total school population	77,355	92,706	106,876	107,723	109,345	103,780	109,198	112,810		124,754	139,838
White enrollment in public schools	45,775	53,175	59,582	58,793	55,345	49,500	47,801	46,736		38,165	24,987
Black enrollment in public schools	19,523	26,974	33,498	34,625	36,666	37,768	43,264	47,980		68,877	97,897
Black proportion of total enrollment	28.9	33.6	35.9	37.0	39.7	43.3	47.6	49.6		64.3	71.5

Source: Constance McLaughlin Green, The Secret City: A History of Race Relations in the National Capital (Princeton, N.J.: Princeton University Press, 1967), p. 309.

withdrawal of white school children from the public schools. Meanwhile the black school population rose from 47,980 to 68,877 between 1950 and 1955. After 1954, de facto school segregation was so advanced that, in effect, a single black system was the sole successor to the dual system, the main difference being that the school system was no longer legally and administratively a separate black system.

The Washington elementary school system is composed of 132 schools: 45 (35 percent) are 100 percent black; 57 (43 percent) are 90-99 percent black; 15 (11 percent) are 50-89 percent black; 10 (18 percent) are 10-49 percent black; and 3 (4 percent) are 0-10 percent black.[33] Passow has shown that in Washington, D.C., between 1950 and 1966 the increase in the black population of schools with 90-100 percent black enrollment was 145 percent (44,817 pupils), whereas in the same period the white population of schools with 90-100 percent white decreased 90 percent (25,674 pupils). He calculated the degree of segregation actually existing in the system by means of a segregation index ranging from total segregation (100) to total integration (0). Within the boundaries of the District of Columbia the segregation score for blacks was 80.[34]

Our main focus in this study is on black elementary-school teachers. We have already seen that enrollments reflect de facto segregation. Is the staff of the Washington school system also segregated? In 1966 there were 3,138 elementary-school teachers in Washington, D.C. Among them 16.7 percent were white, and 83.3 percent were black. Of the black teachers, 91.4 percent taught in schools that were 90-100 percent black; 99.8 percent taught in schools where black pupils were in the majority. Segregation among the staffs of the Washington schools cannot be said to result from residential segregation; instead it reflects the policies of the District Board of Education. Passow, in his study of the Washington public school system, has discussed the system's failure to provide an integrated staff.[35]

For our present purposes the interesting point is that the black teachers under study work in an all-black school system. Although Washington is not unique in this respect (the report of the U.S. Commission on Civil Rights shows that in 1967 65 percent of all black first-grade pupils surveyed in the 24 largest metropolitan areas attended schools with 90 percent or more black enrollment, whereas almost 80 percent of all white first-graders attended schools that were 90 percent or more white), it does offer a setting for study of black teachers' responses in all-black schools, thus permitting us to control for race. Any variations in teachers' commitment and satisfaction that we may find can thus be assumed not to be a function of race. We shall try to answer these questions: What are the various orientations of black teachers in black schools? What kinds of difficulty do they encounter? What are their ideologies, their educational philosophies? What are their sources of professional satisfaction? How strongly are they committed to teaching black children? However, there is still variation among black schools. On what basis shall we compare black schools?

Because of economic separation of social classes and the existence of distinct black social groups, we have decided to categorize schools according to the socioeconomic levels of the residents in the areas that they serve. The data are taken from the 1960 U.S. Census of Washington, D.C., and are the same ones used by Carey in his demographic mapping of the city. Each Census tract was characterized by the median annual family income and by the average number of school years completed. Each school is located in a Census tract, and its enrollment reflects the attributes of the residents of that tract.* Each school is thus first categorized by the median annual family income of the residents of the surrounding Census tract; this median varied from $2,940 to $13,170. The distribution of schools on the median family income of the residents in which the school is located is shown in Table 2.4

TABLE 2.4

Distribution of Schools According to Median Family Income

Median Family Income	Number of Schools	Percentage
Less than $4,000	32	24
$4,000-$4,999	41	31
$5,000-$5,999	21	16
$6,000-$6,999	11	9
$7,000-$7,999	7	5
$8,000-$8,999	6	5
$9,000 and more	13	10
Total	131	100

*The use of the characteristics of the residents of the Census tract to characterize schools may be somewhat biased by the inclusion of older people and couples without children. However, these characteristics were the best available indicators to measure the socioeconomic nature of the schools. Washington being very stratified socially and geographically, it seemed appropriate to use them.

We have also decided to classify the schools according to the average years of education completed by the residents of the areas that they serve. (The decision to include this variable is based on Carey's analysis showing that the median number of school years completed is important in the context of Washington, D.C., demographic patterns and is also an important variable distinguishing the old and new black middle classes.) The median years of education ranged from 7.3 in one track to 13.4 in another. The distribution of schools on the average years completed is shown in Table 2.5.

Based on these two measures of socioeconomic status we can construct an index and locate each school on it.[36] The socioeconomic status (SES) index ranges from 0 for the lowest level to 6 for the highest. The schools were divided into three categories according to SES level: low (score 0-2), medium (3-4), and high (5-6). The distribution of black teachers in these schools is shown in Table 2.6.

In the present study the comparison of black teachers will be based on the varying SES scores of the schools in which they teach. From time to time it will also be appropriate to compare black teachers with white teachers on the same basis. From Table 2.4 above we can see that 41 percent of black teachers compared with 16 percent of white teachers are located in schools of low SES, whereas only 17 percent of black teachers, compared to 58 percent of white teachers, are located in schools of high SES. This divergence suggests another aspect of racial and economic isolation in the public

TABLE 2.5

Distribution of Schools According to Years of Education Completed

Average Education	Number of Schools	Percentage
Less than 8 years	4	3
8 years	15	11
9 years	23	17
10 years	27	21
11 years	21	16
12 years	25	19
13 years	10	8
14 years and more	6	5
Total	131	100

TABLE 2.6

Distribution of Black Teachers by SES of Schools

School SES	Percentage of Black Teachers	Percentage of White Teachers
Low (0-2)	41	16
Medium (3-4)	42	26
High (5-6)	17	58
Total	100	100
	(N=2,419)	(N=499)

schools: an increasing gap in the "economic opportunities" available in white and black schools, in schools with low and high SES.

The differences in "educational opportunities" offered by white and black schools have been widely acknowledged and attacked.[37] As early as 1940, Warner, Loeb, and Havighurst showed that an average of $80 a year was spent on each child's education in the United States.[38] Yet in 10 southern states only $49 was spent on each white child's education and $17 on each black child's education. Judged only in monetary terms, the advantages of white children were three times as great as those of black children. Such differences in educational opportunities in the Washington, D.C., school system have been the subject of lengthy study.

The dual system, as we have seen, consists of two parallel institutions, one for white and one for black children. These institutions were identical as to their organization and number of personnel. The administration and staff of the "colored" schools were all blacks. This segregated organization applied to all levels of the school's program from kindergarten through teachers' college. The dual system* was characterized by many inequalities, most pronounced in the areas of pupil expenditures, school buildings, provisions, and teacher-pupil ratios.

The quality of the dual system competed with that of the white system for some decades. After 1920, however, the inequalities increased and the system gradually deteriorated.[39] The decline was linked to a decline in financial support for the black schools after the black population began to increase, especially through migration from

---

*The dual system of two parallel institutions, one for white children and one for black children, was instituted by law in most southern and border states.

the South. Thus, the Brown decision of 1954 had its effect on a system already deteriorating.

The first investigation of the entire system was conducted in 1947 by George Strayer. He pointed out the differences in the economic resources of black and white schools.[40] Although he stressed that black students are as capable of achieving good academic performances as white students are, he showed the decline in black students' achievements through the years, which he related to lack of money and gradual deterioration of the black school system, partly as a result of the increased black student population. Two years after the desegregation of the school system, conditions in predominantly black schools had clearly worsened. A survey on the effects of desegregation by Ellis Knox showed that the economic gap between white and black schools was increasing but not as a consequence of desegregation.[41] More recently Passow has noted that white schools have higher expenditures per student, are better staffed, and have better facilities than black schools.[42]

Furthermore, comparisons of elementary schools in high- and low- income neighborhoods show a correlation between high income and such teacher characteristics as experience and permanent status. In addition, staff-pupil ratios are lower and expenditure per pupil is higher in the high-income schools. Consequently, increasing numbers of students have serious language and reading difficulties. Pucinski has shown that 60 percent of the District of Columbia's population show reading deficiencies.[43] One of the most critical problems facing the Washington public school system thus arises from its failure to teach most of its pupils how to read. The problem is clearly shown in Table 2.7.

The socioeconomic levels of the schools will thus be used as one of the main context variables in our study--as a measure of both the characteristics of the student body and the pressures that may be impinging upon the teachers. Previous research has shown a difference in the behavior, motivation, and performance of students in low and high SES schools.[44] The findings of these researches will be presented in the next chapter. Other studies have shown how the SES of the student body affects teachers.[45] In addition, as we have seen, schools in low-SES neighborhoods are more likely to be understaffed, to suffer from inadequate facilities, and to have less money. It thus seems legitimate to use school SES as a measure of pressure on teachers. We assume that the lower the school SES, the greater the pressures are.[46] Teachers under greater pressure are more likely to create effective mechanisms for coping and to insulate themselves from failure than are teachers under less pressure. We will analyze for example whether teachers under greater pressure will tend to isolate themselves from the students and to becomes less

TABLE 2.7

Reading Levels at Various Grades in Washington, D.C., Schools

Grade	Percentage Reading at Grade Level	Percentage Reading at 1 or More Years Below Grade Level
Third grade	67.2	32.8
Fourth grade	62.8	37.8
Fifth grade	60.6	39.4
Sixth grade	54.6	45.4
Eighth grade	45.5	54.5

professionally oriented and more oriented toward their peers and toward the agency than will teachers under less pressure. Teachers in low-SES schools will tend to become less client-oriented than will teachers in high-SES schools because students in low-SES schools may not provide sources of professional gratification. The SES of the school is a measure both of the characteristics of the student body and of the level of pressures in the schools.

The assumption that teachers in low-SES schools encounter greater difficulties than do those in high-SES schools can be indirectly tested in our data by teachers' own perceptions of the factors that interfere with teaching and learning in the classroom.

Teachers were asked to list such factors. Among those mentioned we shall study the low level of intelligence of students, students' poor training in basic skills, students' poor home environments, parents' attempts to interfere, too many student absences, large classes, uninterested students, and too much time spent on discipline. Do these factors vary between low-SES and high-SES schools? Teachers in low-SES schools are more likely to report more obstacles in the classroom, thus lending support to the hypothesis that in schools with low SES greater pressures are exerted on teachers than in schools with high SES.

We are speaking here of pressures inside the school. But pressures from the community as a whole and from parents may well be stronger in high-SES schools than in low-SES schools.[47]

Table 2.8 shows that indeed teachers in the low- and medium-SES schools are more likely than those in high-SES schools to perceive that they are facing obstacles in the classroom. The main differences between schools of lower and high SES in the most

TABLE 2.8

Factors That Interfere with Teaching and Learning*
(Percent of teachers who agree on each item)

	All of Sample	Low-SES Schools	Medium-SES Schools	High-SES Schools
Low level of intelligence of students	43%	48%	46%	36%
Poor training in basic skills	57	57	60	53
Poor home environment	76	86	80	55
Parents' attempts to interfere	15	14	16	22
Too many absences	41	50	44	23
Classes too large	65	60	72	69
Students not interested in learning	31	37	33	25
Too much time spent on discipline	62	67	65	56
	(N=2,452)			

*Percentages do not add up to 100 percent because teachers were free to agree with as many items as they wished.

frequent type of obstacle cited are the following: poor home environment, too many absentees, low level of intelligence of students, and too much time spent on discipline. The social and economic conditions of the children are seen as among the most frequent obstacles in the classroom. It is of some interest to note that teachers in all SES levels are not markedly different in the frequency with which they cite discipline as a problem. Among the factors that are cited more often in the high-SES schools are parents' attempts to interfere and classes too large.

The fact that parents of higher SES are more likely to "interfere" than others has been noted. The noninterference of parents in lower-class neighborhoods used to be one of the "advantages" of teaching in a slum neighborhood. However, since the politicization of the problem of community control, this may have changed. It is not surprising that teachers in better schools complain about the size of classes more frequently than in low-SES schools. Indeed, in low-SES schools, the problem of overcrowded classrooms may seem minor compared with problems linked with the social and economic characteristics of the children in the school; in high-SES schools, where such problems are not acute, the problem of facilities in the school may appear more important.

Having classified the schools according to characteristics of the residents of the areas in which they are located and having described the contexts in which black teachers work, we must describe one further characteristic of teachers' working situations. Inside a single school, teachers may be confronted with students of varying academic performance and achievement, as well as level of intelligence. In the Washington, D.C., schools such differences were indeed very distinct because of the use of the tracking system, instituted by Superintendent Karl Hansen. The tracking system was a response to, and means of controlling, the possible downgrading effects of the desegregation ruling and to reassure whites that educational standards would be maintained in the schools. The four "tracks" were actually ability groupings, based on results of intelligence and achievement tests. Once a child had been assigned to one track, he had little chance of reaching a higher one. The lowest track, called "special academic," included students with IQs of 75 or less; the "general" and "regular" tracks were for students with higher test scores. The highest, or "honor," track included students chosen by the teachers and the principal. All the students in a group pursued a similar course of study and achieved similar levels of performance. Despite the inappropriateness of ability and achievement tests for ghetto students and the fact that students learn more from one another than from their teachers, tracking was adopted; social segregation in the schools thus handicapped students from the most impoverished families even further. Their mothers called the tracking system "programed retardation." Coleman has shown how the type of classmate affects students' achievement:

> Attributes of other students account for far more variation in the achievement of minority group children than do any attributes of school facilities and slightly more than do attributes of staff. . . .
>
> The apparent beneficial effect of a student body with a high proportion of white students comes not from racial composition per se, but from the better educational background and higher educational aspirations that are on the average found among white students.[48]

In the present study we shall use the track with which the teache works as a variable in analyzing his attitudes toward students and his perception of them. The tracking system was still in use when the data for this study were collected in 1967. (Since then it has been dropped, in response to attacks by various community groups and following several investigations of its effects on the student body.)[49] Teachers teaching in the lowest track were thus dealing with the most difficult students, those from the most impoverished homes and havin the greatest language difficulties. The general track included student whose performance levels were slightly higher, and the regular track included students whose levels were still higher. The best students were in the honor track. Track thus serves as a crude measure of academic achievement.*

In the next chapter we will present and discuss the concepts that we will be using in the study. We will describe the frame of analysis used to study teachers' responses to problems of functioning in schools.

NOTES

1. This information is based on Constance McLaughlin Green, *The Secret City: A History of Race Relations in the National Capital* (Princeton, N.J.: Princeton University Press, 1967), p. 200.

2. George Carey, "The District of Columbia: Its People and Characteristics," in A. Harry Passow, ed., *Toward Creating a Model Urban School System: A Study of the Washington, D.C. Public School* (New York: Teachers College, Columbia University, 1967), pp. 43-51

3. Green, *Secret City*, p. 8.

4. Wilhelmus Bogart Bryan, *A History of the National Capital*, 2 vols. (New York: Macmillan, 1915-16).

5. Howard Beale, *A History of Freedom of Teaching in Americ Schools* (New York: Octagon, 1966), pp. 111-56.

6. Bryan, *History of the National Capital*, Vol. II, p. 389.

7. Green, *Secret City*, Chapter 4.

8. Bryan, *History of the National Capital*, Vol. II, pp. 525-28.

9. Ellis Knox, *Democracy in the District of Columbia Public Schools* (Washington, D.C.: Judd and Detweiller, 1957), Chapter 1.

---

*In this study we will use the following codes to characterize the tracks where teachers are located according to the achievement level of the students in each track: special academic will have a score of 0, general a score of 1, regular a score of 2. This seemed necessary in view of the misleading labeling of the tracks.

10. Green, Secret City, pp. 73-104.

11. E. Franklin Frazier, Black Bourgeoisie: The Rise of a New Middle Class (New York: The Free Press, 1957).

12. Bryan, History of the National Capital, Vol. II, pp. 635-42.

13. Mary Morton, "The Education of the Negro in the District of Columbia," Journal of Negro Education, Vol. 16, 1947, pp. 325-46; in 1968, however, Congress voted to restore a measure of local suffrage that it took away from Washington in 1874, by authorizing the election of the school board.

14. Gunnar Myrdal, An American Dilemma: The Negro Problem and Modern Democracy (20th anniversary ed.; New York: Harper & Row, 1962), Chapter 31, "Caste and Class," and Chapter 32, "The Negro Class Structure."

15. Quoted in Jack Greenberg, Race Relations and American Law (New York: Columbia University Press, 1959), pp. 32-46.

16. Green, Secret City, p. 200.

17. Joanne Grant, Black Protest: History, Documents and Analyses, Political Perspective Series (New York: Fawcett, 1968), pp. 175-85.

18. Myrdal, American Dilemma, pp. 641, 889-90.

19. See August Meier, Negro Thought in America, 1880-1915: Racial Ideologies in the Age of Booker T. Washington (Ann Arbor: University of Michigan Press, 1964), pp. 85-118, on the rise of industrial education in Negro schools.

20. Ibid., pp. 191-206.

21. Morton, "Education of the Negro," pp. 325-46.

22. Green, Secret City, pp. 267-68, 299.

23. Morton, "Education of the Negro," pp. 334-35.

24. Greenberg, Race Relations and American Law, pp. 213-14.

25. Knox, Democracy in the District of Columbia Public Schools, p. 107.

26. Racial Isolation in the Public Schools, U.S. Commission on Civil Rights, Report of the Commission (Washington, D.C.: Government Printing Office, 1967).

27. Robert Havighurst, "Urban Development and Education System," in A. Harry Passow, ed., Education in Depressed Areas (New York: Teachers College, Columbia University, 1966), pp. 24-45.

28. Colin Greer, "Immigrants, Negroes, and the Public Schools," The Urban Review, January 1969, p. 9.

29. Report of the National Advisory Commission on Civil Disorders (New York: Bantam, 1968). Hereinafter referred to as the Kerner commission report.

30. George Carey, "Demographic Mapping of the District and Its Schools," in Passow, ed., Toward Creating a Model Urban School System, pp. 583-93.

31. Passow, ed., Toward Creating a Model Urban School System, p. 50.

32. The report of the U.S. Commission on Civil Rights done in 1967 (Racial Isolation in the Public Schools; Washington, D.C.: Government Printing Office) shows that of the Negro children enrolled in elementary schools in 75 representative cities studied by the commission, 75 percent of them attend schools where the student bodies are more than 90 percent Negro.

33. From the data collected through questionnaires by Anna Lee Hopson and David E. Wilder on the Washington, D.C., school system: A Study of Teachers in the Public Schools of Washington, D.C. (New York, Bureau of Applied Social Research, Columbia University, 1967).

34. Passow, Toward Creating a Model Urban School System, p. 46.

35. Ibid., pp. 183-86.

36. See Appendix A.

37. Robert A. Dentler, "Barriers to Northern School Desegregation," Daedalus, Winter 1966, pp. 45-63.

38. Lloyd Warner, Robert J. Havighurst, and Martin Loeb, Who Shall be Educated? The Challenge of Opportunities (New York: Harper, 1944), p. 122.

39. Knox, Democracy in the District of Columbia Public Schools p. 17.

40. George D. Strayer, Report for the Congressional Subcommittee on Appropriations (Washington, D.C.: Government Printing Office, 1949).

41. Knox, in Democracy in the District of Columbia Public Schools, shows that "colored pupils per se, do not lower the level of academic work in integrated classes." He also shows that the socioeconomic level of the school affects students' achievement. Black students in schools located in rich neighborhoods are more likely to have higher achievement than black students in poor neighborhoods. He differentiates between race and economic factors.

42. Passow, Toward Creating a Model Urban School System p. 18.

43. A Task Force Study of the Public School System in the District of Columbia as It Relates to the War on Poverty, U.S. Congress, House of Representatives, Committee on Education and Labor (Washington, D.C.: Government Printing Office, June 1966). Hereinafter referred to as the Pucinski report.

44. See Allison Davis, Social Class Influences upon Learning (Cambridge: Harvard University Press, 1950).

45. James Coleman, Equality of Educational Opportunity (Washington, D.C.: Government Printing Office, 1966).

46. Robert E. Herriot and Nancy Hoyt St. John, Social Class and the Urban Schools (New York: John Wiley & Sons, 1966).

47. Howard Becker, "Social Class Variations in the Teacher-Pupil Relationship," Journal of Educational Sociology, Vol. 25, 1952, pp. 451-65. In our study we are dealing only with pressures from inside the schools; pressures coming from the community or from ancillary structures will not be analyzed.

48. Coleman, Equality of Educational Opportunity, p. 309.

49. Passow, ed., Toward Creating a Model Urban School System, Chapter 9.

CHAPTER 3
ANALYSIS OF THE PROBLEMS TO BE STUDIED

We have seen in Chapter 2 the conditions under which the dual school system developed in Washington, D.C., and the functions that it fulfilled for the black community. We have shown that the Washington school system, once respected for serving the needs of the black community, has gradually deteriorated into one of the most troubled systems in the country, plagued by problems that are in varying degrees characteristic of all large American urban centers.[1] The city has become the refuge of poor minorities and rural families. The inner city of Washington has gradually been transformed into slums and ghettos inhabited by poor blacks, whereas the middle classes both white and black, increasingly live in suburbs. Paralleling the changes in the city have been changes in the school system, both quantitative (increased black population, so that 93 percent of public elementary school students are black) and qualitative (the decline in educational standards and the failure to adapt education to the new ghettos, with the result that an increasing percentage of students are unable to read and write). In addition, there have been major organizational problems. Teachers in Washington were accustomed to working under the supervision of black administrators, to having separate school systems for whites and blacks. Since 1954 there has been only one administrative body, and the new approach to the race problem has been based on "color blindness." The pressures upon the Washington system reflect both general and local aspects of the educational crisis in the inner city. As described in Chapter 2, Washington's school system may well be responding to economic, social, and political pressures that are peculiar to it; but the schools and teachers in Washington are also affected by the same forces that are changing all large cities. Washington simply offers a more dramatic example because it has an all-black school system and a stratified black community, whose internal interactions, like the encounters between black professionals and black students of varying socioeconomic status, are one of the main focuses of our study. Teachers must respond to pressures arising from the organizational characteristics of the schools, as well as from the specific kinds of students with whom they have contact. We shall study the mechanisms that teachers use to cope with problems in their relations with students, peers, and the authority structure of the school and the associations of these relations with job satisfaction and commitment to teaching. The main purpose of our study, then, is to analyze teachers' modes of adaptation in ghetto schools of different socioeconomic levels.

In this chapter we present the conceptual framework of the study and the principal analytical tools employed. Although data for treating all the propositions discussed in this chapter are not available because the survey was carried out for other purposes, it is important to view the data that are available in proper theoretical perspective. Indeed, the shortcomings and limitations of the survey data as an aid in understanding problems of functioning in a social setting are significant and will be discussed separately. Some of the limitations of the survey methods were compensated for by very detailed participant observation by several sociologists[2] in elementary schools and other social agencies. As Sieber has pointed out,[3] participant observation is often obligatory in survey research.

The specific limitations of our analysis reflect the facts that the observations were made at only one point in time and that behavior was not measured in detail. Some of our conclusions about processes have been deduced from combinations of related findings and the reports of participant observers in similar settings. We used the latter type of information in several ways: first, as an aid in formulating our hypothesis; second, in interpretation of certain findings (for example, as guidelines for interpreting patterns of positive and negative functioning of the peer group); third, as a check on interpretations based entirely on survey findings; and, finally, to alert us to variations in teachers' attitudes and values connected with assignment to various types of schools.

OCCUPATIONAL SATISFACTION AND CAREER PLAN: SOME OBSERVATIONS

Because one of our main interests is teachers' satisfaction, let us begin with some observations about level of occupational satisfaction and commitment in general. Job satisfaction is one of the more frequently studied variables in sociological research. It is regarded as important because of its correlations with role performance, achievement, and the general effectiveness of the total enterprise, whether factory, army, or welfare agency. It has been studied in connection with organizations, bureaucracies, factories, social agencies, and professions.[4] The morale or climate within an organization or group has been found to be one of the most important variables affecting job satisfaction and in turn the productivity and commitment of the working group. Linked with this finding are those on the contributions of informal relations and the friendship network to job satisfaction, the creation of informal rules and norms, and the establishment of mechanisms for rewarding or punishing adherence to or deviation from such rules and norms.

In the field of education there is still little available research on job satisfaction among teachers. What there is shows that the great majority of teachers are satisfied with their jobs. Mason[5] has noted that "the general level of satisfaction among beginning teachers appears to be high." On most of the items in his survey, two-thirds of all beginning teachers were fairly satisfied. The supplemental studies of teachers in urban public schools conducted for the National Advisory Commission on Civil Disorders,[6] also found that teachers were, on the whole, satisfied with their positions: 88.2 percent of teachers in urban public schools reported satisfaction with their jobs, and about 67 percent wanted to remain teachers. Other studies based on participant observation in schools have also reported high levels of job satisfaction and commitment to teaching. Coleman confirmed this finding in his comparison of black and white teachers.[7] He found that teachers in inner-city schools in general were likely to be satisfied in their current posts, and black teachers specifically were more likely to be satisfied. Redefer, in his study of factors affecting teachers' morale, showed that teachers were generally satisfied with their jobs.[8]

In our study we measured teachers' over-all job satisfaction by means of the question, "All things considered, do you find your present job to be very satisfying, fairly satisfying, not very satisfying, not satisfying?" The general nature of this question implicitly encouraged teachers to evaluate all the positive and negative aspects of their jobs and to combine and weigh them all in an assessment of total job satisfaction. The distribution of responses is shown in Table 3.1. Four-fifths of the black elementary-school teachers in Washington, D.C., were satisfied with their jobs. Our findings thus extend earlier findings about job satisfaction among teachers to black teachers.

That such a high percentage of teachers were satisfied in a system that we know to be characterized by so many serious problems is quite surprising. How can we explain it? In the course of this study we shall investigate several explanations, including the structure of the school and especially the functions of the peer group.

TABLE 3.1

Teachers' Assessments of Over-All Job Satisfaction

	Percentage
Very satisfying	36
Fairly satisfying	52
Not very satisfying	9
Not satisfying	3
Total	100
	(N=2,430)

We have already mentioned that level of workers' satisfaction is sometimes linked with their productivity or effectiveness. Does a high level of satisfaction among teachers correlate with the achievements of their students? Coleman analyzed the effects of certain characteristics of teachers upon students' achievements.[9] His report suggested that although such characteristics of teachers as verbal skills and parents' education were related to students' achievements, they had little effect upon achievement, compared with those of the racial and social backgrounds of classmates and students' own self-confidence.

Relations between teachers and students may be characterized by lack of reciprocal influence.[10] If students are not significantly affected by the types of teachers who teach them, we may well ask whether or not the reverse is true: Is teachers' satisfaction affected by the types of students that they teach, or is it affected mainly by other aspects of their working situation? Teachers' commitment and career plans may be more closely associated with their relations with peers and supervisors than with types of students. If so, another question arises. Why are the occupational satisfaction and commitment of teachers not affected by the students with whom they have contact? Why are teachers insulated from their students? Among other possible explanations we shall study the duality* within the school, as the social organization, the tensions and problems that may arise, and the mechanisms that teachers use to cope with them.

---

*In Chapter 2, "dual system" was used to characterize a form of segregated school system in Washington. By "duality" of the school, we are here referring to a structural characteristic of the school. This latter meaning will figure in this and some later chapters.

We have alluded to teachers' professional commitment* as form of adjustment. Knowing that a high percentage of teachers are satisfied with their jobs, we may ask whether or not they also want to remain teachers. Our measure of their commitment was based on the question, "Which one of these things would you most want to be ten years from now?" followed by eight alternatives, as shown in Table 3.2. Apparently fewer than a quarter of the teachers wanted to be teaching in 10 years later. It is difficult to compare these findings with those of other studies because the wording of the question was different. It is significant, however, that among one sample of beginning teachers 19 percent reported that it was extremely unlikely that they would leave teaching within five years.[11] About the same percentage of Washington elementary-school teachers expected to remain teachers for at least five years. Coleman reported a higher figure. Among his sample of black teachers 45 percent planned to remain in teaching until retirement.[12]

In view of the high percentage of teachers who reported satisfaction with their jobs, this finding raises some questions. Discontent with teaching does not seem to have arisen from the ghetto system

TABLE 3.2

Teachers' Aspirations for 10 Years Later

	Percentage
A classroom teacher in this system	18
A classroom teacher elsewhere	5
An educational specialist	28
A school administrator	11
Teaching at a college	5
To retire	12
To become a full-time housewife	13
Other field than education	9
Total	101* (N=2,452)

*The total percentage does not equal 100% because of rounding of figures.

---

*In our study, "professional commitment" refers to commitment to teaching and not commitment to the educational field in general.

itself, for only 5 percent of Washington's black elementary school teachers wished to be teaching elsewhere, but nearly 40 percent wanted to become either educational specialists or administrators. Whereas the majority of teachers thus seemed committed to the educational field, only a minority were committed to teaching. We suggest that teachers' job satisfaction is based not on achievements in teaching but mainly on other aspects of their jobs, probably those outside the classroom. Indeed, on the basis of our Washington, D.C., survey, Hopson and Wilder suggested that job satisfaction may be more dependent upon conditions of work and supervision than upon performances of students in the system.[13]

THE SCHOOL AS A SOCIAL ORGANIZATION

Conditions in the school that may affect teachers' job satisfaction and commitment to teaching include the structural characteristics of the school. We shall focus on problems of functioning typical of all schools and on substantive problems more specifically associated with ghetto schools. We shall then suggest some possible responses of teachers to these problems. The concept of subculture will be used as one analytical tool for understanding the shared responses of teachers in similar situations, especially in ghetto schools. Indeed, the concept of subculture is important in explaining behavior when groups collectively experience functioning problems.

We shall first describe the characteristics of the school as a social organization and as a social agency, concerned with problems of functioning. We will point to the differences between ghetto and nonghetto schools, introduce the main concepts that will be used in further analysis, and show the limitation of the data available in analyzing the situation in these terms. A review of the research literature shows that the main focuses of educational researchers have traditionally been on the various factors that can affect students' achievements and the quality of learning (for example, ability grouping, teaching methods, and students' socioeconomic backgrounds); characteristics of the student subculture; and processes of interaction between teachers and students in the classroom.[14] That is, all these inquiries have taken individual students and individual teachers as the units of analysis. When interaction processes have been studied, they have usually been isolated in one or two classrooms abstracted from the total organizational context. Wayland has pointed out the importance of using the school as the unit of analysis if we are to understand the interaction processes within.[15] The interrelations of various subunits (like teachers and classroom situations) within this larger unit are of prime importance. In the past decade there has, however, been growing concern with new approaches to studying the schools as global units and investigating students and staff in this larger context. Conceptions of the school as a social organization and as a socializing agency have thus become very important in understanding norms and behavior of teachers. Indeed we must know the institutional contexts in which teachers work, in order to understand the pressures that impinge upon them.

THE DUALITY OF THE SCHOOL ORGANIZATION

The school consists of two major groups: the network of adults and the network of children. The adults enter individually into relations with the children. We may thus view the school as a combination of two systems: one in which adults are associated with one another and one in which teachers relate to children. We shall study the only group that participates in both these systems: teachers.

The school as both institution and social system operates on two levels: that of the classroom and that of the school as a whole. This duality may have important implications for the understanding of teachers' role in the social structure of the school. Recognition that the classroom is a subunit of the school is important in understanding the functioning of the school, but the duality still requires explanation.

In fact, there exist within the institution two separate social systems, that in the classroom and that outside the classroom, that coexist within the school. Each separate classroom is seen as a separate system. Each system has its own, self-contained patterning of interaction, its sets of behavioral norms, and its sets of structured interactions. But, although separate, the two systems do exert mutual influences through the only real link between them: the teachers.[16]

This duality and teachers' pivotal position may affect teachers' behavioral orientations toward both students and peers. First, teacher may have difficulty when the norms of the two systems differ. Second, they may take advantage of the divided school structure to insulate themselves from meaningful contact with students or, conversely, to insulate themselves from control, supervision, and influences originating outside the classroom among peers and supervisors. These possibilities bring us to the concept of visibility of performance.

VISIBILITY OF PERFORMANCE

Visibility of performance, or "observability," is the extent to which adherence to norms and role performances of group members is readily open to observation by others (status inferiors, peers, and status superiors). According to Merton, "Observability is conceived as a property of groups, it directs attention to the ways in which the structure of the group affects the input of information and the output (of response) which thereupon works to exert control."[17] We can ask how "visible" the group of students is to the group of teachers and vice versa.

Teachers' role performances, as well as established norms in the classroom, may have limited visibility among peers and supervisors, thus limiting the control of these groups over the classroom. If such role performances were to become observable to the peer group, we might expect greater control—and a greater tendency among teachers to conform to the norms of the peer group. Because teachers participate in two different systems of structured interaction, they may shift between alternative sets of behavior and norms, depending upon the context in which their performance is visible at any given time.

Our data have provided indicators of teachers' role performances, and we shall study how these performances are correlated with teachers' definition of context.

The concept of visibility is also very important in explaining the emergence and maintenance of a teachers' subculture, which may indeed imply the existence of an interaction process through which members reaffirm group norms and obtain reinforcement and reassurance in return. The subculture is another means of exerting control over the members of a group.

The degree of visibility is thus a major structural characteristic of any social system. Let us now turn to other structural characteristics within the schools. Perhaps the issue can be placed in clearer perspective through a more traditional organizational analysis of the schools.

The school is a special type of organization. It is a bureaucracy to the extent that it has a bureaucratic structure controlling the achievement of specified goals. It is also a socializing agency working to transform human material. And, finally, it is a professional organization, in that many staff members regard themselves as professionals. We shall first discuss the bureaucratic aspects of the school.

THE SCHOOL AS A BUREAUCRATIC ORGANIZATION

The school, like any other bureaucracy, is established according to norms of rationality. There are rules and standards to be followed and both functional and temporal (age-graded) division of labor; indeed, the school, like any producing firm, is geared to achieving a uniform product through a temporal sequence (lasting several years in the school). To attempt even minimal standardization of certified "products," the school must rely on certain routines and uniform criteria for assessing students' performances. Rationalization is thus essential to coordinate and standardize the various elements entering the school system, but its scope is limited by the variability of the human raw materials. Aside from the problem of variation in human "inputs" (that is, in students' characteristics), the school is not organized to deal with the problem of surplus students and has no capacity for "stockpiling products." Indeed, each year a number of students are released into the "market," and waves of new students enter the school, which makes it impossible to hold students at a particular level until they have met expected standards. Limited control over the types of entering students and over the time required to produce certain expected changes renders the school vulnerable and limits its capacity for rationalization.[18]

What are the implications of this structural feature for teachers' role performances and orientations toward students? One is the degree to which teachers must agree to follow standard procedures in evaluating students' performances, procedures that may not be congruent with their own evaluation criteria. To what extent do teachers follow norms of evaluation established by the administration when they seem inappropriate?

THE ROLE OF INTERPERSONAL RELATIONS IN SOCIAL ORGANIZATIONS

The importance of interpersonal relations may vary from one type of organization to another. In the schools interpersonal relations are very important in the achievement of stated goals. Both the bureaucratic organization and the teachers as a primary group operate to further the achievement of given goals. They are not necessarily alternative instruments in such achievement and may well act to complement each other. Litwak and Meyer have presented a typology of bureaucracies based on their theory of coordination between bureaucratic organizations and primary groups.[19] They describe four models of organizations, based on the relative importance of bureaucratic principles and interpersonal relations in achieving organizational goals. The first is called the "rationalistic model" and is characterized by impersonal social relations, detailed rules, a hierarchy of offices, division of labor, relatively unambiguous goals, standardization of tasks, and evaluation of performance based on merit. This type is most familiar in industry and corresponds to that described by Weber. The second model, called the "human-relations model," is dominated by personal social relations and general policies rather than detailed rules and procedures, colleagueship rather than hierarchical structures, broad definition of organizational goals, nonstandardized tasks, and evaluation of performances based on merit. This model has the opposite characteristics from the rationalistic model, except for the mode of evaluation, which is based on merit in both. The third model, the "professional model," incorporates both rationalistic and human-relations elements and occurs when goals dictate both standardized performances and performances requiring interpersonal skills. The fourth model, the "nonmerit model," is characterized by significant intrusion of bases other than merit in evaluation of personnel and performance, such as nepotism, personal friendship, class, race. In the last model there is emphasis on personal, rather than organizational, goals.

In terms of this typology, the school is an example of the professional model, for the bureaucratic organization (rational element) and the teacher as primary group (human-relations element) operate jointly to further the achievement of given goals.[20] The two groups function not as alternative, or incompatible, instruments but as complementary ones. However, at the classroom level, the nonmerit model may predominate. The ineffectiveness of merit as a basis for evaluation may stimulate evaluations based on personal friendship, religion, race, class, or similar factors that are themselves essential in the attainment of teachers' goals in the classroom. In ghetto schools the problem of professional versus bureaucratic orientations may lead to a large gap between the interpersonal factors and professional norms at the classroom level. The behavior of teachers in the classroom may bear little relation to either professional or bureaucratic principles in the school.

Although the classroom is not a self-contained organization but is rather part of the larger unit of the school, the relative importance of bureaucratic and human-relations elements is very different there. Furthermore, the functions of the "personal element" in the achievement of organizational goals may be quite different in the school and in the classroom. This distinction may be important to understanding the pressures of interpersonal norms and bureaucratic principles upon teachers.

The role of interpersonal relations, especially within the peer group, may vary, depending upon organizational structure and inclusion or exclusion of the peer group as a functioning instrument in the achievement of organizational goals. It seems that such organizations as therapeutic hospitals, prisons, and social-welfare agencies use professional peer groups in quite different ways.[21] For example, it seems that the peer group plays no recognized role in prison management, whereas it is explicitly designed to participate in attaining the goals of therapeutic hospitals. In welfare agencies, although the role of the professional peer group is not "official," it is acknowledged and used. In the schools it seems that so far the peer group has not been used to facilitate or promote educational outcomes. Teachers as a group have not yet been organized and defined as a working subunit within the school.

Abraham Zaleznik has shown the importance of interaction in defining a situation: "The management of interpersonal relations consists of establishing a definition and then maintaining it in the ongoing process. The concept or definition of a situation points to the process through which persons select and organize perception of reality as a basis for action."[22] The role of the peer group in an organization may or may not be included in the definition of the working situation and may or may not be functional in producing the organizational "output." On one hand, the peer group may be very important in deflecting the organization from achievement of its goals, thus supporting group members against organizational clients. On the other, the peer group may reinforce institutional norms and commitment to the organization itself. There is also a third possibility, for the peer group may provide a source of gratification in itself, divorced from possible organizational outcomes and from the clients whom the organization is designed to serve. The role of the peer group in an organization may thus have positive, negative, or neutral effects on outcomes.

In this research we shall be able to analyze the role of interpersonal relations, especially among peers, as it affects various aspects of teachers' work and orientation toward students. The role of the peer group may be affected by the dichotomy within the school organization, as has already been pointed out, and may even be a source of tension. Teachers in ghetto schools, because of stronger pressures,[23] may come to put more emphasis on the interpersonal aspects of their work and thus indirectly upon the total organization.

The professional and bureaucratic aspects of school organization are ill adapted to coping with the task of ghetto education. The gap between professional norms and the classroom behavior of teachers may be especially marked in ghetto schools, and we may therefore expect that in ghetto schools the effects of the two-part school organization will be aggravated.

Because interpersonal relations are very important factors in effecting organizational goals, they may be the source of conflicting orientations and values in schools. The teacher may be confronted with two different, sometimes incompatible, sets of demands, from the administration and from students. He must follow bureaucratic principles and use standardized procedures while engaged in particularized student-teacher relationships. These differing demands may create problems unless the scope of bureaucratic principles and impersonal norms is separated or specifically limited.

DISTRIBUTION OF POWER AND RESPONSIBILITY

We have pointed out that the school is also a "professional organization." In addition to the problem of bureaucratic and human-relations principles there are other problems linked with "the distribution of responsibility" in the schools. The concepts of structural looseness and professional autonomy must be defined before we proceed further. Structural looseness is the decentralization of a school's administration, so that the various subunits of the organization are not directly supervised by administrators.[24] Professional autonomy is the reservation of independent judgment to professional workers because of their expert skills and knowledge. As Lieberman has pointed out, "If there is no scope for independent judgment, there is no autonomy and no profession."[25]

The school is characterized by structural looseness and some autonomy of teachers, but the administration is responsible for the quality of the "product." It must provide the market with a certain number of "certified" graduates each year. Because of this responsibility, the administration will try to control the processes related to it. In addition to routine procedures and uniform standards, it may seek to increase its sphere of power and responsibility within the school. Bidwell has mentioned three mechanisms[26] through which the administration tries to impose its control: first, the interweaving of staff orientation with professional norms and local school politics, in order to maximize the commitment of teachers to the goals, methods, and procedures of the school; second, the establishment of standards for student achievement; and, third, increasing bureaucratization of school and classroom activities through imposition of rules that restrict the discretionary sphere of the classroom teacher (for example, less discretion in choosing teaching material for the classroom).

We can see how these mechanisms affect teachers' relations with their students and with peers. We may ask whether or not in ghetto schools these mechanisms are not mobilized intensively or more broadly in an attempt to cope with the severer problems of outcome and educational quality. Bidwell's third mechanism involves the loss of teachers' professional autonomy—a loss that undermines their professional role and that may occur frequently in ghetto schools, where teachers' roles are less well defined to begin with.*

Lieberman analyzed the relationship between the administration and teachers in their professional roles, showing that the teacher has

---

*This idea is discussed in detail later in this chapter.

become a salaried employee, which has led to domination by administrative personnel rather than by professional practitioners:

> The dilemma confronting almost every profession is whether its members shall concentrate on strictly professional works and lose their power to direct it, or learn administration so as to be able to remain in control of it, thus losing the time to practice it.[27]

The tendency to place responsibility for the quality of professional service upon the administration undermines the right of teachers to make professional judgments vis-à-vis their students. The principal, who represents the administration, becomes simultaneously a source of threat to teachers and a source of support for them, for he can use his increasing power within the school to help them or not, to defend them against students and parents or not.[28]

So far we have discussed aspects of the relations between teachers and the principal, who represents the authority structure in the school. We also have gathered data on teachers' perception of the principal's role and whether or not he seems important to them. The role of the principal in schools of varying SES has also been studied by Herriot and St. John.[29] Our data will permit us to see the perceived role and importance of the principal in ghetto schools of varying kinds. We shall study the various functions of the principal in the view of teachers. The relations between principals and teacher are also based upon structural characteristics of the school, especial the two levels of social organization within it.

INDIVIDUAL MODES OF ADAPTATION IN THE SCHOOLS

Teachers' striving for autonomy and a share in control of the school can be viewed as an individual mode of adaptation to the working situation, as a mechanism for coping with problems, based on the structural characteristics of the school and affecting the functioning of the organization and, indirectly, teachers' level of job satisfaction. In our data we have measured both autonomy and the degree of teache participation in decision-making on the operation of the school. We shall analyze how these variables affect relations with the supervisor and how these relations in turn affect levels of teachers' job satisfaction.

Admitting teachers to participation in running the school has bee described by Lieberman as a subtle technique by which the administration gains control of them and compensates them for their loss of autonomy, or perhaps even covers up such a loss:

> When cooperation and participation in the schools occur in a situation characterized by vagueness and ambiguity as to teachers' professional responsibility and autonomy, it degenerates into euphemisms for polite coercion and manipulation.[30]

We can ask the question, Does teachers' participation in running the school reinforce the roles of the peer group and the principal within the school, and, if so, what are the possible consequences for teachers' orientations toward students? We shall also study how autonomy and participation affect job satisfaction in schools with different types of students.

So far we have described and analyzed some of the structural characteristics of the schools and the problems arising from them: duality of the school organization and its consequences for teachers, interpersonal norms and bureaucratic principles, and tensions between professional and institutional orientations.

THE GROUP OF STUDENTS VERSUS THE GROUP OF TEACHERS

We have noted the existence of two main groups within the school: students and teachers. Unlike many organizations the school lacks intermediaries between the two groups, which therefore confront each other directly. At the level of the school as a whole the teacher is a member of a group of colleagues, or peers, with whom he shares experiences and from whom he may receive support in his confrontations with students. How are teachers affected by the student body? At the level of the total school unit the two groups face each other with different, if not conflicting, sets of goals, interests, and demands. Waller has described in detail the generally hostile relations between the two groups:

> Teacher and pupil confront each other with attitudes from which the underlying hostility can never be altogether removed. Pupils are the material in which teachers are supposed to produce results. Pupils are human beings striving to realize themselves in their own spontaneous manner, striving to produce their own results in their own way. Each of these hostile parties stands in the way of the other; in so far as the aims of either are realized, it is at the sacrifices of the aims of the other.[31]

Students as a group may thus be very threatening to teachers as a group. If Waller's observation is valid for American elementary schools in general, then it may be particularly so for ghetto schools. The primary relations between teachers and students actually occur in the classroom in day-to-day interaction, however. And in the classroom the teacher must deal with students alone.

We turn now to analysis of the system within the classroom and to the various adjustment mechanisms that may affect teachers' job satisfaction.

Let us first analyze the nature of the relations between students and teachers in the classroom. How are teachers affected by the types of students that they teach? The nature of student-teacher relations is affected by the characteristics of the student population, which is nonvoluntary and not self-selected. The different processes or recruitment and entry studied by Wheeler, Bidwell, and Wayland[32] suggest that students' participation in the schools is foreign to their own preference, whereas teachers adopt their roles voluntarily.

Waller has shown that in the eyes of children teachers represent the adult world, which imposes a formal curriculum upon children, and they also represent the established order in the school.[33]

In a study of high schools, Gordon[34] found evidence of considerable classroom conflict centering on the incompatibility of teachers' demands and students' desires. Moreover, Gordon found that the penetration of the "students' society" in the classroom affected the balance of power between teachers and students and pushed teachers from reliance on the authority of the office to reliance on the force of personal and affective processes of interaction with students. In this case the priority given to personal and affective ties in the student-teacher relationship springs from the inability to put forward and to perform one's own professional role.

The role of personal relations and the creation of affective bonds between the teachers and the students is made difficult, however because of the authority component of the relation. The frequency of interaction between the teachers and the students does not necessarily increase nor lead to the creation of intimate types of relationships. As Homans put it, "The interaction is kept down to the amount needed for business."[35]

The links that are created between teachers and students have also been referred to in terms of property rights, by McPherson:

"The relationship between superior and subordinate calls for sentiments resembling those attached to property in the sense of exclusive control, jealousy of interference, pride in possession and display."[36]

Despite what Waller describes as the "basic hostility" between teachers and students, according to McPherson teachers may develop forms of emotional attachments to and control over students.[37] Both writers may be correct, for it is possible that teachers respond to students' hostility with heavier reliance upon emotional processes of control than upon their legitimate authority in the classroom, thus minimizing the professional aspects of their role. Relations may develop in this way because of teachers' belief that their students, in some sense their possessions, must conform to expectations.[38] Paradoxically, an emotional bond, involving both like and dislike, may thus grow from impersonal, even hostile, roots and may serve as a channel of control over students.

The survey on which this study is based did not include data on processes of interaction within the classroom, but we do have information on teachers' perceptions and evaluations of their relations with students. Knowing the characteristics of the students, including their social backgrounds and levels of achievement in the classroom, we can analyze the extent to which teachers shaped the interaction on their own terms. We shall study whether or not teachers' perceptions of students reflected their own job satisfaction and to what extent types of students affected this variable.

Many studies have shown that students with different backgrounds do indeed relate to teachers differently and have varying attitudes toward school. Coleman has demonstrated that students from different social classes have different attitudes toward schools and teachers and different levels of motivation and achievement. He has emphasized that children's reports of items in their homes, an indicator of socioeconomic levels, were more related to achievement among blacks than in any other group.[39]

Becker, in his study of social-class variations in teacher-student relations, has described the behavior and attitudes toward work of those who taught pupils from different social classes.[40] Students from both the upper-middle and lower classes were more difficult to deal with than students from the middle class, who were generally more docile, obedient, and disciplined. Students from the upper-middle class were perceived as independent, arrogant, and not hard-working. Students from the lower class and most "slum" children were perceived as more violent, lacking in manners and discipline, less motivated to work, and often uninterested in school. Becker has also reported that teachers in Chicago preferred to teach middle-class children. Slum and lower-class students in particular were regarded as threatening to teachers and unrewarding to teach. In another study Becker has shown that teachers assigned to poor areas sought transfers to "better" schools with middle-class "clienteles."[41] Herriot and St. John have shown that teachers in middle-class schools were more likely to be very satisfied with their jobs than were teachers in lower-class schools.[42]

Wayson has studied the explicit motives that impel some teachers to remain in slum schools.[43] The image of "dangerous" slum children that we have described contrasts with his description of pupils and their relations with teachers in slum schools. He found that teachers in slum schools frequently perceived their students as warm, affectionate, and appreciative and that they enjoyed intimate expressions of personal esteem from their pupils. These teachers doubted that students in higher-status neighborhoods would be as responsive. Wayson listed various types of reasons that teachers gave for staying or leaving slum schools. The second most important reason for staying was personal esteem from the students. The desire for personal recognition may thus be especially important to teachers in slum schools.

What we said earlier about the affective bonds between teachers and students can be linked with teachers' perceptions of their role vis-à-vis students. Wayson reported that teachers who stayed in slum schools were more appreciative of the students and more likely to perceive their roles as encompassing more than the mere transmission of knowledge. Those who chose to stay were likely to say things like, "I'm not only a teacher; I'm also a social worker, a mother, a policeman, a fireman—everything at once." Those who chose to leave tended to reject a broader role.[44]

THE "DEFENSIVE" SUBCULTURE

So far we have described the school as a social organization, emphasizing its duality and the effects on various aspects of its functioning. We have suggested the problems and tensions linked with structural characteristics of the school and the types of clients that the school served and have noted various modes of individual adaptation at both the school and classroom level.

There are also modes of social adaptation, that is, changes effected in the social structure of the school in order to allay anxieties connected with the teachers' role. All teachers in a school share similar stresses and types of experiences, though to different degrees. They participate in interaction within the school and have ways of communicating to one another their experiences and feelings. These facts have led us to look for a possible teachers' subculture, developed to cope with certain kinds of problems, especially the existence of a "society of students." We most probably shall find collective responses to problems arising from teachers' relations with students.

But first we shall explore the concept of subculture and see how it may be applied to teachers. It should be borne in mind that we are using survey data; we are therefore prevented from studying day-to-day interactions involving teachers, but we can discern certain symptoms and outcomes of the subculture. McPherson has given us a great deal of information on the dynamics of teachers' subculture.[45] Because of the nature of our data, then, we shall use the concept of subculture as an analytical tool to clarify patterns found in our analysis. We shall see it as an inferred process stemming from our findings and helping us to understand them.

A subculture is a set of norms, values, and behavior patterns shared by members of a group and distinguishing them as a group within the community or the society. The general conditions for creation of a subculture were explored by Cohen[46] in his study of the subculture of a gang. He defined a subculture as a problem-solving mechanism, a collective effort by actors in the same situation and under the same pressures to adjust and adapt to the problems confronting them.

The types of subcultures and their specific features that can exist in a single society are numerous and varied, but the conditions under which they emerge are limited. Cohen thought that the two main conditions for the emergence of a subculture were effective interaction among its members and shared pressures calling for similar processes of adaptation: "The crucial condition for the emergence of new cultural forms is <u>the existence, in effective interaction with one another, of a number of actors with similar problems of adjustment</u>."[47]

Cohen noted that when several participants in an interaction process are confronted with the same problems, they will gradually evolve group norms, values, and behavior patterns to satisfy their common expectations and demands.[48] The street gang develops when the group of boys does not receive recognition from society or does not share the values and norms of that society; through the gang subculture, members can attain status within the group. Indeed, status problems are largely problems of achieving respect in the eyes of one's peers. If status cannot be achieved in the framework of the larger society, then the only way to achieve it is through elaboration of new sets of norms and values that provide the individual with a new frame of reference shared by others in similar positions. In fact, it may happen that members of a society or group are insecure or dissatisfied <u>as a group</u> with their status in the community or society. One mode of collective adaptation is for individuals who share such problems to "gravitate toward one another and jointly establish new criteria of status, new norms which define as meritorious the characteristics that they do possess and the kinds of conduct of which they are capable."[49]

Semiprofessionals may find that the social class of their clientele "threatens" their own status. For example, welfare workers[50] and policemen who deal with lower-class or ghetto clientele may experience a threat to status because those with whom they deal tend to be less "self-selected" than clients in other milieus—less willing to conform to the official doctrines and expectations of semiprofessionals' training.[51] This often means that semiprofessionals in contact with such clients are led to widen the repertoire of their behavior involved in their work. In turn this may result in vagueness and uncertainty of role definition that threatens the sense of professional status based on official doctrine.

Niederhoffer has furnished insights into the subculture of police, noting that policemen assigned to lower-class areas tend to relinquish professional ethics and norms. Faced with the multiplicity of tasks expected of them, policemen tend to become increasingly pragmatic and less interested in maintaining professional norms. Contacts with a "hostile" clientele also lead to increased solidarity among patrolmen. The greatest satisfactions from police work are based on good relations with peers.[52] Policemen soon develop a complex of rituals, terms and linguistic expressions, and behavior codes that permit them continually to reaffirm their values and to find reassurance among themselves. Each one benefits from sharing these norms, which persist as long as the pressures that have generated them continue.

The young policeman, when first assigned to a lower-class or slum area, experiences "reality shock"—that is, the demoralizing effect upon workers of the discrepancies between their idealistic expectation and reality. It may lead either to such disenchantment that the worker chooses to leave the occupation or to a series of adaptations and adjustments designed to help him cope with job problems. The rookie policeman generally begins with faith in the system and tries to follow the rules and regulations. Then he experiences repercussions not mentioned in the rule book. He is chided by his colleagues for having been so naive as to "follow the book" in the first place.[53] The rookie who remains on the force becomes quickly socialized to the norms of the peer group.

The same process occurs among welfare workers. The beginner is idealistic and unaware of the written and unwritten norms and regulations within the agency. He is also anxious and insecure in dealing with clients. During his first contacts with clients, the beginner too experiences reality shock, which may encourage detachment from clients. Blau has shown that caseworkers begin with strong interest in clients and find some satisfaction with relations with them but that this interest declines and a negative attitude toward clients may appear after several years; but interest may reappear once the workers have acquired enough experience or enough support from their peers to reduce their insecurity.[54]

Reality shock is thus usually temporary for the caseworker. If he remains in the agency he may adapt to the situation by becoming less client-oriented and more peer-oriented. Contacts with clients then become less emotionally threatening. The importance of the peer group in reducing the insecurity of caseworkers is crucial. Friendly relations with colleagues are a source of support.

> Peer group support served to absorb some of the impact of reality shock. The unintegrated worker without such social support, experienced the full force of the reality shock which constrained him to shield his ego by developing a hardened attitude toward clients.[55]

Comparing the effects of experience and of good relations with peers upon caseworkers' orientations toward the agency, Blau noted that experience increases workers' ability to deal with clients while reducing interest in them, whereas good relations with peers increase both concern and ability to deal with clients.

What Blau has described is really the subculture of a group of welfare workers within an agency and the mechanisms linked with it that assist its members in coping with job problems arising from status insecurity.

We have seen under what conditions a subculture emerges and have described some aspects and functions of semiprofessional subcultures. We turn now to application of the concept as an analytic tool, in connection with our study of teachers. First, we note that the preconditions for a subculture are generally present in schools. Teachers do interact in similar milieus and under similar pressures; as we have already seen, they experience role and status insecurity, linked with the structural characteristics of their schools. These pressures, although of the same nature, may vary in intensity with different types of schools and other conditions. For example, teachers working with the lowest track in a low-SES school in Washington, D.C., may have been under greater pressure than were those teaching the highest tracks in high-SES schools. Teachers, like welfare workers and policemen, respond collectively to pressures and evolve norms for coping with professional problems and preserving their professional status, as McPherson has shown:

> Because teachers are constantly dogged by the conviction of failure and by their inability to measure whether or not their methods lead to or away from their goals, . . . they rationalize or create group norms which will provide mutual support and adjustment to the situation.[56]

The existence of a subculture has been described through participant observation by McPherson, Wayson, and Willower.[57] Let us now describe some of the findings. We shall show how teachers rationalize (in the psychological sense) certain professional norms and shall analyze how this process affects job satisfaction and orientation toward students. The perception by teachers that standards are kept and that curriculums meet the needs of deprived children will be studied in connection with teachers' relations with peers. Teachers were asked whether or not they thought that, in their schools, standards were set for the able and whether or not they believed that needs of educationally deprived students were being fulfilled. We shall study how teachers' perceptions of these standards were affected by types of students, as well as by their relationship with peers.

McPherson has given other examples of the functioning of a teachers' subculture. For example, she has examined the role of discipline in the school. Discipline is part of what is called by Willower "onstage behavior" by teachers,[58] behavior that is visible to the peer group. McPherson has argued that onstage behavior, and especially application of disciplinary measures, outside the classroom, offers a means of securing other teachers' approval and enhancing one's self-image. The use of discipline reinforces teachers' mutual support and sense of group membership. Discipline thus may not be only a means of keeping order; it may also be a value for group members.[59] As Waller had already pointed out, "Discipline is a phenomenon of group life. It depends upon a collective opinion."[60]

The role of the peer group is fundamental to teachers' job satisfaction. According to McPherson, "At Adams the teacher turns to colleagues for direction, socialization, support and definition of standards."[61] In addition to providing a common frame of reference and focusing an identity of interests, the peer group exercises some control over new teachers. Reality shock also occurs among teachers, who begin with certain expectations about students, colleagues, and their own performance. Willower, doing a participant observation in a school, has remarked on the importance of the "old guard" in socializing young teachers to the norms of the group.[62] Young teachers at first experience a sense of failure when their expectations are not met, but as they come under the informal control and supervision of older teachers, they adapt their expectations and values in order to receive support and recognition. As an example, Willower mentioned the emphasis in teacher training upon permissive attitudes toward students, which shifts to a more custodial emphasis as teachers are absorbed into the subculture.[63] Similar findings have been reported by McPherson.[64]

Reliance on discipline, toughness, and expectations of hard work from students are thus all part of the teachers' subculture,[65] itself a collective response by teachers to working problems. This response may well involve displacement of the main source of satisfaction from students to peers. A subculture is created in response to pressures on, or status insecurity among, members of a group; we have used the socioeconomic levels of the schools and the tracks in which respondents were teaching as indicators of pressures and strains. We can thus determine whether or not variations in pressures in ghetto schools are associated with greater emphasis on peers and whether or not the existence of a subculture in these schools has especially pervasive effects upon teachers' attitudes. Indeed our review of the literature suggests that the special importance of peer culture may be a distinctive aspect of the "confrontation" between professionals and semiprofessionals, on one hand, and their ghetto "clientele," on the other.

A finding by Herriot and St. John on the effects of SES of the student body upon the role of the peer group is relevant to our research.[66] They discovered that teachers in the lower-SES schools were more likely to be satisfied with opportunities to associate with other professionals than were teachers in the higher-SES schools. Teachers in low-SES schools apparently placed importance upon the satisfaction obtained through interpersonal relations among peers. We may wonder whether, in a parallel to the police, teachers in low-SES schools are more likely to be peer-oriented and more likely to be oriented toward the school.

SUMMARY AND CONCLUSIONS

The importance of the concept of subculture is as a frame of reference for analysis of peer-group dynamics. The influence of the peer group can be functional or dysfunctional in the achievement of organizational goals: It can lead to collective solutions of problems of status insecurity and thus facilitate operation of an organization, but the peer group may simultaneously become in itself a source of gratification and thus fail to aid teachers in coping with work problems. The study of teachers' subculture should include both its functional and dysfunctional aspects.

In this chapter we have described some of the structural characteristics of the school, particularly in the dichotomy within its organization, the possible tensions between professional and institutional norms at both school and classroom levels, and the confrontation between students and teachers as groups. All these factors may contribute to status and role insecurity among teachers. In response, teachers may evolve both individual and collective modes of adaptation to help them cope with work problems. Individual modes of adaptation may reflect teachers' desire for success in the classroom and acceptance by students. Collective modes, including what Cohen has called a "problem-solving subculture," involve sources of reciprocal support within the group in order to preserve the status and role of teachers as a group. The socialization of new teachers to the norms of the group is very important in the maintenance of the subculture.

Having analyzed the school as a social organization and having introduced the concept of subculture as an aid to understanding the mechanisms operating within the school, we may ask again the question with which we started: How can we explain that a great majority of elementary-school teachers in Washington, D.C., were satisfied with their jobs, though only a minority wished to remain teachers? From our discussion it seems that interpersonal relations within the school and the teachers' subculture may well account for this phenomenon. "The society of other teachers," to use Waller's term, may be much more important in affecting teachers' job satisfaction and career plans than their relations with students and the types of students whom they teach. Indeed, in the school that is mainly centered on children, "the society of teachers" seems to offer teachers the opportunity for acceptance on their own terms. Again, to quote Waller "the teacher group comes to constitute a close-knit in-group, a fellowship."[67]

Another answer to the questions was given by an elementary-school teacher, who described her job in the following terms: "I like everything about teaching except the kids."[68] Much of what follows in this book may be considered an exploration of the implications of this remark in the special and significant context of a segregated urban-ghetto school system. The special circumstances that the segregated school system under investigation, that of Washington, D.C., is staffed almost wholly by black teachers will enable us to see whether or not racial differences and ties between teachers and students are themselves significant factors affecting school functioning.

NOTES

1. Robert A. Dentler, Major American Social Problems (Chicago Rand McNally, 1967), Chapters 1, 3.

2. Gertrude McPherson, "The Role Set of Elementary School Teachers" (unpublished Ph.D. dissertation, Columbia University, 1966); W. William Wayson, "Expressed Motives of Teachers in Slum Schools" (unpublished Ph.D. dissertation, University of Chicago, 1966)

Peter Blau, The Dynamics of Bureaucracy: A Study of Interpersonal Relations in Two Government Agencies (Chicago: University of Chicago Press, 1955).

3. Sam D. Sieber, "The Integration of Field Methods and Survey Research" (mimeo., New York, Columbia University, 1969).

4. Blau, Dynamics of Bureaucracy; F. J. Roethlisberg and William J. Dickson, Management and the Worker (Cambridge: Harvard University Press, 1939); Samuel A. Stouffer et al., The American Soldier (Princeton, N.J.: Princeton University Press, 1949); Seymour M. Lipset, Martin Trow, and James Coleman, Union Democracy (Glencoe, Ill.: The Free Press, 1956).

5. Ward S. Mason, The Beginning Teacher: Status and Career Orientations, Final Report on the Survey of New Teachers in the Public Schools 1956-57, Office of Education Circular No. 644 (Washington, D.C.: Government Printing Office, 1961), pp. 79-95.

6. Peter S. Rossi et al., "Between White and Black: The Faces of American Institutions in the Ghetto," Supplemental Studies for the National Advisory Commission on Civil Disorders (Washington, D.C.: Government Printing Office, 1968), pp. 133-45.

7. James Coleman, Equality of Educational Opportunity (Washington D.C.: Government Printing Office, 1966), p. 352.

8. Frederick L. Redefer, "Factors That Affect Teacher Morale," Nation's Schools, Vol. 63, February 1959, pp. 59-62.

9. Coleman, Equality of Educational Opportunity, p. 352.

10. Alvin W. Gouldner, "The Norm of Reciprocity: A Preliminary Statement," American Sociological Review, Vol. 25, No. 2, 1960, pp. 161-76.

11. Mason, Beginning Teacher, p. 102.

12. Coleman, Equality of Educational Opportunity, p. 153.

13. Anna Lee Hopson and David E. Wilder, A Study of Teachers in the Public Schools of Washington, D.C.: (New York: Bureau of Applied Social Research, Columbia University, 1967), p. 153.

14. Sam D. Sieber, Memoranda on Educational Research (New York: Bureau of Applied Social Research, Columbia University, 1966).

15. R. Sloan Wayland, "The Context of Innovation: Some Organizational Characteristics of Schools" (unpublished manuscript).

16. William Waller, The Sociology of Teaching (New York: Wiley, 1932), pp. 7-13.

17. Robert K. Merton, Social Theory and Social Structure (rev. ed.; New York: The Free Press, 1957), pp. 319-23.

18. Stanton Wheeler, "The Structure of Formally Organized Socialization Settings," in Orville Brim and Stanton Wheeler, eds., Socialization After Childhood: Two Essays (New York: John Wiley & Sons, 1967), pp. 83-89.

19. Eugene Litwak and H. J. Meyer, "Bureaucratic and Primary Groups," Administrative Science Quarterly, Vol. 2, June 1966, pp. 31-58.

20. Stanton Wheeler, "Organizational Goals and Social Structure," in Brim and Wheeler, eds., Socialization After Childhood, p. 69.

21. Charles Perrow, "Hospitals: Technology, Structure and Goals," in James March and A. Simon, eds., Handbook of Organizations (Chicago: Rand McNally, 1965), pp. 910-66; Richard A. Cloward et al., Theoretical Studies in Social Organization of the Prison, pamphlet No. 15 (New York: Social Science Research Council, March 1960); Erving Goffman, Asylums: Essays on the Social Situation of Mental Patients and Other Inmates (New York: Doubleday, 1961); Blau, Dynamics of Bureaucracy, pp. 99-142.

22. Abraham Zaleznik, "Interpersonal Relations in Organizations in March and Simon, eds., Handbook of Organizations, pp. 574-614.

23. See Chapter 2 for the definition of pressures.

24. Charles E. Bidwell, "The School as a Formal Organization," in March and Simon, eds., Handbook of Organizations, pp. 1008-10.

25. Myron Lieberman, Education as a Profession (Englewood Cliffs, N.J.: Prentice-Hall, 1956), pp. 481-94.

26. Bidwell, "School as a Formal Organization."

27. Lieberman, Education as a Profession, p. 484.

28. Howard S. Becker, "Social Class Variation in the Teacher-Pupil Relationship," Journal of Educational Sociology, Vol. 25, 1952, pp. 456-61.

29. Robert E. Herriot and Nancy Hoyt St. John, Social Class and the Urban Schools (New York: John Wiley & Sons, 1966), pp. 141-45.

30. Lieberman, Education as a Profession, p. 487.

31. Waller, Sociology of Teaching, p. 196.

32. Wheeler, "Structure of Formally Organized Socialization Setting," pp. 75-79; Bidwell, "School as a Formal Organization"; Wayland, "Context of Innovation."

33. Waller, Sociology of Teaching, p. 196.

34. C. W. Gordon, "The Role of the Teacher in the Social Structure of the High School," Journal of Educational Sociology, Vol. 26 1955, pp. 21-29, reprinted in Gordon, The Social System of the High School (Glencoe, Ill.: The Free Press, 1957).

35. George Homans, The Human Group (New York: Harcourt, Brace & World, 1950), p. 124.

36. McPherson, "Role Set of Elementary School Teachers," p. 280.

37. Ibid.

38. Ibid.

39. Coleman, Equality of Educational Opportunity, p. 302.

40. Becker, "Social Class Variation in Teacher-Pupil Relationship," pp. 453-56.

41. Howard S. Becker, "The Career of the Chicago Public-School Teacher," American Journal of Sociology, Vol. 57, 1952, pp. 470-77.

42. Herriot and St. John, Social Class and the Urban Schools, pp. 88-91.

43. William W. Wayson, "Expressed Motives of Teachers in Slum Schools" (unpublished Ph.D. dissertation, University of Chicago, 1966).

44. Ibid.

45. McPherson, "Role Set of Elementary School Teachers," pp. 213-97.

46. Albert Cohen, Delinquent Boys: The Culture of the Gang (New York: The Free Press, 1961), pp. 49-72.

47. Ibid., p. 59.

48. Ibid., pp. 49-72.

49. Ibid., p. 66.

50. W. Richard Scott, "Professional Employees in a Bureaucratic Structure," in Amitai Etzioni, ed., The Semi-Professions and Their Organization: Teachers, Nurses, Social Workers (New York: The Free Press, 1969), pp. 82-140.

51. Arthur Niederhoffer, Behind the Shield: The Police in an Urban City (New York: Doubleday, 1967), p. 54; Blau, The Dynamics of Bureaucracy, pp. 82-95; Peter Blau, "Orientation Toward Clients in a Public Welfare Agency," Administrative Science Quarterly, No. 3, 1960, pp. 341-61.

52. Niederhoffer, Behind the Shield, pp. 59-89.

53. Ibid., pp. 49-50.

54. Blau, "Orientation Toward Clients," pp. 347-51.

55. Ibid., pp. 354-55.

56. McPherson, "Role Set of Elementary School Teachers," p. 499.

57. Ibid.; Wayson; "Expressed Motives of Teachers in Slum Schools"; Donald Willower, "Teachers' Subculture and Curriculum Change," ERIC File ED 020588 (New York, Teachers College Library, Columbia University), faculty seminar, Temple University.

58. Willover, "Teachers' Subculture and Curriculum Change."

59. McPherson, "Role Set of Elementary School Teachers," p. 175.

60. Waller, Sociology of Teaching, p. 198.

61. McPherson, "Role Set of Elementary School Teachers," pp. 211-12.

62. Willover, "Teachers' Subculture and Curriculum Change," pp. 4-7.

63. *Ibid.*

64. McPherson, "Role Set of Elementary School Teachers," pp. 197-210.

65. Donald Willover, "The School and Pupil Control Ideology," *Pennsylvania State Studies*, No. 24.

66. Herriot and St. John, *Social Class and the Urban Schools*, p. 93.

67. Waller, *Sociology of Teaching*, p. 56.

68. McPherson, "Role Set of Elementary School Teachers," p. 484.

CHAPTER

4

TEACHERS' SOCIAL BACKGROUND AND PROFESSIONAL CHARACTERISTICS: THEIR RELATION TO JOB SATISFACTION AND COMMITMENT TO TEACHING

In this chapter we shall describe the backgrounds and social characteristics of black teachers in the Washington, D.C., elementary school system and analyze the ways in which they are related to the teachers' job satisfaction and commitment to teaching.

In order to understand and analyze teachers' professional roles in the schools, we must take into account three sets of factors. The first is associated with teachers' professional and nonprofessional characteristics. The second is the social structure within the school and the teachers' part in it. The third is the characteristics of the school and especially of the students that it serves. All these factors affect teachers' professional roles, job satisfaction, and commitment to teaching.

In this chapter we shall deal with the first set of factors; in subsequent chapters the other variables will be examined, and the interconnections among all three will be analyzed.

CHARACTERISTICS OF THE BLACK ELEMENTARY-SCHOOL TEACHERS IN THE WASHINGTON, D.C., SYSTEM

The backgrounds of teachers are important to the extent that they may have varying effects on teachers' job satisfaction and commitment to teaching, especially when middle-class black teachers are confronted by lower-class black students. Indeed, teachers' attitudes toward students, their educational philosophies, and their values may be affected by their social origins.

Various authors have studied the impact of background upon various aspects of the teaching profession in general. Charters gave information about nonoccupational statuses of teachers: sex, age, marital status, community of origin, social-class origin, religion, and race.[1] He noted that the modal American teacher in the late 1950s was a married woman between the ages of 46 and 55 and that a great majority of American teachers came from small towns, whic lent a provincial cast to the profession. The parochial outlook of American teachers was also studied by Cook and Cook.[2] Studies of teachers' social origins have been included in broader studies of teachers in various communities or regions. For example, in 1937 White showed that more than half his sample of elementary- and secondary-school teachers in Texas were upwardly mobile.[3] The teaching profession is still an important avenue of social mobility.

The studies done about teachers' background characteristics yield different and sometimes contradictory results. Indeed, the location, type of school system investigated, and time of research may introduce variations. For example the studies done by L. Warn and his group around 1911 in medium-sized communities found that the great majority of the teachers were of middle-class origin.[4] Coffman reported that in his studies done in the same period 52 perc of the nation's teachers came from farm families.[5] Among studies done more recently in large urban centers, one by Wattenberg in 195 shows that among 198 teachers from Detroit 29 percent of those teaching taking in-service training had fathers from unskilled or sen skilled families.[6]

It seems that among teachers' demographic and background characteristics there is much more variability than commonly expec The difference between urban versus rural, between small and medi sized towns and large urban centers, may be significant in understanding these variations.

In the case of black teachers, the problems become even more difficult because of the lack of information about the background of black teachers in different school systems. No analysis of the social backgrounds of black teachers based on a large sample exists.

Because of the difficulties in comparing the findings of teacher background characteristics and of elementary-school teachers in an urban setting with other studies and because of the lack of informati about black teachers on a nation-wide basis or large samples of blac teachers, in this section we will compare the black teachers with the white teachers of the Washington, D.C., school system. We are not doing a comparative study of black and white teachers. We use whit teachers as a point of comparison and only as it helps to show the specific characteristics of black teachers.

The present study gives us the opportunity to study a large group of black teachers in an urban setting. How do their social characteristics differ from those of white teachers and those of the "average American teacher"? Teaching has become a largely female occupation, but it was a male occupation up to the middle of the nineteenth century, when the proportion of males began gradually to decline until in the 1920s it reached its low, 14 percent. The "feminization" of the profession is partly owing to the possibility of reentry after a prolonged absence without the necessity of any additional training or information, women's acceptance of lower salaries than men would accept, the widespread supposition that education of young children is the "natural realm" of women, the increasing importance of the middle classes in a mass society, a desire to supplement family incomes, and the growing proportion of college-educated women in the population. We shall first examine how the social and economic backgrounds of teachers are related to this "feminization" of the professions. Among black teachers in the Washington, D.C., elementary school system 84.5 percent are female and 15.5 percent male. Among whites the proportion of females is even higher, 89.5 percent. A national sample taken in 1960 revealed that 83 percent of all teachers were women. There was little difference between blacks and whites in this respect. Washington's black teachers are, however, generally younger than the white teachers: 71 percent are under 40, compared with 46 percent of white teachers. Throughout the country the average age of teachers was 40 years in 1960 and that for black teachers was between 31 (for men) and 35 (for women).

The distribution of teachers according to age reveals varying patterns of departure from and reentry into the profession. (See Table 4. 1.) The highest percentages of white teachers are at the two extremes of the distribution: in the group less than 25 years old and in the group 56 and more years old. Between these extremes each progressively older group has a lower percentage of members up to the age of 40; then the percentage gradually increases again. Apparently white teachers enter the profession when they are young and unmarried or at least have not yet had children. As teachers marry and have children (a function of age), they generally stop teaching until the children have grown up; then they reenter the profession. This pattern, of course, is that of the female teacher who is not the main wage-earner of her household and whose income is mostly a supplement to that of her husband, making possible a greater share in the products available to society.

Is the same pattern characteristic of the black teachers? The distribution in Table 4.1 suggests not. Black teachers do not seem to reenter the profession after prolonged absences. The percentage of teachers entering the profession increases until about the age of 35 and then gradually diminishes without ever increasing again. How can we interpret this pattern? Does it reflect basic differences between black and white life-styles, different social and economic

TABLE 4.1

Age of Elementary-School Teachers
(percent)

Age	Blacks	Whites
Less than 25 years	12	17
26-30	20	11
31-35	22	10
36-40	15	7
41-45	11	8
46-50	8	11
51-55	6	12
56 and more	5	20
No answer	1	2
Total	100	98*
	(N=2,452)	(N=505)

*Less than 100 percent because of rounding.

realities? Black teachers are younger than white teachers, and they tend to marry earlier. But, among black teachers, getting married or having children does not mean retirement from teaching. We thus come to the question, Are black female teachers the main breadwinne of their families? If they are, then they cannot stop teaching and deprive their families of their main incomes. (The continuation of teaching is made possible by the existence of family and neighborhoo ties.) Our data do not provide direct information on the incomes of these teachers' husbands or on whether or not the teachers are the main sources of income in their families. But we can compare total family income and teacher's income. Family-income figures for bot black teachers and white married teachers are given in Table 4.2. Some difference is apparent. White teachers are more likely to have annual family incomes above $15,000 than are black teachers. Becau there is little difference between teaching salaries for blacks and whites, we may well conclude that higher family incomes among whit mean that husbands are the main breadwinners in these white familie the teaching income may be mainly supplemental for these families. For black teachers the picture is different. We may therefore say that the economic function of teaching is different for blacks and whites.[7]

TABLE 4.2

Total Family Income of
Married Teachers, by Race
(percent)

Family Income	Black Teachers	White Teachers
Less than $10,000	31	35
$10,000-$14,999	40	25
$15,000 and more	29	40
Total	100	100
	(N=2,068)	(N=430)

The age variable is important in our data for two additional reasons. First, comparing older teachers to younger teachers may reveal some intergenerational changes in educational values and general value orientation among teachers. For example, Are young teachers more permissive, more innovative, less elitist, and less academically minded than older teachers? If so, how do these attitudes affect their orientations toward students? Second, age is also related to knowledge and "professionalization." Young teachers may believe that their familiarity with new techniques and current research justifies their wanting to innovate more and makes them better qualified to deal with children than are older teachers. The latter, however, assume the superiority of experience. The role of the "old guard" has been studied by various authors.[8] It is very important in socializing young teachers to the behavior norms of the schools. The relation between older and younger teachers may be a source of tension in the schools.

In this research, however, we will not investigate these matters. Despite the suggestive aspects of age as a measure of such changes, the lack of panel data would introduce excessive ambiguities.

THE TEACHING PROFESSION AS A CHANNEL FOR SOCIAL MOBILITY

The social origins of teachers and the use of the profession as a social ladder are different for white and black teachers. The middle-class origins of most white teachers have been noted by Lloyd Warner,[9] who estimated that 94 percent of American teachers were born into the middle class. Mason showed from 1955 U.S. Census data that among beginning teachers 77 percent came from white-collar families, 19 percent from blue-collar families, and 4 percent from farm families.[10] A study of occupational trends by the U.S. Bureau of the Census yielded the following figures for 1960: Of teachers working in large urban districts 57 percent came from white-collar backgrounds, 34 percent from blue-collar backgrounds, and 8 percent from farms. In social origins black schoolteachers in Washington, D.C., differ from the national norm, as well as from white teachers. (See Table 4.3.) If we subsume under "white collar" the categories of professionals, businessmen, and sales and office workers, we can say that white teachers are twice as likely to come from white-collar families as are black teachers. A majority of black teachers (52.3 percent) come from blue-collar families. Any real comparison seems difficult, however, because of the vagueness of the term "middle class." What do we mean by "middle class"? Can the stable working class be considered part of the lower-middle class? Are semiskilled workers part of the stable working class? If so, 91 percent of white teachers can be said to come from the middle class, as compared to 74.1 percent of black teachers. What is important is that black teachers are more likely than are whites to be drawn from the lower or lower-middle classes, whereas white teachers are more likely to be drawn from the higher levels of the middle class. The social functions of the teaching profession may thus also differ for the two groups.

TABLE 4.3

Social Origins of Teachers, by Race
(percent)

		Black	White
	Professional man	15	24
White	Businessman	11	33
collar	Sales or office worker	9	9
	Skilled worker	28	21
Blue	Semiskilled worker	13	3
collar	Unskilled worker	12	2
Farmer		9	6
No answer		3	2
Total		100	100
		(N=2,452)	(N=505)

The teaching profession seems to be a much more important entrance into the middle class for blacks than for whites.[11] We can classify Washington teachers according to the social distance that they have traveled from their fathers' occupations to their own. We shall thus designate as "stable" teachers whose fathers were professional; as "moderately upwardly mobile" those whose fathers were businessmen, sales or office workers, or skilled workers; and as "highly upwardly mobile" those whose fathers were semiskilled or unskilled workers or farmers. (See Table 4.4.) Black teachers are three times more likely to have high upward social mobility than are whites. For black male teachers, the profession is one of the most important routes into the middle classes, especially since other avenues are often closed to blacks. In Washington, 45 percent of male black teachers are highly mobile compared with 33.8 percent of female black teachers, whereas female teachers are twice as likely to be stable as are male teachers. Because of the relative lessening of economic opportunities and increasing demands, the teaching profession may become still more important for black men.

For white teachers, the profession is still an important avenue of social mobility but mostly within the middle class. Most whites who enter teaching are already members of the middle class, but they often achieve new status: 65 percent of white teachers, compared with 50 percent of black teachers, are moderately mobile.

It would be interesting to investigate what other institutions in the nation are open to blacks as avenues of high social mobility, but that would be beyond the scope of this book. Schools, however, may continue to play a very important role as they recruit more and more blacks from the lower strata of the population. Teaching in black schools is no longer controlled, as it used to be, by the black bourgeoisie. A look at the changes that have taken place in the social origins

TABLE 4.4

Social Mobility, by Race
(percent)

Social Mobility	Black	White
Stable	15	24
Moderately upwardly mobile	50	65
Highly upwardly mobile	35	11
Total	100	100
	(N=2,148)	(N=469)

of Washington teachers over the years may yield additional information. (See Table 4.5.)

Black and white teachers show opposite trends. Whereas the percentage of blacks from blue-collar families keeps increasing, that of whites keeps decreasing. The reverse is true of teachers coming from white-collar, especially professional, families. Among the blacks there has been a decrease in teachers from professional and business families, possibly a result of new career openings for members of the black bourgeoisie or perhaps of alienation from schools staffed primarily by teachers of lower-class origins and increasingly serving slum clienteles. The teaching profession may be becoming less attractive to the black bourgeoisie. It may no longer offer as much prestige as it used to. Among whites the percentage of teachers from professional families (a great majority from teaching families; for example, 36 percent of the beginning teachers studied by Mason came from teachers' families)[12] is increasing. Among teachers less than 30 years old 34 percent come from professional families, which may reflect changes in values among the young. The "opposition" in the social origins of black and white teachers under 30 years of age is very striking. Eighty-one percent of white teachers and only 34 percent of blacks under 30 come from white-collar families, whereas 18 percent of whites and 66 percent of blacks in the same age group come from blue-collar families. Such a disparity in social origins may have important implications for the political and economic functions of schools in black communities. It may also raise important questions concerning the relations between teachers and students.[13] For example, are teachers from the lower class more likely to believe in the educability of lower-class students than are teachers from the middle class? Are they more likely to be authoritarian? Does a cultural gap between lower-class and middle-class blacks exist? If so, what form does it take? We shall treat some of these questions in subsequent chapters.

Besides social origins the education of teachers' parents and the relative financial positions of their families in the community will be included in our index of socioeconomic level of teachers' family backgrounds. The sociological importance of education among blacks has been pointed out by Myrdal. Education has always been the most important factor in stratification among the black population.

> In the Negro community, education is the main factor for the stratification of the Negro people into social classes. The professionals who base their status upon having acquired a higher education form a substantial part of the Negro upper classes. And even in the middle and lower classes, educational levels signify class differences

TABLE 4.5

Social Origins, by Race and Age
(percent)

	Black Teachers				White Teachers			
	Up to 30	31-40	41-50	51 and Over	Up to 30	31-40	41-50	51 and Over
Professional man	15	13	16	25	34	24	17	21
Businessman, sales or office worker	19	19	22	27	47	42	38	45
Skilled worker	32	27	28	29	12	27	26	21
Semiskilled worker, unskilled worker, or farmer	34	40	35	19	6	8	19	12
Total	100 (N=700)	99* (N=806)	101* (N=384)	100 (N=215)	99* (N=131)	101* (N=79)	100 (N=82)	99* (N=165)

*Total differs from 100 percent because of rounding.

in the Negro community. In addition, education has a symbolical significance in the Negro world: the educated Negro has, in one important respect become equal to the better class of white.[14]

Education was for a long time regarded by blacks as the most important means by which to achieve or to gain equality in this country. This perspective was enunciated as far back as 1836 by the Free People of Color of Philadelphia. Already, before the Civil War, education was a path to citizenship.

The education levels of black teachers' parents are shown in Table 4.6. From this table we see that women were more likely to receive higher education than were men; men were more likely than women to have attended only elementary school. Among whites, on the other hand, teachers' fathers were more likely to have received higher education than were their mothers—40 percent of the white fathers had attended college, compared with 30 percent of white mothers.

TABLE 4.6

Educational Levels of Black Teachers' Parents
(percent)

	Father		Mother	
No formal education	1.5		0.8	
Attended elementary school	16.6	32.2	9.5	22.0
Completed elementary school	14.2		11.7	
Attended high school	17.3	37.0	18.1	40.5
Completed high school	19.7		22.4	
Attended college	10.3		13.1	
Completed college	7.7	25.1	11.5	29.3
Went beyond college	7.1		4.7	
Don't know	4.0	6.0	3.7	8.2
No answer	2.0		4.5	
Total	100.3*		100.0	
	(N=2,452)		(N=2,452)	

*More than 100 percent because of rounding.

This sexual difference in education may be an important factor in determining the economic and family roles of black women. Noble, in her study of Negro women's college education,[15] reported that 35.6 percent of all degrees granted by black institutions in 1952 were earned by men. In all institutions the percentage of degrees received by men was 66.6 percent. In contrast the women received 62.4 percent of all degrees in black institutions while in all institutions the percentage of women receiving degrees is 33.4 percent. Education of black women has had priority over education of black men, whereas the importance given to education of white males has been much greater than that for educating white females.

The reasons are numerous, including the traditional black "matriarchal" family type, the likelihood that males will be sent to work very early to secure additional incomes for their families, and so on. But, whatever the reasons, that black women are in a better position to compete on the job market than are black men points to basic differences in the socioeconomic structure of the black and white populations, as well as to differences in family roles.[16]

Four indicators of the socioeconomic status of the teacher's parental family (father's education, mother's education, father's occupation,* and parents' income relative to those of the community) were combined in an index, ranging from 0 to 8. (See Appendix C.) The distribution of black and white teachers on the index is shown in Table 4.7. We see that black teachers are more likely to come from low-SES families, whereas white teachers are more likely to come from high-SES families.

The geographical origins of black teachers are also important. Earlier in this chapter, the possibility was suggested of tension between Washington-born blacks and those from the South. Especially as immigration from the South continued to increase after World War I, the quality of District education declined somewhat and the black school system became somewhat disorganized. Of Washington's black teachers, 45.7 percent were born in the District or within 50 miles of it; 36.3 percent come from southern states; and 16.4 percent come from other parts of the country. Washington's attraction for black teachers may be based on the existence of a large black school system, which provides opportunity for teachers; the city also has

---

*It is well to note the possible distortions that may arise from using the father's occupation as an indicator of socioeconomic status of the black family; the occupation of the mother seems a more significant indicator. Because of the absence of information on the mothers' occupations in our data, however, we have used only the fathers' occupations.

TABLE 4.7

Distribution of Black and White Teachers
on Family SES Scale
(percent)

Family SES	Black Teachers	White Teachers
Low	35	19
Medium	33	31
High	32	50
Total	100	100
	(N=2,303)	(N=491)

many secretarial and administrative jobs open to blacks. It enjoys a large black middle class and an old bourgeoisie. Howard University, one of the main black centers of teacher training, is located in the District.* That many of Washington's black teachers come from the South may be important in the analysis of black teachers' social status and in distinguishing among various groups in the black community. Are black teachers from the South more likely to come from families of low SES than are those born in Washington? Let us examine first the relationship between total family income and geographical origins. (See Table 4.8.)

Black teachers born in Washington are much more likely to have family incomes of $15,000 or more than are teachers from elsewhere, suggesting that black teachers from Washington are more likely to belong to the city's bourgeoisie and to have a higher community status. Black teachers with high family incomes would then also be those who are not the main breadwinners for their families, whereas teachers from the South may more often be the main breadwinners. That the woman is the main provider for the family is a sign of the low status and poor origin of the family. Teachers from other parts of the United States have a similar pattern. Indeed, 46.1 percent of teachers from the South come from semiskilled, unskilled, or farm families,

---

*The reason for taking married teachers only comes from the fact that the total family income is used here as an indicator of social status of the family of the teachers. Unmarried teachers affect the number of teachers in the first category and blur a meaningful difference between teachers from Washington and from the South.

TABLE 4.8

Total Family Income and Geographical Origins
of Married Black Teachers
(percent)

Total Family Income	Washington, D.C.	South	Other Parts of United States
Less than $10,000	9	20	17
$10,000-$14,999	44	51	51
$15,000 and more	47	29	32
Total	100	100	100
	(N=637)	(N=539)	(N=264)

whereas only 25.7 percent of those from Washington do. Teachers from the South and from Washington may represent the values and attitudes of two different worlds. They may differ in their commitment to teaching and in their attitudes toward the students. Teachers from the South are also more likely to be younger and to be male, and they are less likely to remain teachers, than are those born in Washington.

The percentage of teachers from the South in a given school may be an important factor in the relationships among colleagues, which may in turn affect teachers' orientations toward students. We have already suggested that because of changes in the clientele of the schools the percentage of black teachers from white-collar families has tended to diminish. This tendency is also reflected in the shift from a majority of teachers born in Washington to more nearly equal proportions among the younger teachers.

The function of the teaching profession may be different for blacks from the South and from Washington. For the first, teaching may be one of the few available ways to escape rural poverty; for the second, it may be an avenue to additional income and higher status within the middle classes. The increasing numbers of teachers from the South may explain why teachers from Washington increasingly leave the teaching profession. The prestige of the occupation may be lowered by the changes in the social and geographic origins of teachers, as well as of students.

To complete our description of the Washington teachers, we shall examine some aspects of their achieved status. Level and type of education may be important in understanding a teacher's commitment to his profession and his orientation toward students. One measure of educational level is the degree earned. (See Table 4.9.)

TABLE 4.9

Degree Received, by Race
(percent)

Degree Received	Black Teachers	White Teachers
No degree	5	21
B.A. degree	76	58
M.A. degree	19	21
Total	100	100
	(N=2,205)	(N=350)

A national sample of teachers polled by Warkow has shown that 29.8 percent of teachers have no degree.[17] Among the beginning teachers studied by Mason, 12 percent had no degree.[18] In Washington, D.C., the percentage of black teachers with no degree is much lower and that of white teachers with no degree is higher than in the nation generally. The numbers of black and white teachers with master's degrees is very similar in Washington; of the national sample 17 percent had master's degrees, compared with only 5 percent of beginning teachers in Mason's sample, although 22 percent of the latter group had completed some postgraduate work. Altogether, nearly 96 percent of Washington's black teachers have had college education. The reason that white teachers are less likely to have degrees may be that they are generally older and entered the profession when degrees were less frequently required. Table 4.10 compares white and black teachers of various ages as to their level of educational attainment.

Table 4.10 shows that older teachers, both white and black, are more likely than younger teachers to have no degree. However, the proportion of teachers with no degree at all ages is much higher among white than among black teachers. Among teachers aged 30 years or less, 19 percent of the white teachers have no degree, compared with 3 percent of the black teachers. Although certified knowledge and educational degree were less likely to be required some decades ago, it is interesting to note that, even among the younger teachers, white teachers are less likely than black teachers to need certified credentials in order to teach. Of black teachers less than 30 years of age, 92 percent have a college degree compared with 70 percent of white teachers. In other words, nearly all black teachers enter teaching with college education. The need for

TABLE 4.10

Age and Highest Degree Attained, by Race
(percent)

White Teachers

Highest Degree	Age: Less than 30 Years	31-40	41-50	51 and Over
No degree	19	16	12	30
B.A. degree	70	60	66	42
M.A. degree	11	24	22	28
Total	100	100	100	100
	(N=96)	(N=63)	(N=71)	(N=115)

Black Teachers

Highest Degree	Age: Less than 30 Years	31-40	41-50	51 and Over
No degree	3	6	4	14
B.A. degree	92	76	61	53
M.A. degree	5	18	35	33
Total	100	100	100	100
	(N=693)	(N=826)	(N=421)	(N=232)

credentials does not inhibit the entrance of black teachers into the Washington system. It may even suggest an overemphasis on formal education for elementary-school teachers, who may need other kinds of knowledge to deal with urban school problems and especially ghetto school children. The need for certification and the increased emphasis on college education may reflect a more general trend in the country, which may particularly affect black teachers, because for black teaching is an important means of social mobility and inclusion in the society.[19] The table also shows that although black teachers are less likely to enter the profession with a master's degree, they are more likely than the white teachers to acquire one during their teaching careers. The fact that so much emphasis is put on education among black teachers does not tell us anything about the quality or adequacy of college education. Such information was not available in our data. The type of college education received in various teachers' colleges in the South and in Washington are important for understanding the orientation of teachers toward education and their students.

Another measure of teachers' achieved status is years of professional experience. The amount of experience is very important in analyzing various processes within the schools. Indeed, it is linked with knowledge about the school and understanding of the students. Older teachers in a school thus have a certain amount of power over younger ones and can exert pressure. They may well be in a position to set behavior norms for the group and, through indirect channels, to enforce them among younger teachers. Washington, D.C., teachers were distributed according to the number of years of teaching in their present schools, as shown in Table 4.11.

We must note that the school is a socializing agency not only for students but also for teachers.[20] Most teachers' expertise and knowledge come from their experience in the schools. They acquire new professional skills and develop new sets of educational values, as well as of general values, on the job. Socialization to the dominant group norms is a very important process. We are not, unfortunately, in a position to study the changes occurring in a single group of teachers over a specific period; the data in the present study all relate to only one point in time. Because of the difficulties in differentiating between the effect of the socializing process in the schools, the effects of aging per se, and generational change, we will not investigate such aspects in this research.

TABLE 4.11

Years at Present School

Years	Percent
1	22
2	15
3	13
4	9
5	9
6	6
7	5
8	4
9	2
10+	15
Total	100
	(N=2,452)

So far we have discussed background variables in connection with teachers in the Washington, D.C., elementary school system. Black teachers differ in age, social-class origins, geographical origins, and family SES. The function of teaching seems different for whites and blacks. Teaching may have different functions, both social and economic, among the blacks themselves. Among blacks there are strong differences between the middle class and the lower class and between blacks from Washington and those from the South. That white and black teachers are so dissimilar on all our background variables has led us to treat black teachers separately.*

We shall use some of these variables in analyzing the processes of adaptation to teaching in schools of various SES and in comparing the effects of background variables and of interpersonal relations within the schools, to see how they affect teachers' job satisfaction, commitment to teaching, and orientations toward students.

In conclusion, we can say that there are significant differences between the demographic and social background characteristics of black and white teachers. Black teachers are more likely to be younger, women, and married than are white teachers. Black teachers are more likely to come from a blue-collar family or from families of unskilled workers than the white.

The implication of these demographic and social differences may have some significance for the functioning of an urban school system staffed largely by blacks. We have pointed out before that the economic and social functions of teaching may be different for black and for white teachers. The teaching profession is for blacks an important means of social mobility into the middle class. The economic function of teaching for the black family from lower-class origins may be important in understanding some of the issues surrounding the desire to have black teachers teaching black children. In view of the historical role played by the dual system for the black community in Washington, D.C., and of the special importance it had for the middle class, we may ask whether the school system does have similar functions for black teachers from lower-class origins teaching in segregated neighborhoods.

The school and the educational system became, as we said in the first chapter, the center of the controversy in the achievement of "equal rights" for blacks. Today the school has again become the arena of social and political conflicts linked with the problems faced

---

*The differences mentioned among blacks and between black and white teachers only apply in the case of the elementary-school teachers of Washington, D.C.; no inference can be made for blacks and whites in general.

by the black community of the urban slums. It may also manifest some of the tensions among lower-class and middle-class blacks. Our research also shows differences between teachers with a rural background and teachers from Washington, D.C., itself.

In the next section we are going to study how some of the above characteristics of teachers affect their job satisfaction and commitm to teaching.

JOB SATISFACTION AND COMMITMENT TO TEACHING AS RELATED TO TEACHERS' CHARACTERISTICS

In this section we shall study first the relationship between job satisfaction, commitment to teaching, on one hand, and the demographic, social, and professional characteristics of teachers, on the other. Demographic characteristics include sex, age, and marital status; social-background characteristics include social origin and parental SES (ascribed status), present family income (achieved status), and regional origin; occupational characteristics include years of teaching, income from teaching, and level of education.

Previous investigations of social-background correlates of occupational satisfaction among teachers[21] have generally shown that women are more likely than men to be satisfied with teaching, that older teachers are more likely than younger teachers to be satisfied with teaching, that teachers from low-SES families are more likely than those from high-SES families to be satisfied, and, finally, that teachers with higher teaching incomes are more likely than those wit lower ones to be satisfied with teaching.[22]

Our data were taken from a group that had not previously been singled out for this kind of investigation, black teachers.[23] It should therefore be interesting to discover whether or not they differed fron white teachers in the correlates of occupational satisfaction. Knowledge of which teachers are more likely to be satisfied with and committed to teaching may be particularly important in studying the behavior of teachers in ghetto situations. Both white and black teachers are elementary-school teachers.

We have already seen that the social characteristics of black and white teachers are quite different. We now turn to those characteristics most often linked with occupational satisfaction among white teachers; did the same links appear among our sample of black teachers?

Our findings suggest that the relationships between demographi variables and job satisfaction do not differ much from those among white teachers. Whereas occupational satisfaction among white fema teachers is higher than that among white male teachers, in our data the difference was only 3 percent, hardly a significant one. The finding that older teachers are more satisfied than younger ones was also repeated in our data: Of black teachers more than 50 years old 43 percent were very satisfied, compared with only 26 percent of teachers less than 30 years old. Age is an ambiguous indicator, however. The greater satisfaction of older teachers may be linked with length of experience, higher income, changes in social and psychic satisfactions available from teaching over the decades, or characteristics of the life cycle. In this study, however, we are less interested in generational change than in the effects of teaching experiences, and we shall use total number of teaching years in further analysis.

Although it has been shown that single teachers are more likely to be satisfied with their jobs than are married teachers, especially women,[24] we found that black single teachers hardly differed from black married, separated, or divorced teachers: 32 percent (379) of the unmarried teachers were satisfied with their jobs, compared with 34 percent (1,456) of married teachers and 37 percent (295) of those with other marital status.

For social origin and parental SES, we find a slight reversal of the findings for whites: The higher the social origin, the more likely the teacher is to be satisfied. In our sample 38 percent of teachers from professional family backgrounds reported themselves very satisfied with their jobs, compared with 36 percent of those from business families, 34 percent of those from skilled workers' families, and 32 percent of those from unskilled workers' and farm families. Among the reasons for such differences may be that teachers from professional families tend to be assigned to the better (high-SES) schools and thus to be more satisfied. We shall explore this possibility later.

The regional origins of teachers may be of particular interest in Washington because of its geographical location and the traditions and characteristics of the black community, as described in Chapter 2. Black teachers from the South were slightly more likely to be dissatisfied with their jobs. Among teachers born in Washington, 37 percent were very satisfied with their jobs, compared with 33 percent from other parts of the United States, excluding the South, and 30 percent from the South. One may ask whether or not teachers from the South were more likely to be dissatisfied because they were assigned to worse (low-SES) schools or because of differences in life-styles and attitudes that have traditionally distinguished Washington-born blacks and those from the South and may clash in the schools. Achieved status, as we have measured it, showed no relationship with job satisfaction among Washington's black elementary-school teachers.

Among demographic and social-background characteristics the only strong link with job satisfaction was age. Among occupational characteristics teaching income was positively related to job satisfaction in our data, although there was only a small relationship. As to the level of education, our findings showed that the higher the educational level of a teacher, the more likely he was to be very satisfied: 32 percent of teachers with no degree were very satisfied, compared with 34 percent with bachelor's degrees and 40 percent with master's degrees. But, again, earning a master's degree during the course of one's teaching career is closely related to age, and we may therefore be dealing with another spurious relationship. When we control for age, we find the relationship greatly reduced. Experience in schools is evidently a stronger correlate of job satisfaction than is level of education.

Of all the teachers' occupational and other characteristics, only one shows significant correlation with job satisfaction: experience in the schools.

All things considered, one can say that the demographic, social, and professional characteristics of the teachers (with the exception of age and years of teaching) have only a slight relationship to teacher job satisfaction. There does not seem to be any drastic difference from what has been found about white teachers.

Let us now look at the relationship between teachers' characteristics and their commitment to the teaching profession. Of those teachers who expressed a wish to remain teachers 10 years from the date of the study, most were older. As has been noted, our data do not permit us to distinguish directly among the effects of aging and of decisions to remain in teaching based upon level of satisfaction, life-cycle phenomena, generational changes in values, and the possibility that the actual occupational rewards to older teachers (income, influence, control of work, and so on) are greater.

In our data men were more interested than women in obtaining administrative posts, which carry more prestige and higher salaries. Furthermore, black teachers from the lower class were more likely to want to remain teachers than were those from the middle classes; teachers from professional backgrounds were more likely not to want to remain teachers than were those from unskilled workers' families. Teachers from lower-class origins were thus at the same time less likely to be satisfied and more likely to want to remain teachers than were those from middle-class origins—perhaps because the former lacked motivation to seek higher status. It may also be that being a teacher is more prestigious for lower-class teachers in view of the social distance traveled.

It is often claimed that entry into teaching is a much greater social achievement for lower-class than for middle-class teachers.

If we treat the first three columns of Table 4.12 as representing commitment to education, we find that teachers from lower-class origins (approximately 72 percent of those from semiskilled or unskilled backgrounds) were more likely to be committed than were teachers from middle-class origins (approximately 61 percent from professional backgrounds). The finding that teachers from professional families were more interested in retiring or becoming housewives may reflect the ages of teachers in this group. We therefore compared teachers from lower- and middle-class origins who were also less than 40 years old; teachers from lower-class origins were still more likely to be committed to education than were those from middle-class origins.

How does the achieved status of teachers' families affect their commitment to teaching and to education in general? Total family income, including the incomes of both teacher and spouse, is an indicator of social status. In our sample, teachers with the highest family incomes were more likely to want to retire or become housewives than were those with lower family incomes: 35 percent of those with family incomes of $15,000 or more, compared with 19 percent of those with incomes of less than $10,000. Controlling for age, we find that among teachers less than 40 years old 48 percent of those with high family incomes wanted to retire, compared to 30 percent of those with lower family incomes. These findings may indicate that the black middle class, what Frazier called the "black bourgeoisie,"

TABLE 4.12

Career Plans for 10 Years Ahead, and Social Origins (percent)

	Career Plans					
Social Origins	Teacher	Educational Specialist	Administrator	College Teacher	Retired and Housewife	N
Professional	23.2	30.4	7.8	5.6	33.0	(306)
Businessmen	26.5	29.0	10.7	5.9	28.0	(393)
Skilled workers	26.6	30.3	14.4	3.2	25.6	(591)
Semiskilled and unskilled workers	30.9	29.0	12.3	4.9	22.9	(693)
						(N=1,983)

tends to adopt the career patterns, values, and life-styles of the white middle class. The social and economic functions of teaching for blacks of lower-class origins may be very different from those of the "black bourgeoisie" and may affect their career plans differently.

We have already suggested the importance of age and years of teaching. Among teachers with less than 4 years of experience, 21 percent wished to continue, compared with 36 percent among those with 10 to 16 years of experience. Level of education was also related to career plans: Teachers with no degrees or with only bachelor's degrees were equally likely to want to remain teachers or to want to become educational specialists, whereas those with master's degrees were generally interested in becoming administrators.

Teachers with lower teaching incomes (less than $6,000) were more likely to wish to remain teachers than were those with higher teaching incomes (more than $10,000): 30 percent and 23 percent respectively. This finding fits our previous finding that teachers from lower-class backgrounds were more likely to want to continue teaching, for we know that teachers from lower-class origins were more likely to have low family incomes. One reason may be that teachers with low incomes were more likely to be assigned to low-SES schools. Why were such teachers more likely to want to stay in teaching than were those with higher incomes? We have no information with which to answer this question, but one possibility is that teaching income is not one of the most important factors in job satisfaction. In a later chapter we shall return to this problem.

We have noted previously that the relationship between occupational and other characteristics, on one hand, and job satisfaction, on the other, might be affected by the socioeconomic level of the schools to which teachers are assigned.

We must first examine how teachers were distributed among various schools in the Washington, D.C., system, especially whether or not they were randomly distributed among schools of varying SES. We have already shown that 41 percent of black teachers and only 16 percent of white teachers in Washington were assigned to low-SES schools. Conversely, 58 percent of white teachers and 16 percent of black teachers were assigned to high-SES schools. Examining the distribution of black teachers among schools of varying SES we found a slight tendency for teachers from the South to be assigned to low-SES schools and for those from Washington to be assigned to high-SES schools. In fact, 18 percent of black teachers from Washington were assigned to high-SES schools, compared to 12 percent of those from the South. Teachers from low-SES backgrounds were slightly more frequently assigned to low-SES schools: 46 percent, compared with 38 percent of those from high-SES backgrounds. Young teachers, 30 years and less, were not more likely to be assigned to low-SES schools, and only slightly more likely to be assigned to medium-SES schools.

Let us now see how the socioeconomic level of the school affected the relationship between job satisfaction and teacher characteristics. Was job satisfaction affected more by the characteristics of the schools than by those of the teachers?

We have seen that the teachers' ascribed status was related to job satisfaction, that teachers from low-SES backgrounds were more likely to be assigned to low-SES schools, and that those in low-SES schools were less likely than those in high-SES schools to be satisfied with their work.

The simultaneous effects of ascribed status and the SES level of a school on job satisfaction can be seen in Table 4.13. The table shows that, keeping SES of the school constant, the family SES of the teachers does not significantly affect teachers' level of job satisfaction. For example, among teachers in low-SES schools, 38 percent are very satisfied if they come from high-SES families, compared with 32 percent from low-SES families. Among teachers located in high-SES schools, 48 percent from high-SES family backgrounds are very satisfied, compared with 51 percent from low-SES families. Keeping the family SES constant, we see that the SES school level does affect teachers' job satisfaction, especially among teachers from low-SES families.

TABLE 4.13

Job Satisfaction, Teachers' Family SES, and School SES
(percent teachers very satisfied)

	Family SES		
School SES	High	Medium	Low
High	48% (113)*	42% (123)	51% (97)
Medium	30 (303)	35 (304)	31 (297)
Low	38 (256)	30 (258)	32 (336)
Percentage difference	10	12	19

*Actual number

These findings suggest that variations in the background of black teachers and in the SES levels of students in the ghetto schools have little impact upon occupational satisfaction. On common sense grounds, we are surprised at these results, given the wide expectation of "cultural gap" between social classes in the ghetto setting. Although variations and discrepancies between the social origin of teachers and that of students do not seem to affect job satisfaction greatly, this does not mean that there are no differences in social values between these groups. But whatever the differences in values that exist, they do not greatly affect the job satisfaction of black teachers confronting ghetto school children.

SUMMARY AND CONCLUSIONS

Recruitment of black teachers to the ghetto elementary schools of Washington, D.C., was in some respects significantly different from patterns of white recruitment to teaching. The black teachers in Washington were less likely to come from middle-class origins, were more often women (at a time when the over-all representation of men among teachers in general was increasing), and were more likely to be the chief breadwinners of their families. Some of these characteristics were even more marked among younger teachers, suggesting that they may grow even more pronounced as time passes. The historically dominant black bourgeoisie of Washington appeared no longer to dominate the teaching staffs of the public elementary schools serving black students ever since the pattern of race relations had shifted from segregation to "ghettoization."

We do not know how black teachers related to their students in the earlier context. It does appear, however, that more recently rather few of the social and occupational characteristics of the black teachers under study affected their occupational satisfaction or commitment to teaching in the ghetto. Class background, social mobility, and regional origins were unrelated to these aspects of teachers' attitudes; only age seemed linked with them, since older teachers (or those with more teaching experience) expressed greater satisfaction and stronger desires to continue teaching. Of course, the less satisfied and the less committed generally tend to drop out over the years. But it nonetheless remains true that those who had remained in this school system longest tended to be the most satisfied and most certain of continuing to teach, a finding that must be viewed in combination with older teachers' probably greater influence in both formal and informal aspects of school operation. One common expectation—that prolonged exposure to ghetto teaching conditions is linked with lower satisfaction—has not been supported by our data. Nor has the expectation been borne out that a "culture gap" between former and current social status of ghetto teachers—even black ones—would result in relatively low satisfaction and a tendency to leave ghetto teaching. This latter expectation has been subjected to a rather severe test: simultaneous examination of teachers' social origins and of variations in the average SES rating of students in the schools they staff.

These patterns direct our attention away from social background and occupational and personal characteristics of black teachers in Washington in our search for correlates of teachers' reactions to ghetto schools. We must now turn to aspects of the occupational situation, to processes within schools as distinct from social attributes of the contexts in which black teachers encounter ghetto children. For this purpose, survey data are not the most useful materials, but it is in this direction that our findings lead us, and we shall therefore try to examine the possibilities as best we can.

NOTES

1. W. W. Charters, Jr., "The Social Background of Teaching," in N. L. Gage, ed., Handbook of Research on Teaching: A Project of the American Education Research Association, A Department of the National Education Association (Chicago: Rand McNally, 1963), pp. 715-813.

2. L. A. Cook and Elaine F. A. Cook, A Sociological Approach to Education (2nd ed.; New York: McGraw-Hill, 1950), pp. 438-49.

3. Garson McGuire and George White, "Social Origins of Teachers in Texas," in L. S. Stiles, ed., The Teacher's Role in American Society (New York: Harper, 1957), pp. 25-41.

4. Lloyd Warner, American Life: Dream and Reality (Chicago: University of Chicago Press, 1953).

5. L. D. Coffman, The Social Composition of Teaching Population (New York: Teachers College, 1911).

6. W. Wattenberg, "Social Origin of Teachers: A Northern Industrial City," in Stiles, ed., Teachers' Role in American Society, pp. 13-22. About teachers in training, see Charters, "Social Background of Teaching," n. 2, p. 720.

7. Andrew Billingsley, "Family Functioning in the Low Income Black Community," Social Case Work, Vol. 50, No. 10, 1969, pp. 563-72.

8. Gertrude McPherson, "The Role Set of the Elementary School Teachers" (unpublished Ph.D. dissertation, Columbia University, 1966), p. 150; William W. Wayson, "Expressed Motives of Teachers in Slum Schools" (unpublished Ph.D. dissertation, University of Chicago, 1966); Peter Blau, "Orientation Toward Clients in a Public Welfare Agency," Administrative Science Quarterly, No. 3, 1960, pp. 341-61.

9. Lloyd Warner, *American Life: Dream and Reality* (Chicago: University of Chicago Press, 1953), p. 176, reports that "the overwhelming proportion of teachers in the grammar schools and high schools are middle-class, often lower-middle class."

10. W. S. Mason, R. J. Dressel, and R. K. Bain, *The Beginning Teacher*, U.S. Department of Health, Education, and Welfare, Office of Education, Circular No. 510 (Washington, D.C.: Government Printin Office, 1958). The sample includes both elementary- and secondary-school teachers.

11. Howard S. Becker, "Schools and Systems of Stratification," in A. H. Halsey, Jean Floud, and C. Arnold Anderson, eds., *Education, Economy and Society: A Reader in the Sociology of Education* (New York: The Free Press, 1964), pp. 93-104.

12. Mason, Dressel, and Bain, *Beginning Teacher*, p. 14.

13. Howard S. Becker, "Social Class Variation in the Teacher-Pupil Relationship," *Journal of Educational Sociology*, Vol. 25, April 1957, pp. 451-65.

14. Gunnar Myrdal, *An American Dilemma: The Negro Problem and Modern Democracy* (20th anniversary ed.; New York: Harper & Row, 1962), p. 879.

15. Jeanne Lareta Noble, *The Negro Woman's College Education* (New York: Teachers College, Columbia University, 1956).

16. Elliot Liebow, *Tally's Corner: A Study of Negro Streetcorne Men* (Boston: Little, Brown and Company, 1967).

17. Seymour Warkow, "Report for the National Science Foundation on Technical and Professional Manpower" (unpublished), 1965.

18. Mason, Dressel, and Bain, *Beginning Teacher*, p. 22.

19. Talcott Parsons, "Full Citizenship for the Negro American? A Sociological Problem," *Daedalus*, Fall 1965, pp. 1009-54.

20. Stanton Wheeler, "The Structure of Formally Organized Socialization Settings," in Orville Brim and Stanton Wheeler, eds., *Socialization After Childhood: Two Essays* (New York: John Wiley & Sons, 1966).

21. Charters, "Social Background of Teaching," pp. 718-27; Mason, Dressel, and Bain, *Beginning Teacher*, pp. 79-94.

22. Paula Kleinman, "Role Dissensus and Its Correlates in an Educational Setting" (unpublished Ph.D. dissertation, Department of Sociology, Columbia University, 1970).

23. Anna Lee Hopson and David E. Wilder, *A Study of Teachers in the Public Schools of Washington, D.C.* (New York: Bureau of Applied Social Research, Columbia University, 1967), pp. 100-110.

24. Mason, Dressel, and Bain, *Beginning Teacher*, pp. 81-84.

CHAPTER

5

TEACHERS' JOB SATISFACTION AS RELATED TO THE SOCIAL STRUCTURE OF THE SCHOOLS

We have seen that the background characteristics and professional attributes of black teachers were only weakly related to their over-all job satisfaction. Age and teaching experience showed the strongest relationships with it.

In this chapter we shall first analyze teachers' relations with students, peers, and supervisors as these relations affected job satisfaction. We shall seek to learn how various aspects of the social structure of the school were associated with job satisfaction; we shall then examine how teachers' professional attributes separately affected their over-all job satisfaction.

The teaching context may be very important in understanding the high percentage of teachers who reported themselves very satisfied with their jobs. Their roles in the social structure of the school may be more important than their backgrounds and professional attributes in explaining this satisfaction.

CLIENTS, PEERS, AND SUPERVISORS

From the teachers' point of view, the social structure of the school is composed of clients (students), colleagues, and the authorities. Each of these groups may influence teachers differently under different circumstances.

JOB SATISFACTION AND THE RELATIONSHIP WITH THE STUDENTS

Let us first examine teachers' relations with students. Our study did not involve any direct qualitative measures of teacher-student relations, but two questions dealing with teachers' perceptions of students provided at least one indirect measure. First, we asked whether or not the teacher thought that his students liked school; we assumed that the answer to this question also would reflect the teacher's perception of whether or not the students liked him. Second, we asked teachers to evaluate the quality of their students' work, a question that also seemed to tap the extent to which the teacher liked his students.

The distribution of responses to the first question is shown in Table 5.1.

TABLE 5.1

Teachers' Assessments of Students' Liking for School (percent)

Very much	33
Quite a bit	37
Somewhat	23
Not much	4
Not at all	1
No answer	2
Total	100
	(N=2,452)

Seventy percent of the teachers judged that their students liked school at least quite a bit, a very high percentage indeed. This response raises the question of what teachers' perceptions of their students actually mean. How do teachers define their relations with students? This question will be examined in a subsequent section.

The distribution of responses to the second question is shown in Table 5.2. We found that 60 percent of the teachers were at least somewhat satisfied with the quality of students' work, again a very high percentage and even more astonishing in a system in which more than 60 percent of the students had language difficulties and more than half of those in the eighth grade were one or more years behind the average reading level for that grade.[1]

For the moment we shall only suggest some possible explanations. In view of the duality of the school system—which is of two different systems—classroom teachers' professional criteria of

TABLE 5.2

Teachers' Assessments of Students' Work
(percent)

Very satisfied	10
Somewhat satisfied	50
Neither satisfied nor dissatisfied	11
Somewhat dissatisfied	21
Very dissatisfied	5
No answer	3
Total	100
	(N=2,452)

TABLE 5.3

Job Satisfaction and Perception That
Students Liked School
(percent)

	Perception That Students Liked School		
Job Satisfaction	Very Much	Quite a Bit	Not at all
Very satisfying	54	30	17
Fairly satisfying	40	61	58
Not very satisfying	6	9	25
Total	100	100	100
	(N= 767)	(N=862)	(N= 621)

success and failure may be quite different from official ones.* Furthermore, teachers' evaluation of students' achievements may reflect indirect evaluation of their own ability to teach successfully. Is it also possible that teachers reported that their students liked school, in order to protect their own professional status?

In Table 5.3 the relationship is shown between teachers' job satisfaction and their perceptions that students liked school.

*The concept of duality has been defined in Chapter 3. It is a structural characteristic of the school.

From the top row we see that it was a very strong relationship. At the other extreme, unsatisfied teachers were four times more likely to think that their students did not like school than that they did. The direction of the relationship is not, however, clear from these data. We so not know whether teachers were satisfied because their students seemed to like school, or believed that their students liked school because they themselves were satisfied with their jobs. Most likely both processes are at work; we may assume that these variables were mutually reinforcing. We shall return to this question shortly.

We must remember that teachers' professional role is to produce change in students. Professional satisfaction may result from their success in producing such change, but it may also result simply from approval and conformity among students.

Table 5.4 shows how teachers' perceptions of the quality of students' work were related to job satisfaction. Although again we cannot be certain of the direction of the relationship, it is clear that job satisfaction was associated with favorable perceptions of students' work. Student-teacher relations and, more likely than not, job satisfaction seem to have depended upon these positive perceptions, rather than the other way around. Indeed we note that the relationship between job satisfaction and perceptions that students liked school very much (37 percent) was stronger than that between job satisfaction and satisfaction with students' work (21 percent difference). Did the stronger relationship reflect teachers' projection of their own job satisfaction, or did teachers indeed receive more personal gratification from interaction with students than from students' achievements? That teachers were really more concerned about

TABLE 5.4

Job Satisfaction and Perceptions of Quality of Students' Work (percent)

Job Satisfaction	Satisfaction with the Quality of Students' Work: Satisfied	Not Very Satisfied	Dissatisfied
Very satisfied	42	26	21
Fairly satisfied	51	58	55
Not satisfied	7	16	24
Total	100	100	100
	(N= 1,406)	(N= 239)	(N=597)

students' conformity to expectations than about their academic achievements has been reported by McPherson in a study of elementary-school teachers based on participant observation.[2] She reported teachers as saying things like, "If I can just get Richard to sit still this year I will consider it an accomplishment; I don't mind if he does not learn anything, but I wish he would be quiet so that he does not set a bad example for others." But that teachers should be more concerned about nonacademic aspects of teaching does not necessarily mean that they do not receive satisfaction from classroom interaction with students.

JOB SATISFACTION AND PEER RELATIONS

Relations with peers are another aspect of teachers' participation in the social structure of the school. The peer group is the largest such group aside from the student body itself. As we have already noted, the school, unlike many other organizations, has two main subgroups with no intervening hierarchy: students and teachers. All the members of the teachers' peer group share similar professional roles and are under similar pressures, and, of course, they represent the adult world in the school. For most teachers in elementary schools, relations with the peer group probably represent the most important contact with the adult world either outside or inside the school.[3]

We measured teachers' relations with peers by means of a series of five questions on personal and professional contacts among teachers. Respondents were to assess each of various aspects of their relations with their colleagues and to check "strongly agree," "agree," "don't know," "disagree," or "strongly disagree."[4] Table 5.5 shows the percentage of teachers who checked either of the first two alternatives for each of the items. It is interesting that at least half the teachers responded positively to each item, indicating satisfaction with various aspects of their relations with colleagues. As these items are all interrelated, we have combined them in an index of the perceived quality of professional peer relations.

These same items are sometimes used to study teachers' morale or the climate of the school. Various studies in organizational research have shown the importance of workers' morale as a determinant of job satisfaction. Is it equally important for teachers? Table 5.6 shows the relationship between teachers' relations with peers and over-all job satisfaction. The better their relations with peers the more likely teachers were to be very satisfied with their jobs. Teachers who scored high on the peer-relations index were three times more likely to be very satisfied with their jobs than were teachers who scored low on the index.

TABLE 5.5

Percentage of Teachers Who Agreed and Strongly Agreed with Individual Items of Peer-Relations Index

In general faculty relations are satisfactory.	74 (N=2,452)
Teachers at my school share ideas and techniques.	67 (N=2,452)
I feel free to discuss professional difficulties with teachers in my school.	61 (N=2,452)
Faculty at my school share common ideas on educational objectives.	52 (N=2,452)
Teachers at this school have a close and friendly feeling toward one another.	50 (N=2,452)

TABLE 5.6

Job Satisfaction and Peer Relations (percent)

	Peer-Relations Index Score		
Job Satisfaction	High	Medium	Low
Very satisfying	57	37	17
Fairly satisfying	38	54	61
Not satisfying	5	9	22
Total	100	100	100
	(N=525)	(N=927)	(N=802)

We have mentioned in a previous chapter the role of the peer group in facilitating adjustment and adaptation among policemen and welfare workers and have also pointed out the mutual support and recognition provided by peers in similar working situations. Indeed, the existence of a group of colleagues interacting under the same pressures is a necessary condition for creation of a teachers' subculture.

We shall return later on to the role of the peer group in the school and its relative importance in various contexts. For the moment we can point out that the peer group is emerging as an important aspect of teachers' job satisfaction in the school. Indeed we shall note that teachers' relations with peers are much greater in importance than are any of the background characteristics, professional attributes, and school characteristics that we have examined so far.

JOB SATISFACTION AND RELATIONSHIP WITH THE PRINCIPAL

In addition to their relations with students and peers, teachers also interact with the authority structure of the school, particularly the principal. The teachers in our study were asked a variety of questions about their relations, both professional and personal, with principals. Responses were based on the same five-point scale between "agree" and "disagree" that was used for peer relations.[5] The percentage answering in the first two categories for each item is reported in Table 5.7. As with peer relations, the most personal aspects were those with which the teachers were least satisfied. This finding may simply reflect the impossibility of a principal's taking a strong personal interest in every teacher in his school; more likely, structural requirements that a person in authority maintain some distance from his subordinates has been misconstrued by teachers as lack of personal interest.

TABLE 5.7

Percentage of Teachers Who Agreed and Strongly Agreed With Individual Items on Index of Relations with Principal

Item	Percentage
The principal and I get along very well together.	82 (N=2,452)
The principal gives me a fair hearing on any subject I want to bring up.	70 (N=2,452)
The principal tries to be fair and impartial.	66 (N=2,452)
I am entirely satisfied with the amount of appreciation and recognition that I get when I do a good job.	51 (N=2,452)
The principal has a great deal of real interest in me as a person.	46 (N=2,452)

Another possibility is that teachers had various role expectations connected with the principal: He may have appeared not only as an administrator but also as a human-relations expert, a counselor, and an educational specialist. The teacher may have expected, in addition to professional advice and support, intimate contacts and recognition, perhaps even more than students needed from him. Again, the context in which the principal worked may have caused him to emphasize some of his functions over others, a point to which we shall return.

Not surprisingly the second lowest favorable response is also given to the only other item on the list that deals with what the principal voluntarily gives to the teacher. Whereas the lowest score related to nonprofessional recognition, the second lowest related to professional recognition.* Clearly teachers felt the need for professional guidance and advice as well as personal attention from the principal, suggesting the basically conflicting demands that teachers placed on him.

The relations between teachers and principal can also be viewed in terms of the distribution of power and responsibility within the school. That teachers wanted professional advice and better supervision does not mean that they were necessarily willing to relinquish part of their autonomy to the principal; very much the reverse, in fact. The relations between teachers and principals can be reduced analytically to competition for greater shares of power versus maintenance of the status quo. It was possible to document this aspect of teacher-principal relations in our study. Teachers were asked their opinions of what ought to be considered in assigning students to tracks and also what factors actually were considered.[6] Table 5.8 lists the findings. Nearly one-fourth of the respondents thought that principals should have less say in the assignment of students, the single most frequently cited factor.

We interpret teachers' desire to give more weight to students' potential achievements and aspirations as a desire for more voice in the assignment of students, for teachers are those in the position to assess these factors in the context of daily classroom interaction. Such assessment is, in fact, part of their professional function, though

---

*Common failure to meet the teachers' need for such evaluation is further documented by analysis of the fulfillment of occupational characteristics. Among those characteristics most important to teachers but at the same time least satisfied is that they be kept informed of how well they are doing on the job. Of course, the extent to which this demand can be satisfied by the principal without violating the autonomy of teachers may be problematic.

TABLE 5.8

Factors in Assigning Students to Tracks
(percent)

	Should be Given More Weight*
Potential scholastic achievements	14
Levels of aspiration	11
Present scholastic achievements	3
Teachers' judgments	4
	(N=2,362)
	Should Be Given Less Weight*
Principals' judgments	23
Pupils' behavior	10
Parental wishes	10
Socioeconomic backgrounds	6
Race	6
	(N=2,362)

*The percentages do not equal 100 percent because we present only items where there was some difference between factors that ought to be considered and that are actually considered.

in many slum schools increased reliance on specialists in various educational and related problems may alter the situation.

Let us now return to our basic query: How did relations with principals correlate with teachers' over-all job satisfaction? Table 5.9 shows that the two variables are highly related. Among the teachers who are very satisfied with their job, 56 percent are high on relationship with the principal index, compared with 14 percent who are low on the index.

RELATIVE IMPORTANCE OF THE RELATIONSHIP WITH STUDENTS, PEERS, AND PRINCIPAL IN ACCOUNTING FOR TEACHERS' OVER-ALL JOB SATISFACTION

We have noted strong relationships between teachers' satisfaction with their work, on the one hand, and satisfactory relations with

TABLE 5.9

Job Satisfaction and Relations with Principal
(percent)

Job Satisfaction	Index of Satisfaction with Principals High	Medium	Low
Very satisfying	56	36	14
Fairly satisfying	40	58	51
Not satisfying	4	6	25
Total	100	100	100
	(N=839)	(N=678)	(N=737)

peers, satisfactory relations with principals, and favorable perceptions of students, respectively, on the other. We also know that the indexes of peer relations and relations with principals are interrelated. Teachers who are high on the peer-relations index tend also to be high on the relations with principal index. The next question involves the relative importance of these two types of relations in accounting for teachers' job satisfaction. As the scores on the two indexes are interrelated, we must first consider the relationship with job satisfaction of each independently. In Table 5.10 each entry represents the percentage of teachers with a particular combination of scores on the two indexes who were also very satisfied with their jobs. For example, 37 percent of very satisfied teachers had poor relations with their peers and good relations with their principals. Table 5.10 thus reveals that the two variables had independent but additive effects upon job satisfaction. Reading across each row and down each column we see that each trait is related to job satisfaction when the other is constant. For each row and each column we have computed the percentage difference between the extreme categories; this procedure serves as a crude measure of the strength of the association between one factor and job satisfaction when the other factor is held constant.

Comparing the average percentage differences of the columns and the rows, we see that relations with principals were more highly correlated with teachers' job satisfaction that were peer relations. The average difference in the relations with principals was 35.6 percent, compared with an average of approximately 23 percent for peer relations.

There is, however, a further point: The correlation with job satisfaction of one factor increases as that of the other increases. That is, when one is strong, the other shows a greater relationship with job satisfaction than when the first is weak. Peer relations and

TABLE 5.10

Job Satisfaction, Peer Relations, and Relations with Principal
(percent teachers very satisfied)

Peer-Relations Index	Index of Relations with Principals			Percentage Difference Between Extremes
	High	Medium	Low	
High	65% (366)	48% (97)	29% (62)	36
Medium	52 (277)	38 (385)	18 (27)	34
Low	37 (94)	26 (196)	10 (512)	27
Percentage difference	28	22	19	

relations with principals clearly reinforce each other in relation to job satisfaction.

Let us now compare the relative importance of teachers' orientations toward students and satisfaction with peer relations in association with over-all job satisfaction. (See Table 5.11.) Both variables clearly were correlated with teachers' job satisfaction. Keeping satisfaction with students' work constant, we find that the percentage of satisfied teachers increased with better peer relations. Keeping peer relations constant, we find that the percentage increased with satisfaction with students' work. Again the two variables have an additive effect on job satisfaction.

Table 5.11 offers two more valuable pieces of information. First, relations with peers were more closely associated with teachers' over-all job satisfaction than were perceptions that students were doing good work. This is found by comparing the percentage differences for each row and column. It can be seen that the average percentage difference in job satisfaction between low and high peer relations is 25 percent, whereas the average difference between the satisfied and dissatisfied with quality of student work is 16 percentage points.

Second, there is a further story in the percentage differences in the columns and rows of Table 5.11. It will be noted that the effect of one variable on job satisfaction is not affected when the other variables increase. For example, among teachers who are satisfied,

TABLE 5.11

Job Satisfaction, Satisfaction with Students' Work, and Peer Relations (percent teachers very satisfied)

	Satisfaction with Quality of Work		
Peer Relations	Satisfied	Dissatisfied	Percentage Difference
High	54% (732)	38% (348)	16
Low	29 (674)	12 (488)	17
Percentage difference	25	26	

higher peer relations make an impact of 25 percentage points on job satisfaction. Among teachers dissatisfied with the quality of students' work, the impact is the same—26 points. Similarly, among teachers who have unsatisfying relations with peers, the level of satisfaction with the quality of school work yields a percentage difference of 17 points; among teachers with high relations with peers the impact is 16 points.

The two variables, satisfaction with the quality of students' work and peer relations, neither interact nor reinforce each other's effect on job satisfaction. Another way to explain this is to say that peer relations do not serve as a condition for the effect of teachers' satisfaction with the quality of school work; nor is the reverse true.

This finding is not surprising. The world of the teacher in the classroom and the world of the teacher outside the classroom seem to be two separate spheres that do not have joint or cumulative effects on teachers' job satisfaction. This finding supports our analysis of the duality of the structure of the school and of the isolation of the teachers in the classroom.[7] Can we suggest that there are two closed systems within the school? These findings further demonstrate that teachers' relationship with peers is more important in affecting job satisfaction than teachers' satisfaction with the quality of students' work, while at the same time suggesting the existence of two separate systems in the school—one of relationships among adults, the other involving individual teachers and their students.

But teachers tended not to be affected by the outcomes of their teaching efforts (if students' work was unsatisfactory, it was not the teachers' fault!).[8] They may have been more affected by the

TABLE 5.12

Job Satisfaction, Perceptions of Students' Liking School, and Peer Relations
(percent teachers very satisfied)

	Perception That Students Liked School			Percentage Difference Between
Peer Relations	Very Much	Quite a Bit	Not Much	Extremes
High	71% (252)	48% (177)	41% (96)	30
Medium	57 (295)	33 (384)	19 (247)	38
Low	33 (220)	15 (301)	8 (278)	25
Percentage difference	38	33	33	

perceptions that their students liked school—and the teachers themselves. (See Table 5.12.) Keeping peer relations constant, we find that when students liked school most teachers were most likely to be very satisfied. Keeping perception of students constant, we find that better relations were correlated with higher over-all job satisfaction. But peer relations were slightly more strongly correlated with teachers' job satisfaction than was students' liking for school (compare the average percentages of the rows and columns, which are respectively 31 percent and 35 percent).

Furthermore, there seems to have been only a small interaction effect between the two variables in relation to job satisfaction. This table shows that when teachers think that their students liked school very much, quite a bit, or not much, peer relations have about the same effect on teachers' level of job satisfaction. This finding may lend additional support to our proposal of the existence in the school of two separate systems. Thus, peer relations do not interact with teachers' perception that their students liked school in affecting their level of job satisfaction, although they both affect job satisfaction independently.

From Tables 5.11 and 5.12 we learn that peer relations are always more important in affecting job satisfaction than either teachers' perception that the students liked school or their satisfaction with the quality of school work. However, peer relations seem even more important in affecting teachers' over-all job satisfaction when dealing with the quality of students' work, which is a "visible" result of student-teacher interaction and thus more subject to evaluation by the peers. The support of the peers thus becomes more important and more necessary in affecting teachers' job satisfaction. This may suggest that the role of the peer relations varies depending on whether or not teacher-student relations are visible to the peer group.

The two tables also show that although peer relations and teachers' perception that the students liked school and their satisfaction with the quality of school work each affect job satisfaction independently, they do not or only very slightly interact in their impact on job satisfaction. In some sense satisfaction or dissatisfaction in the classroom is somewhat separate from satisfaction that teachers secure outside the classroom. This points to the importance for the teachers of the low visibility of their performances in the classroom. McPherson describes this in the following way:

> The ideal is that each teacher should keep her own teaching to herself within the classroom. That she should not display it . . . and that one teacher should not through interference with another teacher's classroom either reveal her own successful ways or cast doubts on the shaky security of another.[10]

This seems to suggest that while the support of peers may be important for teachers, teachers must be careful to preserve the "privacy" of the classroom; the classroom should be a closed world, not to be controlled by peers.

What happens in the classroom, during the day-to-day interaction between students and teachers, is not directly visible to the peer group. Indeed, in the classroom, where a teacher can apply her own criteria of success and failure to her performance and her students' achievements, her self-image and professional gratifications need not depend on peer relations.[11]

We could perform a similar analysis of relations with principals to see how they are related to job satisfaction in combination with teachers' orientations toward students. In order not to lengthen this chapter unduly, we shall, however, present briefly the results of such an analysis and compare them with those of the preceding one. (See Tables 5.13 and 5.14.)

Comparing the effect of teachers' relations with the principal and teachers' orientation toward the students in affecting teachers' job satisfaction, we find similar results. First, there is an independent effect on job satisfaction of both teachers' relations with the principal and teachers' orientations toward the students. Like satisfaction with peer relations, satisfaction with the principal is always

TABLE 5.13

Job Satisfaction, Satisfaction with Quality of Students' Work, and Relations with Principal (percent teachers very satisfied)

	Satisfaction with Quality of Students' Work		
Relations with Principals	Satisfied	Dissatisfied	Percentage Difference
High	60% (655)	37% (326)	23
Low	25 (751)	13 (510)	12
Percentage difference	35	24	

TABLE 5.14

Job Satisfaction, Perception That Students Liked School, and Relations with Principal (percent teachers very satisfied)

	Perceptions That Students Liked School			Percentage Difference Between Extremes
Relations with Principals	Very Much	Quite a Bit	Not Much	
High	72% (322)	47% (270)	38% (144)	34
Medium	60 (223)	31 (272)	16 (181)	44
Low	23 (222)	14 (320)	8 (296)	15
Percentage difference	49	33	30	

more important in affecting teachers' over-all job satisfaction than is teachers' perception that their students like school or teachers' satisfaction with the quality of students' work. The relative importance of satisfaction with the principal in relation to the quality of school work of students is stronger than for teachers' perception that the students like school. Once again an explanation linking the duality of the social organization within the school to the degree of visibility of teachers-student performances seemed plausible. The main difference from our earlier analysis is that relations with principal and orientations toward the students have an interaction effect on teachers' occupational satisfaction, perhaps indicating the influence of principal upon teachers' classroom performances.

The importance of the principal in affecting teachers' performances has been analyzed by Herriot.[12] In a ghetto school system the role of the principal may be of even greater importance in affecting teachers' performances in the classroom and their over-all job satisfaction. The principal may be in a position to affect teachers' performances in the classroom, more so than the peers. The role of the principal in the ghetto school system may be vital in bridging the gap between the classroom and the school and breaking of isolation of teachers.

SUMMARY AND CONCLUSIONS

Up to this point we have seen that teachers' relationships to the social structure of the school are very important in our understanding their over-all job satisfaction. Teachers' relationship to the students, peers, and principal are all strongly related to their occupational satisfaction. The relationships with the peers and the relationships with the principal emerge as being the most strongly related to job satisfaction. Our findings are congruent with data presented in one of the Supplemental Studies for the National Advisory Commission on Civil Disorders. Conducted in 15 major American cities, it showed that almost 90 percent of teachers in ghetto school systems were generally satisfied with their jobs (including the "very" and the "somewhat satisfied").

> Moreover, reminiscent of the old paradox that the whole is greater that the sum of its parts, they [the teachers] declared themselves more satisfied with their position in general than with any of its aspects. They liked their colleagues next best and flexibility permitted them in the classroom after that.[13]

In fact, 46.2 percent are reported as being very satisfied with their colleagues and 58.2 percent with "flexibility permitted in the classroom." The proportion reporting high levels of satisfaction with the students was lower, 36.6 percent. Thus, in this wide sampling of teachers in urban school systems, we observe—by means of rough measurements, to be sure—the same ordering of priorities as we have more intensively investigated in Washington: primary emphasis upon gratifications derived from the two distinct aspects of the dual social organization that characterizes schools: the "society of teachers," on the one hand, and the classroom, on the other. The students as a separate focus of gratification rank relatively low. In this chapter we have also analyzed some aspects of teachers' orientation toward their students in the classroom. Our intention was not to study the interaction between teachers and students in the classroom; the data available were not well suited for such a purpose. Indeed, we only have information about one side of the relationship: teachers' perception about their students in the classroom. We were interested in analyzing how teachers' perception of their students affected teachers' over-all job satisfaction, and its relative importance compared to other factors.

We saw that teachers' orientations toward the students were affected by their interpersonal relations in the school. Good relations with the peers and principal were related to perception that students liked school, and teachers' job satisfaction was related to the quality of school work. Teachers may want or need support from their peers when facing the students. Peers may be important in helping teachers to cope with problems stemming from the teacher-student interaction.

We have also compared the relative importance of various factors in affecting teachers' over-all job satisfaction. We have seen that when we compare the relative importance of teachers' orientation toward students and peer relations, in affecting teachers' over-all job satisfaction, the latter was more important than the former. When analyzing teachers' orientation toward students in the classroom, we used two indicators: teachers' perception that their students liked school, and teachers' satisfaction with the quality of school work. The relative importance of these factors in affecting teachers' over-all job satisfaction is different. The perception that the students liked school was nearly as important in affecting teachers' job satisfaction as relations with peers. In the classroom, students may well be a source of gratification. Satisfaction with the students in the classroom may be possible because of the structural looseness of the school, which permits teachers to define the classroom situation in their own terms. Our data show that although both the peer group and teachers' orientation toward the students affect over-all job satisfaction independently, their effects do not interact. Satisfaction with the students in the classroom may partly come from the "invisibility" to peers of classroom "performance," which escapes their direct control.

These findings may also point to the existence of two independent sources of teachers' job satisfaction. One is rooted in the day-to-day interaction in the classroom, the other in relationships with the peers outside the classroom. Such findings reflect the duality of the school structure and point to the existence of two distinct systems within schools. We may suggest that although peer relations are important in providing support and help to teachers, they do not interfere with, and are not felt in, the classroom, which is under the control of each individual teacher.[14]

That teachers' satisfaction with the quality of school work of the students is less important than peer relations in affecting teachers' over-all job satisfaction may have a special significance in the case of ghetto school systems. In such settings, it may be of special significance that occupational satisfaction is more rooted in association with other teachers than in educational outcomes.

Teachers' relationships with the principal have also an important impact on their job satisfaction. Satisfaction with the principal is even slightly more important in affecting teachers' over-all job satisfaction than relations with peers.

The principal may be an important link between the classroom and the school organization. We saw that relations with the principal, in contrast to relations with the peers, did interact with teachers' orientation toward the students in affecting teachers' over-all job satisfaction. Thus, one function of the principal in an institution characterized by the duality of its structure may be to diminish the isolation of teachers and reduce the effects of duality.

In the next chapter we will analyze the relationship of teachers' autonomy and participation in the running of the school to teachers' occupational satisfaction.

NOTES

1. A Task Force Study of the Public School System in the District of Columbia as It Relates to the War on Poverty, U. S. Congress, House of Representatives, Committee on Education and Labor (Washington, D.C.: Government Printing Office, June 1966), p. 27. Known as the Pucinski report.

2. Gertrude McPherson, "The Role Set of Elementary School Teachers"(unpublished Ph.D. dissertation, Columbia University, 1966), pp. 250-55.

3. J. Kob, "Definition of the Teacher's Role," in A. H. Halsey, J. Floud, and C. Anderson, eds. Education, Economy and Society (New York: The Free Press, 1967), pp. 558-59.

4. See Appendix C for the peer-relations index.

5. See Appendix D for the construction with the principal index.

6. See Appendix E for the rank order of all the items.

7. See Chapter 3 for some implications of the duality of the school structure.

8. McPherson, "Role Set of Elementary School Teachers," p. 76.

9. Ibid., pp. 107-12.

10. Ibid., p. 171.

11. Ibid., p. 294.

12. Robert E. Herriot and Nancy Hoyt St. John, Social Class and the Urban Schools (New York: John Wiley & Sons, 1966), pp. 141-46.

13. David Boesel, "Teachers in Urban Public Schools," Supplemental Studies for the National Advisory Commission on Civil Disorders (Washington, D.C.: Government Printing Office, July 1968), p. 134. The teacher sample in this study was half white and half black.

14. McPherson, "Role Set of Elementary School Teachers," pp. 86-107.

CHAPTER

6

TEACHERS' AUTONOMY AND PARTICIPATION IN SCHOOLS

In the preceding chapter we saw the association between Washington, D.C., elementary school teachers' interpersonal relations in the school and job satisfaction. We noted that interpersonal relatio and especially peer-group relations, were more important than was any other demographic, social, or occupational attribute in explaining job satisfaction.

We shall now examine another set of factors that may contribute to understanding of the generally high level of teachers' occupational satisfaction. These factors are professional autonomy and participation in running the schools. Professionalism has been defined in Chapter 3 as the ability to apply specialized knowledge at one's own discretion. It also implies membership in a profession, which is itsel defined by various criteria, for example, admission standards, a body of specialized knowledge, necessary training, a code of ethics, control over membership, control over entry into membership, a service idea pride of the members in their profession, and publicly recognized status and prestige.[1]

We shall not discuss the definitions and characteristics of a profession in detail or analyze trends toward conversion of occupatio into professions; these problems have been studied by various authors

Some authors have argued that teaching is not a profession or that teachers are only semiprofessionals.[3] Indeed there seems to be no control by teachers themselves over entry into the occupation and no strong professional commitment, no specialized knowledge. One of the main obstacles to professionalization of teachers is their lack of control over academic matters at the school level.[4] Janowitz has also noted that it is difficult to apply the notion of professionalism to public-school teachers: Unlike professional groups that emphasize and support group practice and close relations among colleagues, teachers are isolated in the classroom.[5]

We have already had occasion to mention the pressures that teachers must cope with in the classroom and in the school at large. We have noted the isolation of the teacher in the classroom, which may be even greater in the ghetto school system. How does professional and colleague support help teachers to cope? In this chapter we shall examine teachers' professional autonomy and sense of participation in decision-making about schools. It is important to keep these two variables separate, for they correspond to very different aspects of teachers' work in the schools. Autonomy is a professional attribute, consisting of control over academic matters in the classroom. Participation in decision-making about the school as a whole is an indirect instrument of control over academic matters in the school. Both autonomy and participation can be viewed as teachers' modes of adaptation in the schools. Can these modes enhance teachers' sense of belonging to the peer group and of "attachment" to the school? Can they be viewed as means of coping with pressures, of overcoming isolation in the classroom and escaping the world of children?

Scope for exercise of professional discretion may or may not be a source of job satisfaction, depending upon the context in which it occurs. It seems reasonable to assume, however, that a sense of having fulfilled a professional role may affect teachers' over-all job satisfaction. Participation in running the schools may also be satisfying as a means of acquiring autonomy and greater control over the working environment.

The definition of teachers' professional role is blurred, and expectations about what they can and ought to accomplish keep changing, as Peterson has shown.[6] For the moment we shall deal not with teachers' professional perspectives but only with autonomy and participation in running the schools.

Autonomy is one of the most distinctive features of a profession and may well define the degree of professionalization of an occupation. We measured teachers' professional autonomy by their perceptions of whether or not they were free to determine textbooks and curriculum for their classes. We used the following item: "Teachers have enough freedom in determining textbooks and curriculum." The distribution of possible responses is shown in Table 6.1. Fewer than half the schoolteachers of the Washington, D.C., system (41 percent) agreed that they were given enough freedom to select textbooks and curriculum.

Autonomy in the classroom may have provided teachers with some gratification and enhanced their professional self-image. We might therefore expect it to be linked with occupational satisfaction. (See Table 6.2.) Table 6.2 tells us that teachers with autonomy are more likely to be very satisfied than teachers with no autonomy. Of teachers who have autonomy, 45 percent are very satisfied, compared to 23 percent of teachers with no autonomy. However, 57 percent of

TABLE 6.1

Distribution on Autonomy Question
(percent)

Strongly agree	10
Agree	31
Don't know	17
Disagree	24
Strongly disagree	16
No answer	2
Total	100
	(N=2,432)

TABLE 6.2

Job Satisfaction and Autonomy*
(percent)

	Perceived Autonomy		
Job Satisfaction	Yes	Don't Know	No
Very satisfied	45	35	23
Fairly satisfied	48	54	57
Dissatisfied	6	11	20
Total	99	100	100
	(N=904)	(N=369)	(N=951)

*The autonomy measure reflects both teachers' perception and their subjective evaluation about having autonomy in the classroom. Thus in this study teachers' autonomy does not reflect any objective measure (due to our lack of information) but a subjective evaluation.

teachers reporting having no autonomy are still fairly satisfied with their job.

Teachers' participation in running the schools was measured by two items, which were combined in an index:[7] "Suggestions that I make for the improvement of my school are given consideration" (teachers could agree, disagree, or say that they did not know); "Do you feel you are given adequate voice in the decisions concerning the assignment of pupils to tracks?" (teachers could answer "yes" or "no"). Forty-five percent of respondents agreed that their suggestions were taken into consideration, and 53 percent thought that they had a voice in assigning students to tracks. About half the teachers thus thought that they participated, in one way or another, in running the schools.

Teachers' participation in running the schools is part of what we call "teachers' orientation toward the agency." Our hypothesis is that such participation is a possible way to achieve professional status.

It is interesting that the percentage of teachers reporting participation was higher than that reporting autonomy. It is clear that teachers' autonomy cannot be taken for granted. We suggest that participation in running the schools may be a means either of enhancing autonomy or of compensating for lack of autonomy. It may also serve to bind teachers to the schools in which they already teach. Consequently, attachment to the agency, both its formal and informal structures, may become greater than that to the profession, especially among teachers working with students from slums; these teachers may find no professional prestige in work with such students and may experience great isolation from other teachers, even while they want professional and peer support.* The desire for professional autonomy may therefore ultimately undermine professional orientation toward clients.

How does participation in running the schools affect over-all job satisfaction? The relationship is shown in Table 6.3. The higher the level of participation, the likelier teachers are to be very satisfied. Of teachers with a high level of participation, 54 percent are very satisfied, compared with 17 percent with a low level of participation.

Comparing the relations between job satisfaction, on one hand, and autonomy and participation, on the other, we find that participation has a greater effect than does autonomy. The percentage difference among those very satisfied is 23 percent for autonomy and 37 percent for participation. This finding supports the earlier hypothesis of the importance of participation in the schools.

We have noted that teachers' autonomy is a professional attribute, whereas participation in decision-making about the schools may be viewed as either a means of control over academic matters in the

---

*Participation in running the schools has lately taken on a political flavor. Indeed the political dimension of the problem of sharing power and responsibility in the schools is a real one. In our research, however, no data were gathered about it. We can deal only with the interpersonal dimension of teachers' participation in the school.

TABLE 6.3

Job Satisfaction and Participation in Running Schools
(percent)

Job Satisfaction	Level of Participation		
	High	Medium	Low
Very satisfied	54	31	17
Fairly satisfied	42	58	58
Dissatisfied	4	11	25
Total	100	100	100
	(N=652)	(N=812)	(N=582)

school as a whole or compensation for low autonomy. Teachers' autonomy and participation ought to be related positively in the first instance and negatively in the second. The relations between the two variables can be seen in Table 6.4. We see that there was a strong positive relationship between autonomy and participation: Teachers who scored high on the participation index were more likely to claim autonomy than were those who scored low on the index. But the direction of the relationship cannot be determined from Table 6.4, for there is probably reciprocal influence between the variables. Teachers with high participation were more likely to have autonomy, and teachers with a sense of autonomy were more likely to participate in decisions.

We have seen that participation and autonomy are interrelated and that both are related to occupational satisfaction. What is the relative importance of these two variables in affecting teachers' job satisfaction, and are their effects mutually independent? Table 6.5 shows their simultaneous effects upon job satisfaction.

The two variables clearly do have independent effects on teacher job satisfaction. Indeed, when participation is kept constant, the percentage of very satisfied teachers increases with perception of autonomy. When autonomy is kept constant, the percentage increases as participation increases.

The percentage differences for columns and rows tell us something about the strength of the relationship between each variable and job satisfaction when the other variable is held constant. The average difference between teachers with low and high participation was 32 percent, whereas that between teachers having and lacking autonomy was 12 percent. Participation in decision-making about the schools was thus much more important than was autonomy in accounting for high job satisfaction. Table 6.5 also gives us information on an interaction effect between autonomy and participation: They tend to reinforce each other. That is, one variable serves as a condition that enhances the effect of the other. Participation in decision-making cannot therefore be regarded as a substitute for professional autonomy

TABLE 6.4

Relationship Between Teachers' Perceived Autonomy and Participation (percent)

	Participation		
Autonomy	High	Medium	Low
Agree	63	40	25
Don't know	16	18	12
Disagree	21	42	63
Total	100	100	100
	(N=653)	(N=812)	(N=582)

TABLE 6.5

Job Satisfaction, Autonomy and Participation (percent teachers very satisfied)

	Participation			Percentage
	High	Medium	Low	Difference*
Agree	41% (124)	25% (95)	14% (363)	27
Don't know	47 (340)	32 (145)	17 (322)	30
Disagree	61 (413)	35 (77)	23 (161)	38
Percentage difference	20	10	9	

*To simplify use of the table, we have computed for each column and for each row the percentage difference between the extreme categories.

in affecting teachers' job satisfaction. Teachers with low professional autonomy were not more prone to participation in running schools. It seems more likely that those who had a role in decision-making experienced greater autonomy as well.

We have already mentioned that in social organizations there is a gradual accommodation of professional norms and standards to occupational norms and standards arising from the specific working situation, as defined by Zaleznik.[8] We have also noted that semi-professionals dealing with lower-class clients tend to become more agency- and peer-oriented and less client-oriented. These general processes may also be at work in the schools. We could interpret the predominance of participation over autonomy as an indication of a tendency to become agency-oriented. Another such indication is the relationship between participation in the decisions about the schools and teachers' relations to principals. Teachers who scored high on the index of relations with principals were more likely to score high on the participation index than were teachers who scored low on relations with principals: 61 percent of teachers with high relations with the principal have a high level of participation compared with 8 percen with low relations with the principal. Participation in running the schools may thus be more than a means of securing autonomy; it may become by itself a means of winning support from principals. It may also correspond to what Lieberman and Bidwell have described as a means of administrative manipulation of control of teachers and of gaining their support for the administration.[9] We do not, unfortunatel have data to test this idea.

The importance of participation in affecting job satisfaction may also result from the fact that contact with adults is limited in schools. Participation with peers in common activities may create opportunities for more extensive peer relations. Waller has describe the important problem of the elementary-school teacher, who has littl sustained contact with adults: "If the teacher is to control understandi it must be by sacrifice of some of his adulthood."[10] Many teachers, especially women, have little contact outside the world of children; indeed there is little difference in this respect between motherhood and elementary-school teaching.

Waller and Kob have analyzed the tensions between the worlds of children and adults, tensions inherent in teaching; they have found that teachers' sense of belonging to the adult world outside the school does not depend upon their profession. They tend to be isolated social As one teacher explained, "Outside the classroom I have nothing to say."[11] The teacher is wholly absorbed in the child's world. The professional sphere, especially of the woman teacher, is organized around the child; women's nonprofessional lives are also frequently centered on children. Such teachers perform only a "guest role" in adult society, which may explain why the peer group in the school comes to seem so important and why participation in running the school may appear to open possibilities of institutionalized interaction among adults. Indeed, participation in decision-making about the schools gives teachers a chance to approach problems from an adult point of view. Issues, discussions, and even language are different from those in child-centered classrooms. Participation may thus compensate for some of the psychological and social isolation between children and adults. It may also increase teachers' interaction and communication with peers. If participation in decision-making has this function, then we should find it related to peer relations. And, indeed, Table 6.6 shows that the better the relations with peers, the more likely is high participation. Of teachers high on the peer relations index, 54 percent are also high on participation, compared with 14 percent of teachers who are low on the peer-relations index. Of course, teachers' participation may grow out of interaction, and, conversely, they may have to interact to influence decision-making; we therefore assume that the two variables have reciprocal effects and possibly reflect the need to escape from classroom isolation.

As participation and peer relations are both related to job satisfaction and are also highly interrelated, the question arises whether or not they have independent effects upon job satisfaction. Table 6.7 shows that they do, that each affects job satisfaction when the other is held constant. We also learn that peer relations are slightly more important than is participation in affecting job satisfaction. Finally, participation and peer relations have no interaction effect upon job satisfaction. Apparently the two variables are interchangeable

TABLE 6.6

Participation in School and Peer Relations
(percent)

Participation	Peer-Relations Index Scores		
Index Scores	High	Medium	Low
High	54	35	14
Medium	34	42	42
Low	13	23	45
Total	101*	100	101*
	(N=484)	(N=840)	(N=731)

*Higher than 100 percent because of the rounding of figures.

TABLE 6.7

Job Satisfaction, Peer Relations, and
Participation in Running School
(percent teachers very satisfied)

Participation-Index Scores	Peer-Relations Index Scores High	Medium	Low	Percentage Difference
High	68% (263)	48% (290)	37% (99)	31
Medium	48 (158)	36 (354)	16 (300)	32
Low	42 (62)	21 (193)	10 (327)	32
Percentage difference	26	27	27	

means of securing higher job satisfaction outside the classroom. Thus 42 percent of the teachers with a low level of participation and high peer relations are very satisfied while 37 percent with the opposite combination—high level of participation, poor relations with peers—are very satisfied.

To sum up, participation in decisions about running the schools may have various purposes for teachers. First, it is likely to enhance a sense of autonomy; second, it is likely to promote some attachment or loyalty to the organization beyond the confines of the classroom; third, it may reinforce peer relations. We saw at the beginning of the chapter that autonomy was related to job satisfaction. It may also have been associated with peer relations. Let us see to what extent peer relations and teachers' sense of autonomy were associated. The better the peer relations, the more likely teachers were to perceive themselves as autonomous. Among teachers who are high on the peer-relations index, 63 percent perceived that they have autonomy, compared to 26 percent who are low on the peer-relations index. Good relations with colleagues may thus be viewed as a support for teachers' sense of autonomy.

We have already seen that both perceived autonomy and peer relations were related to job satisfaction. How did they affect it in combination, and what was the relative importance of each? Table 6.8 shows that these variables affected teachers' job satisfaction independently but that relations with peers were more important than was autonomy. This finding suggests that there may have been a

TABLE 6.8

Job Satisfaction, Peer Relations, and Autonomy
(percent teachers very satisfied)

Perceived Autonomy	Peer-Relations Index Scores			Percentage Difference
	High	Medium	Low	
Agree	37% (120)	32% (336)	13% (448)	24
Don't know	62 (72)	32 (165)	23 (132)	39
Disagree	64 (330)	43 (412)	22 (202)	42
Percentage difference	27	11	9	

shift in the source of job satisfaction from classroom to peer. Why autonomy was less important than peer relations can be understood in the light of processes accounting for the "deprofessionalization" of teachers, as described by Lieberman.[12]

Autonomy was also associated with teachers' relations with principals; the latter had greater effects on job satisfaction, but there was also an interaction effect between the two variables.

Previous findings about interpersonal relations in schools suggest that both autonomy (a professional attribute) and participation (a structural characteristic of the school) vary significantly with the character of interpersonal relations within the school; both may serve as forms of control over individual teachers. Conformity with the peer group and the preferences of the principal may thus be rewarded; indeed good relations with peers and principals were more important in job satisfaction among Washington teachers than were participation and especially autonomy.

The results reported in this chapter suggest the greater importance of participation over autonomy in affecting job satisfaction. It was suggested that participation increased teachers' autonomy, promoted an "attachment" to the school, and contributed to peer relations. In a ghetto school system it may have even greater importance and may lead to further isolation of teachers from students. Professional autonomy seems relatively unimportant to job satisfaction among ghetto teachers. It may be used by administrators as a form of control, and the professional desire for autonomy may thus ultimately undermine professional orientation toward clients.

We turn now to the socioeconomic level of the school, the context in which these relations occur.

NOTES

1. See Appendix F, prestige rating.

2. For example, A. R. Carr-Saunders, Professions: Their Organization and Place in Society (Oxford: The Clarendon Press, 1928); Everett C. Hughes, "Profession," Daedalus, Vol. 92, Fall 1953, pp. 655-68; William J. Goode, "Community Within a Community: The Professions," American Sociological Review, Vol. 25, 1960, pp. 902-14.

3. William J. Goode, "The Theoretical Limits of Professionalization," in Amitai Etzioni, ed., The Semi-Professions and Their Organization (New York: The Free Press, 1969), pp. 267, 286.

4. Myron Lieberman, Education as a Profession (Englewood Cliffs, N.J.: Prentice-Hall, 1956), pp. 44-55.

5. Morris Janowitz, Institution Building in Urban Education (New York: The Russell Sage Foundation, 1959), pp. 29-32.

6. Warren Peterson, "Teachers Amid Changing Expectations," Harvard Educational Review, Vol. 25, 1954, pp. 106-17.

7. See Appendix G for the construction of the index.

8. Abraham Zaleznik, "Interpersonal Relations in Organizations," in James March and A. Simon, eds., Handbook of Organizations (Chicago: Rand McNally, 1965), p. 588.

9. Lieberman, Education as a Profession, p. 485; and Charles E. Bidwell, "The School as a Formal Organization," in March and Simon, eds., Handbook of Organizations, pp. 1003-9.

10. William Waller, The Sociology of Teaching (New York: Wiley, 1932), p. 59.

11. Ibid., p. 60; J. Kob, "Definition of the Teacher's Role," in A. H. Halsey, J. Floud, and C. Anderson, eds., Education, Economy and Society (New York: The Free Press, 1967), p. 559.

12. Lieberman, Education as a Profession, p. 489.

CHAPTER

7

THE SOCIOECONOMIC CONTEXT OF THE SCHOOL AND TEACHERS' ROLE IN ITS SOCIAL STRUCTURE

We have seen in previous chapters the importance of the interpersonal relations within the schools; we have singled out the peer group as more important in affecting teachers' occupational satisfaction than either professional attributes or satisfaction with students' work.

Teachers do not, however, all teach in the same types of schools. In Chapter 2, we classified Washington elementary schools according to the socioeconomic levels of the residents in the areas that they serve, and we explained our use of such levels as indicators of the problems and pressures that teachers encountered. We shall now ask in what ways the socioeconomic characteristics of the students affected the social structure of the school and the teachers' role in it. More specifically, we shall explore how school SES affected teachers' relations with students, peers, and the authority structure of the school.

Previous studies have shown that the SES of the student body affects various aspects of the teacher's job besides his attitude toward students. Herriot and St. John found that teachers in low-SES schools were less likely to be satisfied than those in high-SES schools.[1] Becker noted that teachers in low-SES schools wanted to be transferred to better schools in middle-class neighborhoods.[2] He presented a model of horizontal mobility, in contrast to the usual model of vertical mobility, reflecting teachers' greater interest in achieving transfers to higher-status schools than in attaining higher professional or administrative status within low-status schools.

In our study we found that teachers in low-SES schools were indeed less likely to be satisfied. (See Table 7.1.) Almost half the teachers in high-SES schools were very satisfied, compared with about a third in low- and medium-SES schools. The percentage

TABLE 7.1

Job Satisfaction and School SES
(percent)

Job Satisfaction	School SES		
	High	Medium	Low
Very satisfied	46	32	33
Fairly satisfied	45	55	55
Not satisfied	9	13	12
Total	100	100	100
	(N=350)	(N=953)	(N=920)

difference was not very great, but it was worth noting. It has been widely assumed that a major source of dissatisfaction among teachers in "slum" schools is the types of students that they must teach and the nature of relations between students and teachers. As we have already discovered, teachers reported a greater number of obstacles in low-SES schools—for example, students' poor home environments, too much time spent on discipline, and students' poor training in basic skills—than in high-SES schools.[3]

Effects of school SES were, however, also modified in various ways by the tracks to which teachers were assigned within the school. The tracking system in use during the survey of the Washington, D.C., schools, included four levels, as we explained in Chapter 2. In our study of black elementary-school teachers we have used tracks as crude measures of classroom achievement but have omitted the honor track because only 24 black teachers out of a total of 2,452 teachers were assigned to it. We shall use data from the regular, general, and special academic tracks in our analysis of teachers' attitudes toward students. From the lowest (special academic) to the highest (regular) track there were differences in students' IQs and achievement levels within each grade.

Let us first see to what extent the tracks to which teachers were assigned affected occupational job satisfaction. Our findings are presented in Table 7.2, which shows a weak relation between teachers' job satisfaction and the tracks in which they were teaching. Among teachers who were very satisfied there was no linear relation at all. Teachers in the general track were the least likely to be very satisfied with their jobs, 29 percent, compared with 33 percent in the special academic track and 36 percent in the regular track.

Among teachers who were dissatisfied with their jobs 16 percent were teaching in the special academic track, 16 percent in the general track, and 10 percent in the regular track. There was no apparent patterned association between over-all job satisfaction and tracks in which teachers were teaching. Let us turn to how teachers' orientations toward students were affected by school SES and tracks in which they were teaching.

TEACHERS' RELATIONS WITH STUDENTS AND SCHOOL SES

Although we do not have any direct data on teacher-student relations in Washington's elementary schools, we do have data on teachers' perceptions of students. Let us see how the socioeconomic levels of the schools affected teachers' perceptions of their students' liking for school and satisfaction with students' work. Our findings are shown in Tables 7.3 and 7.4.

Table 7.3 shows that teachers in high-SES schools were more likely to perceive their students as liking school very much than were teachers in low- or medium-SES schools. Of teachers in high-SES schools, 43 percent thought that their students liked school very much, compared to 32 percent in low-SES schools. What is most surprising is not the relatively low correlation between perceptions of students' liking and SES level but the high percentage of teachers in each type of school who thought that their students liked school

TABLE 7.2

Job Satisfaction and Track
(percent)

		Track	
Job Satisfaction	(2) Regular	(1) General	(0) Special Academic
Very satisfied	36	29	33
Fairly satisfied	54	55	51
Not satisfied	10	16	16
Total	100	100	100
	(N=1,132)	(N=637)	(N=207)

TABLE 7.3

Teachers' Perception of Students' Liking for School, by School SES (percent)

Students' Liking for School	School SES High	Medium	Low
Very much	43	33	32
Quite a bit	37	40	37
Somewhat, not much, and not at all	20	27	31
Total	100	100	100
	(N=351)	(N=954)	(N=918)

TABLE 7.4

Teachers' Satisfaction with Quality of School Work, by School SES (percent)

Satisfaction	Index of School SES High	Medium	Low
Very satisfied and somewhat satisfied	69	61	62
Neither satisfied nor dissatisfied, somewhat dissatisfied, and very dissatisfied	31	39	38
Total	100	100	100
	(N=348)	(N=948)	(N=918)

very much or quite a bit. That such perceptions were slightly related to school SES no doubt reflected differences in social origins of the students.

Indeed we expect students from middle-class homes to enjoy school more than do students from lower-class homes. Many studies[4] have confirmed that school and teachers mean different things to students from middle-class and lower-class homes.[5] For middle-class students school is an extension of home, where similar values and behavior are expected, a challenge corresponding to their experiences outside; they are motivated to work through approval and encouragement from both teachers and parents. For lower-class students the reverse is true. They do not find continuity between home and school; they are caught between different values and different kinds of pressures in the two settings;[6] the school experience and what is taught often do not make sense to students and thus cannot be applied outside the school.

Table 7.4 reveals an even lower correlation between SES level and teachers' satisfaction with students' work than we found between SES level and perceptions that students liked school. Of teachers in high-SES schools, 69 percent were satisfied with the quality of students' work, compared to 62 percent in low-SES schools. Authors like Havighurst, Loeb, Davis, and Coleman,[7] to mention only a few, have demonstrated that students' achievements and performance are primarily affected by their social origins. How then was it possible that the social origins of their students affected Washington teachers' satisfaction with school work so slightly? The percentage of teachers in all types of elementary schools who were satisfied with their students' work was very high, more than 60 percent. That school SES only slightly affected teachers' perception of students' liking school and their satisfaction with students' work may suggest that their perceptions were less influenced by the social characteristics of the students in the ghetto system than by their own definition of the situation. To quote Coleman, "We do not observe any systematic tendency for teachers' professional commitment to be affected by the composition and characteristics of schools in which they teach."[8]

But school SES may not be the appropriate variable in analysis of student-teacher relations that occur mainly in the classroom. The characteristics of students with whom the teacher was in direct contact may have affected him more than did the general socio-economic level of the school. Let us see how the track in which the teacher worked affected his perception of students' liking for school and his evaluation of student work. The relation between teachers' perceptions that their students liked school and track can be seen in Table 7.5, which shows that teachers in the regular track were

TABLE 7.5

Perception That Students Liked School and Track
(percent)

Perceptions That Students Liked School	Track		
	(2) Regular	(1) General	(0) Special Academic
Very much	37	28	25
Quite a bit	41	40	32
Somewhat and not much	23	33	44
Total	101*	101*	101*
	(N=1,131)	(N=640)	(N=207)

*Percentages exceed 100 percent because of rounding.

likelier to think that their students liked school very much than were teachers in the special academic track. Of teachers in the regular track, 37 percent thought that their students liked school very much, compared with 25 percent in the special academic track. What seems surprising is that, even among teachers in the special academic track, more than half perceived their students as liking school at least quite a bit. Among teachers who perceived their students as liking school somewhat or not much, 44 percent were assigned to the special academic track and 23 percent to the regular track.

The tracks to which teachers were assigned significantly affected their perceptions that students liked school. Did teachers' satisfaction with quality of students' work also vary according to track? Our findings are presented in Table 7.6, which shows that there was a relation between satisfaction with students' work and track.

Teachers in the regular track were likelier to be satisfied than teachers in the special academic track, 69 percent compared with 52 percent. At least half the teachers were, however, satisfied with the quality of their students' school work, still a very high figure. The tracks with which teachers worked were thus clearly more closely associated with their perceptions of students than was school SES. But the differences were not very great. Whatever the track, there was still a high percentage of teachers who were satisfied with the quality of students' work and thought that their students liked school very much.

TABLE 7.6

Satisfaction with Students' Work and Track
(percent)

	Track		
Satisfaction with Students' Work	(2) Regular	(1) General	(0) Special Academic
Very satisfied and satisfied	69	52	52
Neither satisfied nor dissatisfied, somewhat dissatisfied, and very dissatisfied	31	48	48
Total	100	100	100
	(N=1,130)	(N=636)	(N=207)

The tables discussed so far seem to have shown a marked difference in perceptions between teachers in high-SES schools, on one hand, and in medium- and low-SES schools, on the other, and between those in the regular track, on one hand, and those in the general and special academic tracks, on the other. Now we ask what the simultaneous effects were of school SES and track on teachers' job satisfaction. SES characterizes the large and complex unit called the "school," whereas track specifies the types of students whom teachers confronted in the classroom. Table 7.7 shows the simultaneous independent effects of track and school SES on job satisfaction. School SES had greater effects on job satisfaction than did track. For example, among teachers who worked in the special academic track, 26 percent of those who were very satisfied were assigned to low-SES schools, compared with 48 percent assigned to high-SES schools, suggesting that the social characteristics of the students with whom they were in day-to-day contact were less important in affecting teachers' job satisfaction than were over-all characteristics of the schools.

We shall use both measures (school SES and track) in further analysis, depending upon the aspect of student-teacher relations that we are studying.

TEACHERS' RELATIONS WITH PEERS AND SCHOOL SES

Many studies have examined students' social origins only in connection with student-teacher relations, but the school is a social

TABLE 7.7

Job Satisfaction, School SES, and Track Among
Very Satisfied Teachers
(percent)

School SES	Track: (2) Regular	(1) General	(0) Special Academic
High	47 (204)	36 (83)	48 (25)
Medium	30 (496)	30 (258)	36 (80)
Low	37 (414)	27 (289)	26 (99)
Percentage difference	10	9	22

organization in which interaction processes and interpersonal relatio
are important in achieving organization goals, and we may therefore
expect that all elements of the social structure will be affected
whenever part of it is.

There has been little research on the effects of school SES
upon the social structure of the school. We shall attempt here to
fill some gaps by examining its effects upon teachers' relations with
peers and principals. The variations in peer relations in schools of
different SES are shown in Table 7.8, which reveals that school SES
was indeed associated with teachers' peer relations. Teachers in
high-SES schools were likelier than teachers in low-SES schools to
have very good peer relations. Of teachers in high-SES schools,
35 percent scored high on the peer-relations index, compared with
21 percent in low-SES schools. Apparently more difficult working
conditions and more "difficult" children undermined peer relations.
Can we assume that dealing with lower-class children generated
greater conflict and tension among teachers? Perhaps schools
serving lower-class students in general face new problems for which
there are no ready solutions or traditional remedies? A wider range
of disagreement on the most appropriate ways to deal with such
problems may exist among teachers; because such a situation calls
for new teaching techniques and new organizational responses, the
greatest tension may exist between older and younger teachers, who

are likelier to uphold different methods and philosophies of teaching. All these factors may explain why teachers in low-SES schools in Washington were likelier to have poor peer relations.

TEACHERS' RELATIONS WITH PRINCIPALS AND SCHOOL SES

Let us turn now to variations in the correlation between school SES and teachers' relations with principals. Considering our analysis of teacher-principal relations in Chapter 5 and our suggestion that principals in low-SES schools had greater shares of responsibility for and power over both administrative and academic matters, we might expect teacher-principal relations to have been closely associated with school SES. Herriot and St. John have pointed out that principals in low-SES schools had different functions than did those in high-SES schools: "In many respects the teachers in schools of high SES can perform at high level, irrespective of the performance of the principal, whereas in schools of lowest SES, their performances may depend on his."[9] The role of the principal is clearly of crucial importance in a ghetto school.

Becker has reported another important function of the principal in such a school.[10] Whereas in middle-class schools teachers tend to confine disciplinary problems to the classroom and to punish children themselves (values shared by teachers and parents ensure parental support), teachers in lower-class schools send troublesome

TABLE 7.8

Teachers' Relations with Peers and School SES (percent)

Index of Peer Relations	Index of School SES		
	High	Medium	Low
High	35	22	21
Medium	42	42	40
Low	23	36	39
Total	100	100	100
	(N=334)	(N=951)	(N=931)

TABLE 7.9

Teachers' Relations with Principal and School SES
(percent)

Index of Relations with Principals	Index of School SES		
	High	Medium	Low
High	38	33	31
Medium	33	30	30
Low	29	37	39
Total	100	100	100
	(N=354)	(N=957)	(N=931)

children to the principals for correction in an effort to avoid alienati[illegible]
children and parents.

The role of the principal in a low-SES school is ambiguous, for, as we saw earlier, teachers may require his help and guidance while at the same time fearing loss of professional responsibility. In this study we have been able to measure teachers' perceptions of the importance of their own role and that of the principal within the school. Teachers were asked, "To the best of your knowledge, in most cases who actually participated in the decisions regarding the assignment of pupils? Counselor, principal, teachers, others." In low-SES schools 58 percent of the teachers perceived that the princi-pal was the main participant, whereas 39 percent thought that teache[illegible] were. In high-SES schools the corresponding figures were 50 percer[illegible] and 48 percent. At the same time that teachers in low-SES schools were likely to think that principals had too much to say in assigning pupils they expressed desires for more personal supervision. They were likelier to place importance on being kept informed of how well they were doing and more dissatisfied with the amount of such feed-back that they received than were teachers in high-SES schools.

The variations in teachers' relations with principals in Washin[illegible] ton elementary schools of varying SES can be seen in Table 7.9. As we might have expected, teachers in low-SES schools were likelier t[illegible] have poor relations with principals than were those in high-SES schools. Of teachers in low-SES schools, 39 percent ranked low on the index of relations with principals, compared with 29 percent in high-SES schools.

Lieberman, Bidwell, and Herriot and St. John[11] have independently analyzed the dynamics of teacher-principal relations and have suggested that principals are increasingly in control of academic matters and that teachers' professional role tends to diminish, especially in the undefined working situations typical of low-SES schools.

TEACHERS' AUTONOMY, LEVEL OF PARTICIPATION, AND SCHOOL SES

Our research has suggested how school SES affects teachers' sense of autonomy and perceived participation in decisions about running the school.[12] Variations in teachers' autonomy in schools of different SES are shown in Table 7.10. Teachers in low-SES schools were indeed less likely to have a sense of autonomy than were teachers in high-SES schools. Autonomy was also very strongly related to teacher-principal relations. Teachers who experienced very good relations with principals were more likely to have autonomy—and the converse. Is it possible that the hope of autonomy was used as an instrument of control over teachers, that increased autonomy was a reward, especially in low-SES schools?

Participation in decisions about operating the schools was also lower among teachers in low-SES schools (31 percent reported low participation) than among those in high-SES schools (20 percent reported low participation). This variable was also highly related to teachers' relations with principals: 61 percent of teachers who reported high satisfaction with principals also reported high levels of participation in decisions about running the schools, compared with 8 percent of those who reported low satisfaction with principals. Although we do not know the direction of this relationship, it may be that Lieberman was correct in describing autonomy and participation as instruments of subtle manipulation of teachers by administrators and thus as indirect sources of control. (See Chapter 6.)

PATTERNS AMONG THE RESULTS

All the findings discussed so far reveal consistent patterns: The level of school SES is never strongly related to teachers' job satisfaction, relationships with peers and principal, and sense of autonomy and participation. The strongest relationship is found between relations with peers and school SES. It shows a difference of 11 percent. The level of school SES thus seems to play a relatively small role in affecting various aspects of teachers' work. Teachers in low-SES schools were more likely to be dissatisfied with their

TABLE 7.10

Teachers' Autonomy and School SES
(percent)

Autonomy	Index of School SES		
	High	Medium	Low
Some	50	43	41
None	50	57	59
Total	100 (N=352)	100 (N=945)	100 (N=909)

students, more likely to have poor relations with their peers and principals, and less likely to have autonomy and to participate in decisions about running the schools.

From these findings two major conclusions emerge. First, school SES was related to all aspects of teachers' interpersonal relations, autonomy, and participation in the schools. Teachers' interpersonal relations with peers were more affected by school SES than were those with the students and principals. We saw in Chapter 5 that peer relations were among the most important in afffecting teachers' job satisfaction. Now we learn that they were also the most dependent upon the global context in which they developed (as attested by the percentage difference between low- and high-SES schools, which was greater for peer relations than for any other variable studied). Second, teachers in low-SES schools not only had to deal with more "difficult" students and under more difficult conditions but were also "penalized" socially, in that they more frequently suffered poor peer relations, and professionally, in that they were less likely to enjoy autonomy and a share in decisions about running the schools. We can thus easily understand why teachers in low-SES schools were somewhat less likely to be very satisfied with their jobs than were those in high-SES schools.

JOB SATISFACTION AS AFFECTED BY SCHOOL SES, INTERPERSONAL RELATIONS, AND PARTICIPATION

So far we have analyzed variations in teachers' relations within the school social structure, autonomy, and participation according to school SES. In Chapter 5 and 6 we examined the extent to which these factors were associated with teachers' occupational satisfaction and noted the importance of interpersonal relations. Because school SES; teachers' relations with students, peers, and principals; and teachers' participation and autonomy are all related to job satisfaction, we must study their effects independently.

In Chapter 5 we examined the association between job satisfaction and two indicators of teachers' relations with students: their perceptions that students liked school and their satisfaction with the quality of students' work. Let us see how such relations varied according to two aspects of context: social composition of the student body and the track in which the teacher worked. Our major concern will be to show the different effects of these two aspects on the responses of teachers to the ghetto situation.

We have found that job satisfaction was affected by both school SES and teachers' perceptions that students liked school. What were the simultaneous effects of these two variables upon job satisfaction?

Table 7.11 shows, first, that when SES is kept constant, the percentage of very satisfied teachers increases with teachers' perceptions of students' liking for school. Keeping these perceptions constant, we see that the higher the SES, the more likely teachers were to be very satisfied. Both variables thus had independent effects on teachers' job satisfaction. Second, comparing the average percentage differences for rows and columns (crude measures of the association of one variable with job satisfaction when the other is

TABLE 7.11

Job Satisfaction, Relations with Students, and School SES
(percent teachers very satisfied)

	Perception That Students Liked School			
School SES	Very Much	Quite a Bit	Not Much	Percentage Difference
High	64% (151)	42% (129)	17% (70)	47
Medium	50 (313)	26 (378)	19 (262)	31
Low	54 (294)	29 (344)	15 (278)	39
Percentage difference	10	13	2	

TABLE 7.12

Job Satisfaction, Perception That Students Liked School, and Track
(percent teachers very satisfied)

Track	Perception that Students Liked School			Percentage Difference
	Very Much	Quite a Bit	Not Much	
Regular	55% (417)	29% (459)	15% (255)	40
General	49 (176)	25 (252)	18 (208)	31
Special academic	55 (51)	41 (66)	16 (90)	39

kept constant), we can see to what extent each variable accounts for teachers' level of job satisfaction. The average percentage difference in the columns is 8.2, in the rows 39. The perception that students liked school was thus about four times as important as was school SES in affecting teachers' job satisfaction. Finally, Table 7.11 reveals that the two variables not only had additive effects upon job satisfaction but that they also interacted to reinforce each other's effects. For example, school SES had a stronger impact on job satisfaction among teachers who thought that their students liked school very much than among those who thought that their students liked school very little.

We have noted that track was also related to teachers' perceptions that students liked school. Table 7.12 shows the combined effect on job satisfaction of teachers' perceptions and of the tracks in which they were teaching. The former, rather than the latter, mainly accounted for teachers' job satisfaction. The patterns of perception among teachers in the regular (highest) and special academic (lowest) tracks were very similar in relation to job satisfaction.* Job satisfaction among teachers in the general track was less affected by perceptions that students liked school.

Among teachers who thought that students liked school very much or not at all, there was no linear relation between track and

*As the number of teachers working with the special academic track was small, we must interpret this finding with caution.

job satisfaction. Teachers in the general and special academic tracks were equally likely to be very satisfied with their jobs, whereas those in the regular track were less likely to be very satisfied. It is difficult to interpret these findings because of the nonlinear nature of these relationships. In order to throw some additional light on the impact of track and school SES, however, we shall consider how they affect the relation between teachers' satisfaction with the quality of school work and over-all job satisfaction. Perceptions that students liked school may have reflected subjective evaluations based on various criteria, including students' conformity to teachers' expectations. This possibility may partly explain the absence of pattern among the associations in Table 7.12. Asking teachers about the quality of students' work may have revealed a more uniform basis for evaluation of students.

First, let us see how school SES affected the relation between satisfaction with quality of school work and over-all job satisfaction. Our findings are shown in Table 7.13. The patterns revealed are similar to those in Table 7.11. Both school SES and satisfaction with quality of students' work affected job satisfaction independently. The latter variable accounted for a greater part of job satisfaction than did the former, and both interacted to influence job satisfaction.

Teachers' satisfaction with the quality of students' work also had a greater impact on job satisfaction in high-SES schools than in low- and medium-SES schools: 23 percent compared to 17 and 19 percent respectively. In high-SES schools teachers who were very

TABLE 7.13

Job Satisfaction, Satisfaction with School Work, and School SES
(percent teachers very satisfied)

	Satisfaction with Students' Work		
School SES	Very Satisfied and Satisfied	Not Satisfied and Dissatisfied	Percentage Difference
High	55% (262)	32% (124)	23
Medium	40 (598)	23 (371)	17
Low	41 (598)	22 (371)	19
Percentage difference	14	10	

TABLE 7.14

Job Satisfaction, Satisfaction with Students' Work, and Track
(percent teachers very satisfied)

Track	Very Satisfied and Satisfied	Neither Satisfied nor Dissatisfied	Dissatisfied and Very Dissatisfied	Percentage Difference
Regular (2)	40% (777)	33% (96)	23% (257)	17
General (1)	37 (331)	15 (88)	22 (214)	15
Special academic (0)	50 (108)	24 (33)	11 (66)	39

satisfied with their jobs were likelier to be very satisfied with students' work and dissatisfied with the students' work at the same time than were very satisfied teachers in medium- and low-SES schools. Teachers in high-SES schools may have had both "better" students and higher standards and expectations in connection with them.

Let us now look at the effects of track, as shown in Table 7.14. This classroom context had a very different impact on job satisfaction than did school SES, a measure of school context. Keeping track constant, we find that satisfaction with the quality of school work affected teachers' job satisfaction but that teachers in the regular and general tracks were much less affected than were those in the special academic track (as can be seen from comparison of the percentage differences in the rows). The percentage differences between teachers who were satisfied with students' work and those who were dissatisfied were 17 in the regular track, 15 in the general track, and 39 in the special academic track. We see then that teachers in the last (lowest) track were likelier to be affected by their perceptions of the quality of school work; 50 percent were very satisfied with their jobs and with the quality of students' work, but only 11 percent were very satisfied with their jobs and dissatisfied with the quality of students' work. How can we explain that teachers in contact with the most "difficult" students were so satisfied with the quality of school work?

Again it is likely that teachers' modes of evaluation, their criteria of achievement in the classroom, depend upon their expectation perceptions of, commitment to, and understanding of students. Even teachers dealing with difficult children may find success with them very gratifying as long as that success is not measured by standard achievement tests.[13] Indeed, teachers working in the special academic track were most likely to deny that achievements corresponded with their assessments of student performance. Perception and satisfaction with students' work may be different from, sometimes even opposed to, the "official norm" of achievement; and the interaction between students and teachers may offer gratifications unrelated to purely academic performance. In the classroom itself teachers are able to evaluate their own success in promoting social and intellectual change in students.

It is difficult to find any consistent pattern between the variables in Table 7.14. But the "objective characteristics" of students— as represented by the tracks—were clearly less important in explaining job satisfaction than were teachers' own perceptions of the quality of students' school work. Another way to explain this finding is to suggest that teachers had their own ways of defining the classroom situation and their own criteria of success and failure.

Teachers' perceptions of students' liking for school and satisfaction with the quality of students' work may thus have been a function more of their own definitions of the classroom situation than of the characteristics of their students. Indeed, how else could we explain that teachers dealing with the most "difficult" students, with those who had the lowest level of academic achievement, were as likely to perceive that their students liked school very much as were teachers dealing with more academically oriented students—and more likely to be satisfied with the quality of these students' works?

It is possible that teachers working in the lower tracks lowered their academic standards of evaluation and changed or adapted their expectations of students. Teachers' level of satisfaction would then have been a function of their own norms and expectations. Teachers working in the higher tracks, as we have mentioned, were dealing with students defined as more able. They may have had higher expectations and standards for school work, which may explain why they were less satisfied with it, even when they thought that students were doing good work. Their frame of reference would have been different from that of teachers working with less able students.

That school SES and track affected teachers so differently may also reflect the two levels of school organization.[14] That measures based on the social origins of students at the broader school level, compared with similar measures at the classroom level, affected teachers differently, suggests that norms and patterns of interaction at the two levels may also have been different. Teachers were less affected by students' characteristics in the classroom than by school

SES. At the school level there was some association among students' social origins, teachers' perceptions that students liked school, and teachers' satisfaction with the quality of school work. But at the classroom level there were no linear relationship.

If teachers tended to define the classroom situation in their own terms, then the relation between job satisfaction, on one hand, and teachers' perceptions that students' liked school and satisfaction with the quality of school work, on the other, could be explained in a new light. Indeed, in Chapter 5, we speculated about the direction of such a relationship. The additional information that we now have on teacher-student interaction suggests that teachers were likely to be satisfied when students conformed to their definitions of the classroom situation (whatever they might be) and that at the same time they evaluated their own performances according to their expectations from students, which in turn affected over-all job satisfaction.

The association between teachers' orientations toward students and job satisfaction was affected differently by track and by school SES. It seems possible that the two levels of school organization and the isolation of teachers in the classroom may have accounted for the lesser importance of track in over-all job satisfaction.

Of course, teachers' definitions of the classroom situation are not necessarily either adequate or appropriate to the specific needs of students: Most of the time what teachers demand is conformity.

JOB SATISFACTION, PEER RELATIONS, AND SCHOOL SES

Let us turn now to analysis of the relationship between job satisfaction and teachers' relations with peers and principals in schools of varying SES. We have already seen that all these variables were related to teachers' over-all job satisfaction. We now ask what was the relative importance of peer group and school SES in determining teachers' over-all job satisfaction. Table 7.15 shows that both did affect job satisfaction independently. Indeed, keeping peer relations constant, we find that the percentage of very satisfied teachers increased with school SES; keeping SES constant, we see that the percentage of very satisfied teachers increased with better peer relations. The table also shows that peer relations were more important in affecting job satisfaction than was school SES. Teachers with good peer relations in low-SES schools were three times as likely to be very satisfied than were teachers with poor peer relations in high-SES schools. Finally, the table reveals mutual reinforcement between SES and peer relations in their impact on job satisfaction.

TABLE 7.15

Job Satisfaction, Peer Relations, and School SES
(percent teachers very satisfied)

School SES	Peer-Relations Index Scores: High		Medium		Low		Percentage Difference
High	60%	(123)	45%	(146)	18%	(81)	48
Medium	54	(207)	34	(401)	17	(345)	37
Low	55	(190)	37	(371)	17	(359)	38
Percentage difference	11		8		1		

Teachers in high-SES schools were likelier to be affected by peer relations than were teachers in medium- and low-SES schools (as can be seen from a comparison of the percentage differences in the rows). The percentage difference for teachers in high-SES schools was 48, whereas it was only 37 and 38 in medium- and low-SES schools, respectively. How can we explain such differences? It may be that teachers in high-SES schools had different standards of evaluation for their peer relations, or perhaps there was some other source of reinforcement of good peer relations. There may have been elements in the climate of high-SES schools that permitted peer relations to exert a stronger impact on job satisfaction. One possibility is that high-SES schools had a socially and regionally more homogeneous population of teachers. Teachers from Washington itself were more likely to be assigned to high-SES schools than were teachers from the South. When we measure the schools by percentage of Washington-born teachers, we see that teachers assigned to schools where half or more of the faculty had been born in Washington were twice as likely to have good peer relations as were teachers assigned to other schools. (See Table 7.16.)

Teachers who had lived in Washington all their lives were more likely to have shared the same experiences and values.[15] Schools in which the faculty included a majority of such teachers were apt to have high social homogeneity, which in turn contributed to satisfactory peer relations.

TABLE 7.16

Proportion of Washington-born Faculty and Peer Relations (percent)

	Washington-born Faculty			
	30% and Less	31-40%	41-50%	51% and More
Percentage of teachers scoring high on peer-relations index	15 (350)	26 (630)	28 (820)	36 (430)

Another factor may also have come into play. High-SES schools were characterized by higher percentages of older teachers and of teachers who had longer teaching experience in the system. When we classify schools by the average number of years teachers had spent in the system, we have the results shown in Table 7.17.

The longer that teachers had been in the Washington, D.C., system, the likelier they were to have known one another; perhaps as important, the likelier they were to have internalized both the formal and the informal norms of the schools. We must remember that a school in which the average length of teaching service is less than four years has had considerable turnover. Through the years teachers have either left for more desirable posts or have left the system entirely, and the school has had to depend upon newcomers to the system. As teachers in such schools tend to be relative strangers to one another, it is not surprising that they score low on the peer-relations index. These two factors may help to explain why peer relations had greater impact on job satisfaction in high-SES schools. Let us turn now to teachers' relations with principals in schools of varying SES.

TEACHERS' RELATIONS WITH PRINCIPALS

We have seen that both teachers' relations with principals and school SES were related to job satisfaction. What were their independent effects? Our results are shown in Table 7.18. The independent effect of each variable can be seen from a glance at the association between it and job satisfaction when the other variable is held constant. Relations with principals were much more important than was

TABLE 7.17

Average Years Teaching in System
(percent)

	Less than 4	5-6	7-8	9 and More
Percentage of teachers scoring high on peer-relation index	18 (493)	21 (782)	23 (518)	34 (399)

TABLE 7.18

Job Satisfaction, Relations with Principal, and School SES
(percent teachers very satisfied)

School SES	High	Medium	Low	Percentage Difference
High	67% (133)	46% (115)	20% (102)	47
Medium	54 (313)	33 (280)	12 (360)	42
Low	54 (284)	35 (278)	14 (258)	40
Percentage difference	13	11	6	

school SES. The average percentage differences in rows and columns were 43 and 10, respectively. Relations with principals were thus four times as important in accounting for teachers' job satisfaction as was school SES. Finally, school SES and relations with principals had an interaction effect upon teachers' job satisfaction. When one variable was present to a strong degree, the other had even greater impact on teachers' job satisfaction.

So far we have seen that teachers' relations with peers and principals were more important in accounting for teachers' job satisfaction than was school SES. Although both kinds of relations had greater impact on teachers' job satisfaction in high-SES schools, they were important at all SES levels. Interpersonal relations in schools were thus crucial to teachers' job satisfactions.

TEACHERS' AUTONOMY AND PARTICIPATION IN SCHOOL

We saw in Chapter 6 that autonomy and participation in running the schools were strongly related to teachers' job satisfaction. We have also mentioned that job satisfaction was affected by school SES. Let us examine the independent effect on job satisfaction of autonomy and participation, on one hand, and school SES, on the other. Table 7.19 shows the relation between teachers' perceived autonomy and job satisfaction in schools of varying SES; Table 7.20 shows the relation between teachers' participation in school decisions and job satisfaction in schools of varying SES.

Table 7.20 reveals that both school SES and teachers' sense of autonomy affected occupational satisfaction and that the former was the more important. The higher the school SES, the more likely perceived autonomy was to have an impact on job satisfaction. The percentages were 28 for high-SES schools, 22 for medium-SES schools, and 19 for low-SES schools. As in most of the other tables in this chapter, the main difference is between high-SES schools, on one hand, and low- and medium-SES schools, on the other.

Table 7.20 reveals the same pattern again: Both teachers' level of participation and school SES affected job satisfaction independently, but, in high-SES schools, participation had the stronger effect.

TABLE 7.19

Job Satisfaction, Perceived Autonomy, and School SES
(percent teachers very satisfied)

	Perceived Autonomy			
School SES	Agree	Don't Know	Disgrace	Percentage Difference
High	58% (176)	39% (56)	30% (116)	28
Medium	43 (401)	33 (157)	21 (385)	22
Low	42 (368)	35 (150)	23 (385)	19
Percentage difference	16	4	7	

TABLE 7.20

Job Satisfaction, Participation, and School SES
(percent teachers very satisfied)

School SES	Level of Participation			Percentage Difference
	High	Medium	Low	
High	63% (125)	40% (141)	23% (70)	40
Medium	54 (280)	24 (338)	17 (240)	37
Low	48 (260)	33 (327)	15 (241)	33
Percentage difference	15	7	8	

The percentage difference was 40, compared to 37 in medium-SES schools and 33 in low-SES schools.

SUMMARY AND CONCLUSIONS

In the first part of this chapter we introduced school SES and examined how it affected various aspects of teachers' interpersonal relations, autonomy, and participation in running the schools. We noted that teachers in low-SES schools were more likely to be dissatisfied than were those in high-SES schools and that they were less satisfied with the quality of students' work and less likely to think that their students liked school. Their relations with peers and principals were less likely to be good. Finally, they were less likely to perceive themselves as enjoying autonomy and participating in decisions about the schools. On all grounds teachers in low-SES schools were thus at some disadvantage, compared with teachers in high-SES schools. Not only did they teach lower-class students, who often are more "difficult," but they were also penalized socially (in their interpersonal relations) and professionally (in their participation and autonomy).

In the second part of the chapter we examined the relations between job satisfaction, on one hand, and teachers' relations with students, peers, and principals and their autonomy and participation, on the other, in schools of varying SES. Indeed, we isolated the independent contribution of each of these latter factors as it affected job satisfaction. In each instance school SES and the paired variable contributed independently to job satisfaction. Second, we noticed that school SES was always much less important in accounting for job satisfaction.

Third, we noted that the relation between teachers' job satisfaction and any one of the variables under study was specified by school SES; it was stronger in high-SES schools and weaker in low-SES schools. Teachers in low-SES schools were thus always less likely to be satisfied than were teachers in high-SES schools. The difference in job satisfaction between teachers in high- and low-SES schools was most marked in association with peer relations. We suggested that the difference could have arisen from the greater liklihood that faculties in high-SES schools were socially and regionally homogeneous and included higher proportions of teachers who had been in the system for a long time.

Finally, this chapter has given us the opportunity to compare track and school SES in relation to teachers' orientations toward students in schools of varying SES. Such analysis and comparison suggested that teachers were affected differently by the classroom characteristics of their students and the social characteristics of the students in the school as a whole. We suggested that, because of the two levels of school organization and the isolation of teachers in the classroom, students' classroom characteristics were much less important in affecting teachers' job satisfaction than were teachers' perceptions that students liked school and teachers' satisfaction with the quality of school work. We suggested further that this condition might have arisen because teachers were able to define the classroom situation in their own terms. Indeed, teachers in the special academic track (the lowest track) appear to have been more satisfied when they perceived their students as doing well.

These observations suggest that ghetto teachers' occupational satisfaction is frequently based upon definitions of the professional situation that are not grounded in the academic progress of students, especially in the lowest-SES schools and the lowest tracks.

NOTES

1. Robert E. Herriot and Nancy Hoyt St. John, Social Class and the Urban Schools (New York: John Wiley & Sons, 1966), pp. 84-102.

2. Howard S. Becker, "The Career of the Chicago Public School Teacher," American Journal of Sociology, Vol. 57, 1952, pp. 470-77.

3. See Chapter 2.

4. For example, Howard S. Becker, "Social Class Variations in the Teacher-Pupil Relationship," *Journal of Educational Psychology*, Vol. 25, 1952, pp. 451-65.

5. Allison Davis, "Cultural Factors in Remediation," *Educational Horizons*, Summer 1965, pp. 231-51.

6. Martin Deutsch, "The Disadvantaged Child and the Learning Process," in Harry Passow, ed., *Education in Depressed Areas* (New York: Teachers College, Columbia University, 1966), pp. 161-79.

7. Lloyd Warner, Robert J. Havighurst, and Martin Loeb, *Who Shall be Educated?* (New York: Harper, 1944); Allison Davis, *Social Class Influences upon Learning* (Cambridge: Harvard University Press, 1950); James Coleman, *Equality of Educational Opportunity* (Washington, D.C.: Government Printing Office, 1966), pp. 217-330.

8. Coleman, *Equality of Educational Opportunity*, p. 350.

9. Herriot and St. John, *Social Class and the Urban Schools*, p. 144.

10. Becker, "Career of the Chicago Public School Teacher."

11. Myron Lieberman, *Education as a Profession* (Englewood Cliffs, N. J.: Prentice-Hall, 1956), pp. 282-87; Charles E. Bidwell, "The School as a Formal Organization," in James March and A. Simon, eds., *Handbook of Organizations* (Chicago: Rand McNally, 1965), pp. 1003-9; Herriot and St. John, *Social Class and the Urban Schools*, pp. 141-57.

12. These two variables were described in Chapter 6.

13. Gertrude McPherson, "The Role Set of Elementary School Teachers" (unpublished Ph.D. dissertation, Columbia University, 1966).

14. See Chapter 3.

15. See historical analysis in Chapter 2.

CHAPTER

8

TEACHERS' PROFESSIONAL STANDARDS: THE CREATION OF COLLECTIVE BELIEFS

In Chapter 3, we examined the conditions under which a subculture originates and the factors that keep it going. In Chapter 7, we described how the social structure of the school affected teachers' job satisfaction in Washington, D.C. Social structure is also very important in the solution of problems of functioning as described by Cohen.[1] In this chapter we shall show how teachers' participation in a system of social interaction affected how they dealt with their problems. We have suggested that teachers face a series of problems linked with the structural characteristics of the schools and with the types of students they teach. Now we shall try to show how the peer group contributed to defining teachers' professional standards in the Washington public elementary schools. The existence of group standards among teachers implies a common frame of reference that permits each teacher to share norms with the other members of the group. To what extent were teachers' attitudes toward professional standards associated with their relations with their peers?

The questionnaire yielded information only about teachers' perceptions of whether or not professional standards were upheld in the schools. There was no question about how academic standards were maintained and how the needs of "deprived" children were fulfilled. But other available data suggest the problematic nature of maintaining standards in a ghetto school system. Both Passow and Pucinski have given information on the achievements of students in Washington, D.C., school system.[2] Passow noted that mean achievement scores tended to follow socioeconomic and racial patterns. (The information was given for students at every school level.) Those of students in the Washington system were below the national norm. The percentage of dropouts was very high, and the inability of a majority of the students to read and write was also reported by Pucinski. The inadequacy of the curriculum was Pucinski's main concern, but he also noted the problems of working conditions and inadequate means for serving.

We shall begin by examining to what extent teachers' perceptions that professional standards were maintained was related to their occupational satisfaction. Then we can see how far peer relations affected these perceptions and the association between them and job satisfaction.

In their professional roles, teachers in general are confronted with two sets of demands in connection with the academic abilities of students: that the able ones be kept to appropriate standards and that the curriculum also meet the needs of "deprived" students. These two sets of professional demands are not necessarily incompatible but receive different relative emphases among different types of teachers in different schools.

Let us first see how Washington's black elementary schoolteachers perceived their schools in terms of these two sets of demands. To the statement, "High academic standards are maintained in my school for the able students," teachers could respond "strongly agree," "agree," "don't know," "disagree," or "strongly disagree." Table 8.1 shows the distribution of the answers.

More than half thought that such standards were being kept up in their schools. (Notice that the question applied only to the schools in which the respondents themselves were teaching.) The issue is an important one, for evaluation of a school and of its teachers by

TABLE 8.1

Black Teachers' Perception That Standards Were Maintained for the Able

	Percent	N
Strongly agree	10	246
Agree	41	998
Don't know	27	675
Disagree	14	333
Strongly disagree	4	104
No answer	3	96
Total	99*	2,452

*Less than 100 percent because of rounding.

TABLE 8.2

Black Teachers' Perception That Curriculum Satisfied Deprived Children's Needs

	Percent	N
Strongly agree	8	183
Agree	36	878
Don't know	13	331
Disagree	29	699
Strongly disagree	12	307
No Answer	2	54
Total	100	2,452

the community, parents, and other schools often turns on it. But whether or not academic standards are maintained may be linked with the type of students that the school serves. Teachers in high- and low-SES schools may thus differ in their perceptions: Indeed, 66 percent of the teachers in Washington's high-SES schools thought that standards for the able were being preserved, compared to 48 percent in low-SES schools.

Although upholding such standards is the task of each individual teacher in the classroom, all teachers must cope with it, or at least acknowledge it as a problem, a very real one in a school system characterized by a generally low level of student achievement. It has been described thus by one teacher in a slum school: "I am afraid maybe my standards are going down. I think my academic standards definitely are changing. You see, you just can't hold these children to the same standards you would if you have children from the suburbs and I don't like that this happens."[3] It is clear that keeping up standards for the able is both an individual challenge and a collective problem in the school.

Black teachers were also presented with the following statement: "The curriculum in my school meets the needs of underprivileged and culturally deprived* children." Again they could respond "strongly agree," "agree," "don't know," "disagree," or "strongly disagree." The distribution of responses is shown in Table 8.2.

---

*We use the term "culturally deprived" because it was used in the questionnaire. Nevertheless, we would have liked to avoid the value judgments inherent in it.

Approximately equal numbers of teachers agreed and disagreed. Again we have information only on teachers' perceptions of the curriculum where they were actually teaching and no direct measure of the adequacy of the curriculum itself.

How to meet the needs of the deprived is one of the most fundamental problems in ghetto education. Yet little has been accomplished in terms of existing programs or methods for dealing with slum children. The needs of these children have been studied in detail, but solutions and methods are still in the experimental stage. In Washington a 1966 survey revealed that 54.5 percent of eighth-grade students read at one or more years below grade level.[4] It emphasized the specific needs of children whose values and concerns are different from those of middle-class white children.

Teachers have been aware of the importance of the needs of deprived students. Most, however, do not have the specialized training to respond adequately. Specialists, officials, and the community at large may emphasize the needs of the deprived without providing teachers with the means to cope with them.

In Washington, D.C., the problem of the deprived was very acute for all teachers because of the great majority of such children in the schools. Indeed, the greater part of the teachers' professional role was focused around deprived children.

In trying to meet professional standards for both able and deprived students most teachers are likely to experience individual failure, but they may respond to the problem collectively, defining a frame of referecne in which failure is no longer experienced as such. To use Cohen's words, " 'failure' can be transformed into something less humiliating by imputing to others fraud, malevolence or corruption, but this means adopting new perspectives for looking at others and oneself."[5] McPherson described the same process of collective redefinition, in which teachers shift the blame from themselves to students. As one teacher at Adams School reported, "We teach, that is our job. If students don't want to learn it is not our fault."[6]

Teachers may indeed be able to cope with or solve the problem by redefining their frame of reference, but what we want to know now is how far such solutions can be inferred from knowledge of teachers' interpersonal relations within the school and how far they affect teachers' job satisfaction.

First, let us see how perceptions that professional standards were being met were related to job satisfaction; then we shall introduce characteristics of the students and peer relations. The relation between job satisfaction and perceptions that academic standards were kept for the able can be seen in Table 8.3.

Teachers who thought that high academic standards were maintained in their schools were more likely to be very satisfied

TABLE 8.3

Job Satisfaction and Perception That Standards Were Maintained for the Able (percent)

Job Satisfaction	Standards Kept for the Able		
	Agree	Don't Know	Disagree
Very satisfied	44	30	16
Fairly satisfied	50	55	58
Not satisfied	6	15	25
Total	100	100	99*
	(N=1,139)	(N=635)	(N=403)

*Because of rounding, total is less than 100 percent.

TABLE 8.4

Job Satisfaction, Perception of Standards for the Able, and School SES (percent teachers very satisfied)

School SES	Perception of Standards			Percentage Difference
	Agree	Don't Know	Disagree	
High	54% (225)	36% (77)	26% (42)	28
Medium	42 (485)	23 (267)	14 (166)	28
Low	40 (422)	33 (280)	15 (185)	25

than were teachers who did not think so: 44 percent compared to 16 percent. We have already noted that teachers in high-SES schools were more likely to perceive the schools as maintaining standards for the able than were teachers in low-SES schools—and also that SES was related to job satisfaction. The initial relationship may thus have been affected by the SES of the school in which the teacher worked, but the relation between perception of standards and job satisfaction was not as Table 8.4 shows. Keeping school SES constant, we see that the relation between job satisfaction and perceptions of standards was not affected. Teachers were more satisfied when they thought that their schools maintained high standards for the able, but their satisfaction was not affected by the "objective" characteristics of their students. The same processes of collective definition seem to have been at work in schools of varying SES. The percentage difference between teachers who agree and those who disagree of different school level is roughly the same.

We have already suggested that teachers in a process of interaction and coping with similar problems will put forth a collective response. We may therefore expect that teachers' perceptions that standards were being kept up for the able were associated with their peer-group relations. Table 8.5 shows that the relationship was a strong one. Of those who scored high on the peer-relations index, 75 percent agreed that standards were kept in their schools, compared with 32 percent of those with low scores (the percentage difference was 43).

Because of this strong relationship, that between job satisfaction and perception of standards may be analyzed in a new light: The peer group may have been crucial. We can therefore raise the question whether or not perception that high academic standards are maintained depends upon the quality of peer relations. It may represent a group standard.

The influence of peer relations on the association between job satisfaction and perceptions of standards can be seen in Table 8.6, which shows that, in fact, peer relations specified that relation. The initial relationship was weakened at all three levels of peer relations. However, we can see that the lower the peer relations,

TABLE 8.5

Perception of Academic Standards and Peer Relations
(percent)

High Academic Standards Kept	Peer-Relations Index Scores		
	High	Medium	Low
Agree	75	57	32
Don't know	19	29	36
Disagree	6	14	32
Total	100	100	100
	(N=519)	(N=893)	(N=776)

TABLE 8.6

Job Satisfaction, Perception of Standards for the Able, and Peer Relations (percent teachers very satisfied)

Peer-Relations Index	Perception of Standards Agree		Don't Know		Disagree		Percentage Difference
High	60%	(390)	56%	(100)	31%	(20)	29
Medium	42	(504)	35	(258)	21	(127)	21
Low	23	(245)	16	(277)	11	(248)	12

the more likely that the relation was more strongly reduced. Comparing the percentage difference among the rows (crude measure of the association between satisfaction and perception of standards), we see that it is of 12 percent when scores of the peer-relations index are low, of 21 percent when they are medium, and of 29 percent when they are high. The higher the scores on the peer-relations, index, the more likely that it will affect the relation between perception of standards and teachers' job satisfaction. In addition among teachers who agreed that high academic standards were being kept up, 23 percent were very satisfied, compared with 11 percent among those who disagreed. Among teachers with high peer relations, 60 percent of those who agreed and 31 percent of those who disagreed were very satisfied. Although school SES did not affect the initial relationship, as we saw in Table 8.4, peer relations did, as shown in Table 8.6.

In the light of our general knowledge about the role of interaction among people who must cope with the same problems under similar conditions, we might suggest that teachers' perceptions that academic standards are maintained for the able is a collective belief that functions to preserve their sense of professional status by changing their frame of reference. If teachers' belief that academic standards are kept up is supported by the peer group, they are likely to be very satisfied independently of the characteristics of the students. Their satisfaction is the result of a process of collective rationalization. Agreeing that high academic standards are maintained makes it possible for teachers to displace responsibility for students' inability to learn to the students themselves. If teachers' collective belief is a collective answer to their difficulties in keeping up standards for the able, the same process may occur, even more so, in response to difficulties meeting the needs of deprived children.

Again we must emphasize that we do not know to what extent academic standards were actually maintained and the needs of deprived students met in Washington schools, for these elements were not measured in our study. It seems probable, however, that, given the characteristics of these schools, as described in Chapter 2, the problems no doubt confronted them all, in varying degrees. What we can analyze here is teachers' perceptions that standards for the able were maintained and needs of the deprived met, and we can examine the results of teachers' collective solutions to these two problems of functioning. Indeed, we have shown that perception of academic standards was related to school SES.

Providing adequate curriculum for deprived children may be an even greater problem than keeping up standards for the able and may thus also call for collective solution. Although about 40 percent of our teachers believed that the curriculum met the needs of deprived students, the task force study of the District of Columbia public school system gave very detailed analysis and assessment of accomplishments in this area. It showed that, although there have been important efforts to introduce remedial programs, few students have benefited from them.[7]

The problem of how to respond to the needs of deprived children is pervasive. Most teachers and most schools are not equipped to deal adequately with it, although official philosophy may emphasize the necessity of doing so. Again every teacher faces the problem in the classroom, and it is a general concern of the school as a whole. How do teachers function in such a setting? Again we may expect that teachers sharing similar experience and involved in an interaction process will evolve a collective response in the form of a shared definition of the situation.

We shall proceed as in our examination of teachers' perceptions that standards were kept up for the able. The perception that the curriculum met the needs of deprived students in the school may have been a source of job satisfaction in that it reflected the successful performance of one aspect of the professional role. The relation between job satisfaction and perceptions that the curriculum met the needs of the deprived can be seen in Table 8.7.

Teachers who perceived their schools as meeting the needs of deprived children were more likely to be very satisfied with their jobs than were teachers who did not think so: 48 percent compared with 20 percent. Meeting the needs of deprived children, which is a function of the school, was also a source of gratification for teachers.

TABLE 8.7

Job Satisfaction and Perception That Curriculum Met Deprived Children's Needs (percent)

Job Satisfaction	Agree	Perceptions Don't Know	Disagree
Very satisfied	48	33	20
Fairly satisfied	45	57	60
Not satisfied	7	10	19
Total	100	100	99*
	(N=981)	(N=308)	(N=926)

*Less than 100 percent due to rounding.

TABLE 8.8

Job Satisfaction, Perception That Curriculum Met Deprived Children's Needs, and School SES (percent teachers very satisfied)

School SES	Agree	Perceptions Don't Know	Disagree	Percentage Difference
High	57% (164)	36% (61)	35% (118)	22
Medium	46 (418)	30 (141)	17 (331)	29
Low	46 (391)	34 (101)	19 (410)	27

We may ask whether teachers' perception that the needs of deprived children are met are affected by the school SES. We find no significant difference in the perceptions of teachers located in schools of various SES, in contrast to our findings about standards for the able. Of teachers in low-SES schools, 44 percent thought that the curriculum met the needs of deprived children, compared with 48 percent in high-SES schools.

The relation between job satisfaction and perceptions that the needs of the deprived were met was slightly affected by school SES, as shown in Table 8.8. In low- and medium-SES schools the relation was a little stronger than in high-SES schools. Perceptions that the curriculum met the needs of the deprived may have been more important in affecting job satisfaction in low-SES than in high-SES schools. We will discuss this finding later in the chapter. Table 8.8 also suggests that the social characteristics of the student body had much less effect on job satisfaction than did perceptions that the curriculum meets deprived children's needs.

From this table we learn that, keeping SES constant, the relationship between teachers' perception of the needs of the deprived and job satisfaction is rather similar at the three levels of school SES. Looking at the percentage differences of the rows (again used as a crude measure of association between job satisfaction and perception that the curriculum meets the needs of deprived children), we see that there is no great difference between schools with low,medium, and high school SES, although, in medium- and low-SES schools, teachers' job satisfaction is slightly more affected by the belief that they are met.

If we keep in mind that dealing with such needs is a common problem, shared by all the teachers of a school, we may expect teachers' perceptions to be related to peer relations.

We have also to keep in mind that successfully teaching slum children implies an understanding of the values and behavior of these children, use of specialized methods, and access to appropriate material and other resources.[8] Teachers in ghetto schools may be finding it increasingly difficult to teach children to read and write. Teachers' inability to perform successfully their professional role may lead to feelings of insecurity and threats to their professional role and status, even though, as we have seen, a majority of our teachers were satisfied with the quality of their students' work! This apparent contradiction can be explained by teachers' collective redefinition of the frame of reference, so that individual sense of failure was replaced by simultaneous mutual recognition of set standards by which performances could be defined and evaluated.

In the light of these considerations, let us just analyze the association between peer relations and perceptions that the curriculum met the needs of deprived children and then let us see to what extent variations in peer relations affected the association between job satisfaction and such perceptions.

Table 8.9 shows that the better the relations with peers, the likelier it was that teachers would agree that the curriculum met the needs of deprived children; 61 percent with high-peer relations scores thought so, and 27 percent did not. How can we explain that such perceptions were so strongly related to peer relations when we know that school SES and the tracks in which they taught did not cause

TABLE 8.9

Peer Relations and Perceptions That Deprived Children's Needs Were Met (percent)

Perceptions	Peer-Relations Index Scores High	Medium	Low
Strongly agree and agree	61	50	27
Don't know	15	15	12
Disagree and strongly disagree	24	35	61
Total	100	100	100
	(N=520)	(N=918)	(N=789)

any variation or meaningfully affect the relation between job satisfaction and perceptions? Such perceptions may have reflected teachers' collective rationalization, their adherence to a collective belief. Such rationalization introduces a new frame of reference, which permits teachers to cope with the problem and to preserve their sense of professional role; it thus may affect their occupational satisfaction. Peer relations become very important, for the acceptability of an idea to one person depends upon its acceptability to others in the group.

The peer group would thus permit and reinforce collective beliefs among teachers, which would in turn affect teachers' job satisfaction. If this is so, then the association between teachers' job satisfaction and perceptions that the curriculum met the needs of deprived children ought to have been affected by the nature of peer-group relations. The influence of the peer group on the relation between job satisfaction and perceptions that the curriculum met the needs of deprived children is presented in Table 8.10. This table shows that peer relations did indeed specify the initial relationship. For teachers with less satisfactory peer relations, the initial relationship between need of deprived and job satisfaction was less than half that for teachers with more satisfactory peer relations. We have already seen that perceptions about the curriculum for deprived students were correlated with peer relations. Now we see that both interacted to affect teachers' job satisfaction.

The creation and maintenance of a subculture is linked with processes of constant reinforcement and reaffirmation of shared beliefs and standards. We may say that peer relations are a condition for the creation of a problem-solving subculture leading to collective beliefs, which in turn may reinforce group relations, as long as there is a common problem. The peer group, thus, affected perceptions that deprived children's needs were being met, which situation, in turn, may have affected the quality of peer relations.

Two aspects of ghetto teachers' professional functioning—perception that standards were being kept up for the able—gave rise to shared beliefs among teachers. They were part of an adaptive process within a problem-solving subculture, a means by which teachers could preserve a sense of professional standards and achieve high job satisfaction. We have described a process in which ghetto teachers' perceptions were affected not by objective characteristics like school SES but by their peer relations. In addition, we have shown that the relation between job satisfaction and perceptions that professional standards were being met was specified by the quality of peer relations. We may say that these perceptions represented collective rationalizations about organizational problems that teachers were unable to solve but that were linked with successful performance of their professional roles: maintenance of standards for the able and meeting the needs of deprived children

TABLE 8.10

Job Satisfaction, Perceptions That Curriculum Met Deprived Children's Needs, and Peer Relations (percent teachers very satisfied)

Peer-Relations Index Scores	Perceptions Agree	Don't Know	Disagree	Percentage Difference
High	65% (316)	33% (77)	41% (125)*	24
Medium	47 (457)	32 (136)	24 (321)	23
Low	26 (208	19 (95)	13 (480)	13
Percentage difference	39	14	28	

*Keeping high peer-relations constant, we notice that the relationship between perception of the needs of deprived and job satisfaction is not linear. It reduces the percentage difference.

under ghetto conditions. Teachers faced with such problems, which they cannot successfully resolve, find it necessary in some way to protect their professional status and role from the "threat" posed by failure to satisfy professional standards. Teachers in the same setting dealing with the same problem will evolve a collective response. In our example teachers' perceptions were really collective beliefs and may have served to protect their professional status. At the same time they reinforced peer relations and permitted teachers to be satisfied with their jobs, whatever the characteristics of their students.

If the creation and maintenance of collective beliefs under such conditions helps to preserve professional standing and enhance job satisfaction, adherence to such beliefs should vary as a function of the apparent gap between professional standards and school functioning. The process of collective definition of the situation, as a function of an occupational subculture based on peer relations, should, for example, be more prominent in situations in which it is more difficult to meet the educational needs of deprived children. In such an organizational context, the collective belief that such needs are being met in the schools becomes more imperative, to the degree that they are not, in fact, being met. As a partial test of this reasoning and a further extension of the analysis, we shall turn to the effects of variations in the social-class composition of ghetto student bodies upon teachers' belief that the needs of deprived children are being met.

We have said that the perception that the curriculum meets the needs of deprived students was not related to the school SES. At the same time we pointed to information documenting the Washington system's inability to meet the needs of the deprived in most of its schools. If, however, the perception that the needs of the deprived are met reflects a collective belief—as a response to teachers' inability to cope with the needs of the deprived—such beliefs ought to be more pronounced in schools dealing with lower-SES students. In such schools, it is even more difficult to meet the needs of the deprived children, and their teachers have to cope with the problems arising from such a situation, involving a sense of failure and insecurity. Because of the inability of teachers to respond adequately to the needs of the deprived and the official ideology about the importance of taking into account the needs of the deprived, teachers in low SES schools might be compelled to adhere more strongly to collective beliefs about their success in order to escape a sense of professional failure and insecurity.

In such situations, the peer group ought to be of prime importanc in finding a solution, in the form of a collective belief, that will give teachers support and reassurance. This search may lead, to use

TABLE 8.11

Teachers' Perception That Curriculum Met Needs of Deprived Students, Peer Relations, and School SES (percent teachers who think that the curriculum meets the needs of the deprived)

School SES	Peer Relations Index High	Peer Relations Index Medium	Peer Relations Index Low	Percentage Difference
High	53% (120)	52% (147)	36% (80)	17
Medium	60 (206)	52 (396)	26 (340)	34
Low	68 (189)	47 (367)	27 (352)	41
Percentage difference	15	5	9	

Cohen's words, to "mutual exploration and joint elaboration of a new solution."[9]

Let us see to what extent variations in the SES of schools affect the existence of shared beliefs among teachers. Let us analyze the relationship between teachers' perceptions that the needs of the deprived are met and peer relations in schools of varying SES. The results are found in Table 8.11.

This table suggests that, indeed, the lower the school SES, the more likely that peer relations will play an important role in insulating teachers from a sense of failure. In low-SES schools, teachers' relations with peers are comparatively more important in affecting teachers' perceptions that the needs of the deprived are met. Looking at the percentage difference between contexts of low and high satisfaction with peer relations at the three SES levels, we see that the percentage differences increase regularly from the high-SES schools to the low-SES schools. In the high-SES schools, the percentage difference is 17, in the medium-SES schools 34, in the low-SES schools 41.

In the low-SES schools it is more difficult to meet the needs of deprived children while at the same time the pressures to do so are greater. Teachers in such situations need to create a shared frame of reference, a shared belief, that might alleviate a sense of inadequacy, of failure.[10] Thus, in such schools, the character of peer relations has a greater effect on teachers' perceptions of their success. Another way to interpret the finding is to suggest that teachers in low-SES schools have at the same time to rely more heavily on the peer group and to conform to the norm of the group if they are to receive mutual support and reaffirmation from the peer group.

In low-SES schools, 68 percent of teachers perceived the curriculum as meeting the needs of deprived students if they have high scores on the peer-relations index, compared with 27 percent with low scores. We may suggest that conformity to the norms of the group is much stronger in low-SES than in middle- and high-SES schools. This might have important implications when analyzing the problem of change in slum schools and the diffusion of innovation. In such a context, various informal forms of control by the peer group are such that any individual innovation or nonconformist behavior might be more difficult to achieve than in higher SES schools. The satisfactions attained through peer association more heavily influence teachers' definition of the professional situation. In such a context, "relational dependence"[11] becomes crucial because it is rewarded and valued by others in the group, and it is also a way to achieve security and acceptance in the group. We suggest that in order for teachers to preserve their professional role and status, they have to elaborate collective beliefs about professional norms. They do not seem to be creating new norms or new standards but rather preserving existing ones.

As we can see from Table 8.11, in the high-SES schools the role of the peer group is much less important in affecting teachers' beliefs that the needs of the deprived are met. In such a situation the "threat" to the professional role and status of the teachers in not fulfilling these professional standards is less conducive to the creation of collective beliefs because the apparent gap between the needs of deprived being met and the functioning of the school is smaller.

However, we may wonder if the preservation of high academic standards for the able is not perceived by teachers in high-SES schools as being more of a problem than in low-SES schools. One would think that whereas in low-SES schools the shared concern of teachers under the same pressures is to provide a collective response to problems linked with the deprived children, in high-SES schools teachers might share a concern about preserving high academic standards. The processes described here would be similar to those ascribed to low-SES schools. In this case, however, the "threat" to professional norms would come from the inability to keep high academic standards for the able, in schools where such standards might be expected to be kept.

So let us look at the relationship between job satisfaction and teachers' perception that high academic standards are being kept for the able in schools of varying SES. The results can be seen in Table 8.12.

Table 8.12 tells us that the higher the school SES, the more likely that peer relations will play a more important role in affecting teachers' perception that high academic standards are kept for the able. Looking at the percentage difference in the rows, it is 48 in the case of high-SES schools, 45 in medium-SES schools, and 35 in low-SES schools. At all school levels, the more satisfying the peer relations, the more likely that the teachers perceived that high standards are being kept for the able, but the link is stronger in high-SES schools. We suggest that although the problem of keeping high standards for the able is a problem faced in some form by many schools, it is especially marked in high-SES schools. Thus teachers in a process of interaction and faced with the same problem develop collective responses. In high-SES schools 85 percent of teachers with high scores on the peer-relations index think that high standards are kept for the able while only 37 percent with low peer relations think so. In this example, as in the case of the needs of deprived students, we can see a cumulative effect of school SES and quality of peer relationships on collective beliefs of teachers that define their situation. In this case, the threat to professional norms being stronger in high-SES schools, it will elicit a stronger need for a

TABLE 8.12

Standards Kept for the Able, Peer Relations, and School SES (percent teachers very satisfied)

	Peer Relations			
School SES	High	Medium	Low	Percentage Difference
High	85% (123)	65% (145)	37% (80)	48
Medium	78 (203)	57 (384)	33 (333)	45
Low	66 (188)	55 (358)	31 (346)	35
Percentage difference	19	10	6	

collective solution in order to preserve the professional status and role of the teachers.

SUMMARY AND CONCLUSIONS

In this chapter we have analyzed some sources of teachers' perceptions of their professional functioning in various types of ghetto schools. Teachers' occupational satisfaction is, indeed, higher where teachers perceive that professional standards—keeping standards for the able, meeting the educational needs of the "deprived"—are being met. However, the SES of schools' students—an indicator of the degree to which the educational problems of the ghetto prevail—is not linked to this relationship.

Thus, we were led to seek for the sources of variation in teachers' perception in this ghetto school system in areas other than the characteristics of the students. We found, to begin with, that the more satisfied the teachers were with their relationships to other teachers (index of peer relations), the more likely they were to see professional standards as being met. This finding led us to expect that satisfying peer relations should contribute to higher job satisfaction—an expectation confirmed by the data. Thus, the relationships of teachers to each other appear as more significant in affecting both occupational satisfaction and evaluation of professional functioning, within ghetto schools, than variations in the characteristics of the students.

We were thus led to ask why peer relations are so important. We suggested that in ghetto schools the question of meeting professional standards poses problems of a special order for teachers. We then employed average SES of schools' students as a context within which to examine the interplay of peer relations and teachers' definition of the professional situation. We saw, then, that satisfying peer relations play functionally equivalent roles in affecting teachers' perceptions in ghetto schools of relatively high and low SES.

Thus, in low-SES schools—where a main professional problem is meeting the needs of the "deprived"—more satisfying peer relations are linked to a perception that these needs are met. In high-SES schools—where a main professional problem is keeping standards for the able—more satisfying peer relations are linked to a perception that these standards are kept. We inferred, therefore, that satisfying peer relations among ghetto teachers have special impact on teachers' definitions of their situation where the gap between professional standards and the actual functioning of the schools is greatest.

We interpreted these patterns throughout as manifestations of the "society of teachers," to use Waller's term, and of a "problem-solving subculture," to use Albert Cohen's. In this case, the problems are defensive and adaptive ones stemming from the situation of teachers in a ghetto school system. We suggested that the teachers, facing a common problem of defining their professional situation and protecting their self-esteem while in interaction with each other, develop group standards by means of which they evaluate their situation. The role of satisfying peer-relations—more important than the actual characteristics of students—was analyzed as reflecting this process.

An important consequence of the existence of such a subculture among ghetto teachers is that teachers may be satisfied with their jobs because of—and evaluate their professional performance as a function of—their interaction with each other rather than with their students. Thus, peer relations, rather than relations with students, may come to be a major source of satisfactions and of definitions of professional success.

In the next chapter, we will carry out further the analysis of peer relations in ghetto schools of different student SES and further explore the functions of a teachers' subculture in these settings.

NOTES

1. Albert K. Cohen, Delinquent Boys: The Culture of the Gang (New York: The Free Press, 1961), p. 55.
2. A. Harry Passow, ed., Toward Creating a Model Urban School System; A Study of the Washington, D. C. Public Schools (New York: Teachers College, Columbia University, 1967); and A Task Force Study of the Public School System in the District of Columbia as It Relates to the War on Poverty, U.S. Congress, House of Representatives, Committee on Education and Labor (Washington, D.C.: Government Printing Office, June 1966)—referred to here as the Pucinski report.
3. Quoted in William W. Wayson, "Expressed Motives of Teachers in Slum Schools" (unpublished Ph.D. dissertation, University of Chicago, 1966).
4. Pucinski report, p. 29.
5. Cohen, Delinquent Boys, p. 54.
6. Gertrude McPherson, "The Role Set of Elementary School Teachers" (unpublished Ph.D. dissertation, Columbia University, 1966), p. 96.
7. Passow, ed., Toward Creating a Model Urban School System, pp. 273-80.

8. Bernard Mackler, "Up from Poverty: The Price for 'Making It' in a Ghetto School" (unpublished manuscript given at the Seventh Annual Conference of Urban Education, Teachers College, Columbia University, New York, 1969).

9. Cohen, Delinquent Boys, p. 60.

10. Ibid.

11. Albert K. Cohen, Deviance and Control (Englewood Cliffs, N.J.: Prentice-Hall, 1966), p. 86.

CHAPTER

9

THE PEER GROUP AND TEACHERS' ORIENTATIONS, EVALUATIONS, AND COMMITMENT TO TEACHING

In Chapter 8 we described collective responses and solutions to problems shared by teachers. Among the solutions that we investigated were redefinition of the situation and collective rationalizations. Adherence to such rationalizations enabled teachers to be satisfied with their jobs, although they were teaching in one of the worst ghetto school systems in the country. We pointed out that in such organizational contexts collective beliefs become more imperative, to the degree that they do not in fact correspond to reality. For example, when both groups of teachers had good relations with their peers, teachers in the lowest-SES schools were more likely than those in high-SES schools to perceive that the needs of the deprived were being met. These processes and the creation of collective beliefs and group standards formed part of teachers' "defensive subculture."

In this chapter we intend to examine further aspects of teachers' peer relations within the same conceptual framework established in the preceding chapter, using the concept of subculture to interpret the pattern of our findings. We shall study the relative importance of peer relations in schools of varying SES in association with, first, teachers' custodial orientation; second, their comparisons of their own schools with other public schools in the country in terms of educational quality; and, third, their commitment to teaching in the Washington, D.C., elementary schools.

TEACHERS' CUSTODIAL ORIENTATION

We have mentioned that the creation and maintenance of a subculture constitute a collective response to some form of "status threat." We have also shown that such responses vary, depending upon the necessity of preserving status and the intensity of the threat. Among ghetto teachers in our study, responses took the form of collective rationalization to permit belief that professional standards were being maintained.

In Chapter 3, we noted that one structural characteristic of schools is the confrontation of two main groups: students and teacher We also described various features of student-teacher relations, emphasizing their hostile and emotional components. The problems of discipline and maintaining order raise, in our research, interesting questions. In a ghetto school system—and in slum schools in general- the problem of discipline is linked with the problem of teachers' authority, and therefore teachers may see discipline as a means of preserving their authority, legitimacy before the students, and professional status in the eyes of peers.

Depending upon the type of students, the threat to teachers' professional authority and, accordingly, their responses may vary. Problems of discipline and teachers' authority are experienced in some way by all teachers and thus may lead to both individual and collective responses. We might expect that in low-SES schools, wher discipline problems are more severe and teachers' authority more likely to be questioned, teachers' responses would tend to take collective forms.

Before discussing how we tested this idea in our research, we shall say a bit more about discipline and authority. Authority is an aspect of the teachers' classroom role necessary to accomplish educational tasks. The teacher's authority in the classroom is not unchallenged, because of the diverging, and sometimes conflicting, needs and demands of teachers and students, and therefore subordination of one group to the other cannot be escaped.[1]

The problem of discipline is different. Keeping order inside an outside the classroom is not inherent in the teachers' role and is neither a necessary nor a sufficient condition for performing educatio tasks—as teachers' authority and role legitimacy are. The professio role of the elementary-school teacher is focused mainly on providing children with basic intellectual and social skills. The relative priori given to these goals has varied from time to time and place to place.[2] The function of keeping order inside and outside the classroom seems recently to have taken on new importance because of changes in conditions in the school and changes in the student population. One of the most frequent complaints from teachers involves the time and effort required to keep order. The problem of classroom discipline was reported in our data as one of the most important obstacles to teachi and learning. Among elementary-school teachers in Washington, D.C 75 percent complained that too much time was spent on discipline in the classroom.

Comparing the social composition of student bodies, we found that in low-SES schools teachers were most likely to complain of spending too much time on classroom discipline: 67 percent compared with 56 percent in high-SES schools.[3] But the problem was widespread in all the schools.

Becker listed three spheres that are important in teachers' discussion of adjustment to their students: teaching itself, discipline, and moral acceptability. He related discipline to students' social-class backgrounds. In low-SES schools the problem of discipline took much of the teachers' time, energy, and patience, distracting them from their primary function of teaching.[4]

McPherson, from her participant observation in an elementary school, described the extent to which teachers expected students to conform to their demands and felt insecure when they encountered resistance. Such insecurity even increased when teachers were dealing with lower-class students because of misunderstandings and value clashes. "The pupils most concerned about fairness and justice are those who are less privileged, less successful and often less well behaved. The teacher often sees these pupils as infringing [upon] her rights, being unfair to her."[5]

Discipline was described by Waller as a means of preserving teachers' definition of the classroom situation as an established order to which students must conform. Discipline becomes a means of control, "a way of getting the teachers' definition of the situation accepted and the wishes carried out without a direct clash of wills between teachers and students."[6] What most teachers expect of students is conformity to an established order. Discipline may also have other functions. McPherson showed how discipline was used to isolate teachers from the pressures and demands of students.[7] Discipline may be an important means of preserving teachers' authority, in the struggle to ascertain one's own status, and legitimacy in the classroom. We shall return to this point.

Attitudes toward discipline may also reflect a teaching philosophy in which students are expected to control their own daily behavior. Discipline may be supposed to form "character" and good habits that will last students through life.[8] Such a conception of discipline is likeliest when problems of keeping order are not severe; it reflects the desire of middle-class parents to have their children learn good manners in school.

But conceptions of discipline are many and vary from one context to the next. It may be viewed as a way to control and manipulate students and to isolate teachers from them or as a means to establish status and legitimacy in the eyes of students. The conception may also arise from an educational philosophy centered on formation of character. None of these conceptions of discipline is exclusive, and all may, in fact, affect teachers simultaneously.

Discipline has still another and most important meaning in the schools. In the strict sense it is a means of keeping order inside and outside the classroom. More broadly, it may represent a general student-control orientation. In the school that Willover studied, the prevailing norm was "strictness."[9] Pupil control was the dominant pattern in all aspects of student-teacher relations. McPherson also reported emphasis on strictness.[10]

We might expect teachers to receive support and gratification if they conform to norms. McPherson reported that teachers would go out of their way to scold students publicly, in front of other students.* Willover reported the importance of punishment outside the classroom as part of teachers' "on-stage behavior." Visibility of various types of punishment or forms of strictness can be very important in gaining the support of the peer group.[11] Discipline may become a way to bolster professional status and authority in the eyes not only of students _but also of peers_, especially in slum schools.

Indeed, in slum schools the problem of preserving or maintaining teachers' authority is often reduced to mere maintenance of order inside and outside the classroom. The maintenance of order is by definition a secondary function of teachers but may become their main function in slum schools. It is thus once more crucial as a mainstay of teachers' professional authority. Strictness may come to reflect a collective solution to the problem of maintaining authority, which no teacher can escape. We may thus ask whether or not the norm of strictness, the student-control ideology, is a salient aspect of teachers' subculture in the schools. To what extent does it affect teachers in schools of varying SES?

We do not have any direct measures of Washington, D.C., teachers' use of discipline; we have only indirect measures of their attitudes toward discipline in general. They were presented with the item, "Obedience and respect for authority are the most important virtues children should learn." They could respond "agree," "don't know," or "disagree." The distribution of responses is shown in Table 9.1. About half the Washington elementary-school teachers thought that obedience and respect for authority were the most important virtues that children could learn, whereas only a few more than a quarter of the teachers disagreed. The percentage of teachers who agreed or who did not know seems quite high.

---

*Wayson told the story of a teacher who was having lunch in the staff dining room when a student came to ask her advice. Instead of listening, the teacher very loudly complained about the student's behavior in the classroom.

TABLE 9.1

Responses to Obedience-and-Respect Item

	Percent	N
Agree	48	1,175
Don't know	20	493
Disagree	27	656
No answer	5	128
Total	100	2,452

We have described variations in the percentages of teachers in low-, medium-, and high-SES schools who complained that they spent too much time on discipline. We have also given examples from other studies of the effects of students' social class on teachers' custodial orientation. In our research, however, there was barely any difference in the percentages of teachers in low-, medium-, and high-SES schools who thought that obedience and respect for authority were the most important virtues that children should learn. This lack of variation was intriguing. Perhaps teachers in schools of different SES defined obedience and respect for authority differently. The track in which teachers were teaching did not affect this attitude either, although teachers in the special academic track were slightly more likely to think that obedience and respect were most important.

The characteristics of the students thus did not seem to affect teachers' orientations toward the question of discipline. Let us, however, carry this analysis a step further and study the simultaneous effects of peer relations and students' characteristics upon teachers' orientations toward the problem of order.

We have already noted that the problem of order and discipline may stimulate collective responses in the form of collective norms or strictness. If classroom stresses threaten teachers' sense of professional role and status, then these collective responses may evolve through processes similar to those described in Chapter 8. From our previous discussion and findings, we already know that in low-SES schools peer relations were an important factor in the creation of collective beliefs among teachers, for in such schools the problems of authority and discipline could not be separated; discipline had become a legitimate means of securing and preserving teachers' authority.

Let us look at the relation between the belief that obedience and respect are the most important virtues and peer relations in schools of varying SES. The results are shown in Table 9.2. Peer relations had different importance in low-, medium-, and high-SES schools. Looking at the percentage difference in the rows of the table (a crude measure of association between peer relations and teachers' emphasis on obedience and respect), we see that the percentage difference was the highest in low-SES schools. In low-SES schools the difference between very satisfied teachers with low and high peer relations is 12, in the medium-SES schools 3, in the high-SES schools -1. This showed that in low-SES schools the peer group had a greater impact in affecting teachers' concern over obedience and authority. In low-SES schools good relations with peers was conducive to student-control ideology, while it did not play such a role in medium- and high-SES schools. Fifty-seven percent of those who scored high on the peer-relations index, compared with 45 percent of those who scored low, agreed that obedience and respect were most important. Although the percentage difference is not great, it takes on additional meaning within our general framework because it is congruent with our previous findings. We may thus suggest that in low-SES schools teachers' authority was more threatened and teachers themselves were more likely to adopt a student-control ideology in order to preserve their own sense of professional role and status. Discipline had become a means by which not only to keep order and facilitate school functioning but also to satisfy group norms and thus win approval.

In medium-SES schools peer relations barely influenced the student-control ideology, whereas in high-SES schools it does not do

TABLE 9.2

Belief in Authority, Peer Relations, and School SES
(percent teachers emphasizing obedience
and respect for authority)

School SES	High	Medium	Low	Percentage Difference
High	47% (123)	49% (148)	48% (83)	-1
Medium	52 (207)	47 (402)	49 (348)	3
Low	57 (192)	49 (372)	45 (367)	12

so at all. But these latter findings do not necessarily mean that discipline and authority problems did not exist in these schools. They were simply not a salient aspect of teachers' subculture, as they were in low-SES schools. Such differences may have been caused by the distinction, in high-SES schools, between authority and discipline. Or discipline problems may have involved simply teaching students good manners and good habits, as Waller has suggested, rather than keeping order per se.[12]

Teachers in low-SES schools were more likely to adhere to a student-control ideology, which was both conditioned and reinforced by peer relations; they may thus have tended to overemphasize disciplinary problems and methods, widening still further the social and psychological gap between teachers and students.

Willover described several aspects of the control ideology, including maintenance of order, distrust of students, and a punitive, moralistic approach.[13] We do not have comparable information for Washington, D.C., but we have some data on teachers' educational philosophies and general values. The control ideology was associated with a "practical" orientation in educational philosophy. The correlation between teachers' belief in obedience and authority, on one hand, and the primary educational goal of preparing students to find better jobs, on the other, was $\underline{r} = .253$. The belief that any man with ability and willingness to work has a good chance of being successful these days, regardless of race and religion, was also correlated with this goal ($\underline{r} = .213$), as was the belief that most people with enough will power will raise themselves from poverty ($\underline{r} = .207$).

There was indeed a relation among a control-oriented approach to discipline, a practical educational philosophy, and optimism about the prospects of individual social mobility despite obstacles. It is not our intention to study those values in different contexts; we simply note their overlap among teachers in a ghetto school system.

We have no additional data on the control ideology, or the norm of strictness, in relation to the teachers' subculture. Our findings do, however, suggest the various uses and meanings of discipline, especially the salience in low-SES schools of teachers' emphasis on obedience and respect for authority. This emphasis may have been engendered by contact with students, who may have seemed to threaten teachers' authority in the classroom and the school at large. Let us now turn to another aspect of peer relations in schools of varying SES.

TEACHERS' COMPARISONS OF THEIR SCHOOLS WITH OTHER PUBLIC SCHOOLS IN THE NATION

How did teachers' peer relations affect their comparative perceptions of their schools and other public schools in the nation?

They were asked, "As far as giving a good education is concerned, compare your school with other public schools in the United States; do you think that your school is better than most, about the same as most, not as good as most?" The criterion specified was educational accomplishment in the school. The distribution of responses is shown in Table 9.3.

From this table we see that only one-fourth of the teachers thought their schools poorer than most schools in the country in terms of educational outcome. The majority rated their schools about the same as most others. From these figures it seems that elementary-school teachers in the Washington, D.C., system had a rather positive, perhaps uncritical, view of their schools. Again we refer to the Passow and Pucinski reports.[14] That 73 percent of the teachers found their schools at least as good as most other schools in the country reflected either their unawareness of decay in the Washington system and their unfamiliarity with schools outside Washington or unwillingness to acknowledge the failure of their own schools and the Washington system as a whole to provide quality education. A failure of the system and its schools is also a failure of the teachers to educate children adequately. We shall investigate to what extent teachers may have changed their frame of reference in order to evaluate their schools positively, using a criterion other than educational outcome as the basis for comparison.

Let us begin by examining the variations as related to school SES. The findings are shown in Table 9.4. Teachers in high-SES schools were likelier to rate them better than most, whereas teachers in low-SES schools were likelier to rate them not as good. In Chapter 2 we saw that at the school level there was indeed a correlation between school SES and various measures of achievement, educational facilities, and school characteristics like student-teacher ratio,

TABLE 9.3

Teachers' Comparative Ratings of Their Own Schools

	Percent	N
Better than most	14	354
About the same as most	59	1,154
Not as good as most	24	588
No answer	3	65
Total	100	2,161

TABLE 9.4

Comparative Ratings of Schools and SES
(percent)

Rating	School SES High	Medium	Low
Better than most	26	13	12
About the same as most	61	63	60
Not as good as most	13	24	28
Total	100	100	100
	(N=345)	(N=938)	(N=905)

TABLE 9.5

Comparative Ratings of Schools and Peer Relations
(percent)

Ratings	Peer-Relations Index Scores High	Medium	Low
Better than most	26	13	8
About the same as most	63	67	54
Not as good as most	11	20	38
Total	100	100	100
	(N=518)	(N=910)	(N=791)

percentage of permanent teachers, and percentage of teachers with masters' degrees. In Washington, D.C., high-SES schools were likelier to provide quality education than were low-SES schools. Our previous analysis of factors related to teachers' satisfaction, particularly peer relations, raises the question of how far such relations affected teachers' perceptions of comparative educational outcomes in their schools and others. Let us examine the association between teachers' comparisons and peer relations. The findings are presented in Table 9.5, which shows that teachers who scored high on peer relations were indeed likelier to rate their schools at least equal to others than were teachers who scored low. We may ask the question, "Were teachers' comparisons more affected by peer relations than by the schools' actual performance in providing good education?" We have seen that Washington teachers' perceptions of satisfying the needs of deprived children were barely affected by the actual characteristics of the students but reflected a collective response to a problem encountered by all teachers. We also noticed that this response, which took the form of a collective rationalization, was greater in schools where the needs of deprived children were least likely to be met.

We may now ask whether teachers did not also collectively redefine their frame of reference in order to change the basis of their evaluations and therefore to avoid a sense of failure. Using the same logic as before, we may expect the peer group to have influenced teachers' definition of the situation in low-SES schools, where the possibility of providing good education was less. These teachers would have been likelier to take interpersonal relations rather than actual educational accomplishment as bases for judgment. Again we suggest that teachers avoided a sense of failure by changing the frame of reference within which they compared their schools with other public schools. This process was possible because they shared similar experiences and interaction processes and necessary because they felt insecure about their professional role and status.

In order to test this idea, let us examine the association between teachers' comparative ratings of their schools and peer relations in schools of different SES. Table 9.6 tells us, first, that peer relations

TABLE 9.6

Comparative Ratings of Schools, Peer Relations, and School SES
(percentage rating their schools low)

School SES	Peer-Relations Index Score			Percentage
	High	Medium	Low	Difference
High	7% (121)	13% (144)	24% (80)	17
Medium	12 (202)	21 (397)	36 (339)	24
Low	13 (190)	21 (360)	44 (355)	31
Percentage differences	6	8	20	

were more important than school SES in affecting teachers' comparisons (compare the average percentage differences of the rows and columns). It also shows that the two attributes nevertheless did affect teachers' judgments independently. Table 9.6 mainly shows the importance of peer relations in affecting teachers' evaluation, in schools of different SES. We see that the lower the SES, the more likely that peer relations played an important role. Comparing the percentage difference (in the rows) of teachers' rating of their schools in contexts of low and high satisfaction with peer relations, we see that it is 31 in low-SES schools, 24 in medium-SES schools, and 17 in high-SES schools. The impact of peer relations in affecting teachers' evaluation of their school was stronger in the low SES schools. Of teachers with low peer relations, 44 percent rated their school negatively, compared with 13 percent with high peer relations. Thus, peer relations were a more important basis for teachers' evaluations of their schools in low-SES schools than in medium- and high-SES schools. Furthermore, teachers in high-SES schools who scored low on peer relations were twice as likely to rate their schools low as were teachers in low-SES schools who scored high on relations with peers.

Although we saw, in Chapter 7, that peer relations were less likely to be good in low-SES schools, they nevertheless played a more important part in ratings by teachers in low-SES schools than in ratings by teachers in high-SES schools. That is, although conditions characteristic of low-SES schools were less conducive to good peer relations, those relations were more critical in such schools than in high-SES schools.

In Chapters 8 and 9 we have shown in four instances the significance of peer relations in determining teachers' adjustments to the problematic aspects of teaching in ghetto schools. Thus, in ghetto schools of relatively low-SES student composition, satisfying peer relations were associated with the view that curriculums met the needs of the deprived, with pupil-control orientations, and with favorable evaluations of the educational success of one's own school compared with others in America. In ghetto schools of relatively high-SES student composition, keeping standards for the able is particularly problematic; in these schools, satisfying peer relations were linked with teachers' perception that such standards are kept. This pattern of findings suggests the existence of a teachers' subculture with both defensive and adaptive functions. Thus, in the low-SES schools, the existence of satisfying interpersonal relationships among teachers seems linked to a definition of the professional situation that is indeed gratifying for teachers faced with serious problems of professional functioning: The curriculum is seen as adequate, pupils are to be controlled, and their schools' achievements are evaluated well, compared to others'. Such a pattern may help to explain why and how so high a proportion of teachers in this ghetto school system are satisfied with their jobs (88 percent) and with the quality of their students' work (60 percent).

If teachers in low-SES schools are more likely to rely on peer relations for professional satisfactions, peer groups may be more cohesive in such schools. Conformity and adherence to collective beliefs become both more necessary and more rewarding. Under such circumstances, teachers' desires to remain in the schools should reflect the extent of satisfaction with peer relations. Let us turn to this question, examining teachers' career plans in greater detail.

TEACHERS' CAREER PLANS AND SCHOOL SES

In Chapter 3, we noted that, although the great majority of Washington's elementary-school teachers were satisfied with their jobs, only 18 percent wanted to remain teachers in the system 10 years later. We suggested that teachers were less satisfied with intrinsic than with extrinsic aspects of their professional role. We are now going to examine factors within the school that may have affected teachers' desire to remain in the system.

We also noted, in Chapter 7, that teachers in low-SES schools were likelier to want to stay in the system than were those in high-SES schools (32 and 24 percent, respectively). This surprising observation may take on new meaning in the light of our discussion about the importance of the peer group in low-SES schools.

Let us first see to what extent teachers' career plans were affected by the school SES. From Table 9.7 we can see that teachers in low-SES schools were more likely to want to stay where they were than were teachers in higher-SES schools. Of teachers in low-SES schools, 32 percent wished to be teaching in the same system 10 years later, while only 24 percent of teachers in high-SES schools hoped to. This finding is somewhat surprising. Indeed, why should anyone want to stay in a low-SES school, where, according to our data, teachers were less rewarded and satisfied? We shall try to suggest some of the possible reasons in this chapter.

First, let us remark on the association between teachers' perceptions that their students liked school and their desire to remain in the schools 10 years later, which is shown in Table 9.8.[15] The socioeconomic level of the school does not seem to have affected the association between teachers' perceptions that students liked school and their desire to remain in the system. The only exceptions occurred among teachers who perceived that students liked school quite a bit. For example, among teachers who thought that their students liked school very much, 37 percent wished to remain in the system if located

TABLE 9.7

Teachers' Career Plans and School SES
(percent)

	School SES		
	High (5-8)	Medium (3-4)	Low (0-2)
To teach in present system	24 (56)	29 (179)	32 (198)
To teach in another system, or become specialist or administrator	76 (173)	71 (440)	68 (431)
Total	100 (N=229)	100 (N=619)	100 (N=629)

TABLE 9.8

Career Plans, Perceptions of Students' Liking School, and School SES
(percent wishing to remain teachers)

School SES	Very Much	Quite a Bit	Not Much	Percentage Difference
High	36% (98)	13% (86)	24% (42)	12
Medium	37 (201)	28 (238)	21 (178)	16
Low	37 (192)	33 (240)	24 (192)	13
Percentage difference	1	20	0	

in low-SES school, while 36 percent wished to if located in high-SES school. What counts is their perception that they were successful. Furthermore, keeping SES constant, we see that the impact of teachers' perception that their students liked school is very similar in low, medium, and high-SES schools. Look at the percentage difference (the rows) between teachers who thought that their students liked school very much and those who thought that they did not like school. Among those who wished to remain teachers, the difference is 12 percent in high-SES schools, 16 percent in medium-SES schools, and 13 percent in low-SES schools.

Such findings are reinforced when we look at how teachers' satisfaction with the quality of students' work affects teachers' desire to remain in the system, in schools of various SES. Table 9.9 shows that the satisfaction with the quality of students' work has more impact on teachers' desire to remain in low-SES schools. Looking at the percentage difference in the rows between satisfied and less satisfied teachers who wish to remain, we see that the difference is the largest in the low-SES schools. This may be explained by inferring that teachers in low-, medium-, and high-SES schools have different evaluations and expectations about students. Quality of work and high standards, as we have seen, may be more of a problem for teachers in high-SES school. Therefore, the teachers may be less likely to be satisfied and more likely to react to the qualitative changes in the educational system of Washington, D.C., than teachers in low-SES schools.

TABLE 9.9

Career Plans, Satisfaction with Students' Work, and School SES
(percent wishing to remain teachers)

	Satisfaction with the Quality of Students' Work		
SES	Satisfied	Neither Satisfied nor Dissatisfied	Percentage Difference
High	25% (156)	24% (63)	1
Medium	31 (375)	26 (239)	5
Low	34 (399)	26 (222)	8

Let us turn to other factors that may have been associated with teachers' desire to remain in the system 10 years later. Teachers' peer relations again attract our attention. We have already shown their special importance in engendering collective responses to problems of status insecurity.

We have to keep in mind that when analyzing teachers' career plans, we are asking them about future plans. Thus the future reference of teachers' career plans might be affected differently than the present reference to teachers' job satisfaction.

To what extent did peer relations in schools of different SES affect teachers' desire to remain teaching in the system 10 years later? The answer can be seen in Table 9.10, which indicates that school SES and peer relations had independent effects on teachers' desire to remain in the system and that peer relations were more important (see average differences in rows and columns). Comparing teachers who are high on the peer-relations index, we can note in low-SES schools 43 percent wished to remain in the system compared with 33 percent in high-SES schools. The table also shows that peer relations had slightly more effect on teachers' desire to stay in low- and medium- SES than in high-SES schools (compare percentage differences in the rows). Although the percentage differences are not great, they follow the pattern of findings established in Chapter 8. Although peer relations were less likely to be good in low- and medium-SES schools, their relative importance affecting teachers' desire to stay was greater, as shown in Table 9.10.

TABLE 9.10

Career Plans, Peer Relations, and School SES
(percent who wish to remain teachers)

School SES	Peer-Relations Index Score: High	Medium	Low	Percentage Difference
High	33% (84)	21% (89)	16% (56)	17
Medium	42 (134)	29 (263)	21 (222)	21
Low	43 (120)	35 (248)	23 (261)	20
Percentage difference	10	14	7	

That the school SES has a smaller impact on the relations between peer relations and desire to remain in the system than in all previous relations might be due to the fact that, while occupational satisfaction refers to current position, staying in the system might refer to future positions in different schools.

We suggest the possibility that schools' "retaining power" varied according to peer relations. Our findings imply that the peer group engendered a greater sense of belonging in low-SES than in high-SES schools. Wayson, in his study of motivations of teachers in slum schools, mentioned "group belongingness" among the most important for black teachers.[16]

Though peer relations affected teachers' desire to stay, especially in low-SES schools, they may have been supplemented by other factors. We saw in Chapter 6 that participation in decision-making about running schools was strongly related to teachers' job satisfaction, as well as to peer relations. In Chapter 3, we noted that semiprofessionals are likely to become more agency-oriented and less client-oriented,[17] especially when confronted by a lower-class clientele.[18] As a partial test of this hypothesis for teachers, we are therefore going to examine how such participation was related to teachers' desires to remain in schools of varying SES. Greater involvement in aspects of the administrative functioning of the schools is viewed as a manifestation of teachers' orientation toward the agency.[19] Table 9.11 shows that both school SES and level of participation have independent effects on teachers' desire to remain in the schools. We

TABLE 9.11

Career Plans, Participation in Decisions, and School SES (percent wishing to remain teachers)

School SES	Level of Participation: High	Medium	Low	Percentage Difference
High	25% (87)	23% (93)	32% (41)	-7
Medium	38 (192)	26 (213)	16 (153)	22
Low	39 (170)	29 (228)	25 (164)	14
Percentage difference	-14	-6	7	

already knew that the higher the school SES, the likelier teachers were to rank high in participation. Now we learn in addition that participation had different effects in low- and medium-SES schools, on one hand, and in high-SES schools, on the other. In the former there was a positive correlation between participation and desire to remain teachers, whereas in the latter the correlation was negative. Even though teachers in high-SES schools were likelier to perceive themselves as participating in decisions about the schools, such activities had negative effects on their desire to remain teachers. In low- and medium-SES schools, where teachers were less likely to perceive themselves as sharing in such decisions, participation was more important in desires to remain. The function of participation may have been quite different in the two types of schools. First, as we have noted, participation may have been an important means of acquiring greater autonomy, but teachers in high-SES schools were likelier to have autonomy, and participation may have been correspondingly less important. Second, students in high-SES schools—middle-class students—may have been more rewarding to teach, so that teachers would have needed less reward from administrative quarters. Administrative tasks may in fact have been, as Table 9.9 suggests, more a burden than a source of gratification for teachers.

In low- and medium-SES schools, on the contrary, participation may have given teachers a greater sense of control over their working environment, an especially important sense in view of their greater insecurity, resulting from contact with students.

Peer relations and participation in school decisions were more important in affecting teachers' desires to remain in the system than were school SES, especially in low- and medium-SES schools.

SUMMARY AND CONCLUSIONS

In this chapter we have analyzed the role of the peer group in varying socioeconomic contexts, concentrating on three areas likely to reflect the existence of a teachers' subculture. We extended the analysis in Chapter 8 to test the possibility that collective mechanisms were used to cope with threats to status in the schools. We expected that in low-SES schools, where threats to teachers' professional role and status, and resulting insecurity, were likely to be strongest, peer relations would be a more significant aid in coping with problems of functioning.

It seems that the problems of functioning and therefore the role of peer relations may have been quite different in low-SES and high-SES schools. We have seen that discipline and authority had different meanings in different SES contexts. In high-SES schools it seems that discipline problems did not give rise to a defensive subculture because they were not confounded with problems of teachers' authority. In low-SES schools, however, discipline problems apparently encouraged a student-control ideology based on the use of discipline to maintain teachers' authority, which was threatened in those contexts. Emphasis on order and the norm of strictness may have become a salient aspect of the teachers' subculture in low-SES schools. One possible result may have been a tendency among teachers in low-SES schools to overemphasize discipline in order to achieve support and recognition from peers.

Another area of investigation was teachers' evaluations of the schools' educational performance. We noted that teachers in high-SES schools were likelier to rate their schools high than were teachers in low-SES schools. Peer relations were more important than school SES in affecting these perceptions, but peer relations had their greatest effects in low-SES schools. Teachers interacting under the same pressures may have redefined their working situation in order to shift the main focus from students' characteristics and educational achievements to teachers' own good relations with peers. Such findings support our hypothesis about the existence of a teachers' subculture that may permit teachers to be satisfied with their jobs and with students' work in a ghetto school system.

The third area of inquiry was teachers' commitment to teaching in the system. Their perceptions that students liked school, their peer relations, and their participation in school decisions were all important in accounting for desires to stay in the system. Teachers in low-SES schools, however, were likelier than teachers in high-SES schools to want to remain. Among the factors that might explain this surprising finding was that in low- and medium-SES schools peer relations and participation in running the schools were more important in affecting teachers' desire to remain teachers.

Although teachers in low- and medium-SES schools were less likely to have good peer relations or to perceive themselves as participating in school decision-making, peer relations were more important in low- than in high-SES schools in affecting teachers' custodial orientations, ratings of their schools, and career plans.

We have studied various types of collective solutions by teachers to problems of functioning in ghetto schools. Our findings suggest that such solutions result from a teachers' subculture with marked adaptive and defensive features.

NOTES

1. William Waller, The Sociology of Teaching (New York: Wiley, 1932), pp. 306-10.

2. Lawrence A. Cremin, The Transformation of the School: Progressivism in American Education 1876-1957 (New York: Vintage, 1961), pp. 330-53.

3. See Chapter 2, Table 2.8.

4. Howard S. Becker, "Social Class Variation in the Teacher-Pupil Relationship," Journal of Educational Sociology, Vol. 25, 1952, pp. 453-61.

5. Gertrude McPherson, "The Role Set of Elementary School Teachers" (unpublished Ph.D. dissertation, Columbia University, 1966).

6. Waller, Sociology of Teaching, p. 203.

7. McPherson, "Role Set of Elementary School Teachers," pp. 250-56.

8. Waller Sociology of Teaching, p. 310.

9. Donald Willover, "The School and Pupil Control Ideology," Pennsylvania State Studies, No. 24, p. 15.

10. McPherson, "Role Set of Elementary School Teachers," pp. 88-91.

11. Willover, "School and Pupil Control Ideology," pp. 6-8, 15.

12. Waller, Sociology of Teaching, p. 310

13. Willover, "School and Pupil Control Ideology," p. 17.

14. A. Harry Passow, ed., Toward Creating a Model Urban School System: A Study of the Washington, D.C. Public Schools (New York: Teachers College, Columbia University, 1966); and A Task Force Study of the Public School System in the District of Columbia as It Relates to the War on Poverty, U. S. Congress, House of Representatives, Committee on Education and Labor (Washington, D. C.: Government Printing Office, June 1966)—the Pucinski report.

15. Teachers' orientation toward students was discussed in Chapter 5.

16. William Wayson, "Source of Teacher Satisfaction in Slum Schools," Administrator Notebook, Vol. 24, No. 9, 1966, p. 3. Wayson remarked that white teachers do not carry over these peer relations outside the school, whereas black teachers generally do. The informal groups created in the schools are thus perpetuated in the community, which may in turn reinforce peer relations *in* the school. We have no data on this point, however.

17. Abraham Zaleznik, "Interpersonal Relations in Organizations," in James March and A. Simon, eds., Handbook of Organizations (Chicago: Rand McNally, 1965), pp. 592-96.

18. Peter Blau, "Orientations Toward Clients in a Public Welfare Agency," Administrative Science Quarterly, No. 3, 1960, pp. 349-50.

19. See Chapter 6.

CHAPTER

10

CONCLUSION

In this study we have explored some aspects of social dynamics in ghetto schools: specifically, how black elementary-school teachers in the Washington, D.C., system coped with problems and adapted themselves to functioning in such a ghetto system. We focused our research on middle-class teachers' contact with increasing numbers of ghetto students. What type of relations between teachers and students emerged under such conditions? How did teachers respond to the students who confronted them in the classroom and in the school at large?

The encounter between middle-class black teachers and ghetto schoolchildren took on special importance in Washington, where there is an old and stratified black community: 90 percent of the students and more than 80 percent of the teachers were black. Comparing the old, "dual" Washington school system and the segregated system of the 1960s makes us aware of the fundamental changes that had occurred in the black community and its schools. The Washington school system is and has always been segregated, either by law or as a result of patterns of residential segregation (in fact, as we have shown, after 1954, District public schools experienced a drastic reduction in white enrollment). The main difference between the old and new segregated systems involved organization and ability to provide black children with some education. The existence of an all-black system parallel to the white system in organization and curriculum had for many years given Washington's black community a sense of pride and commitment to the education of black children. Even after financial and organizational problems became more cumbersome, teachers' commitment to educating black children was very high, as reported by Knox.[1] Demographic and social trends in the District gradually changed this black institution, geared to providing black children with adequate education, to what can be characterized as a "superghetto" school system.

Washington's "black bourgeoisie" had been the most active group in organizing, operating, and defending the dual system. Resistance to desegregation among the middle class had economic, ethnic, and even psychological sources. Most of the teachers in the dual system came from middle-class families. Teaching was a respected occupation, in both black and white communities. We do not have information about relations between middle-class teachers and students in the dual system, but the disparity in their social origins may well have increased with the successive waves of poor rural blacks from the South.

Today black teachers are no longer recruited mainly from the middle class. Among black elementary-school teachers in Washington in 1967, 66 percent came from blue-collar families. A community that had been articulated in various social classes and in which the black middle class formed a great majority had developed stronger social and residential barriers between the inner-city ghettos and the suburbs of the black middle class. The black community of Washington is so divided socially and residentially that we found it useful to differentiate according to the average levels of education and income in the areas that the schools served.

Among the problems under investigation was that of relations within the schools between teachers and students of varying social origins. The culture-gap hypothesis leads to postulation of culture clash and resulting misunderstandings between middle-class teachers and lower-class students. That the values of these two groups are different is clear. Their possible clash in the schools arouses questions about race and social origin: To what extent are disparities between the class origins of black teachers and black students linked with problems of functioning in the schools? In the Washington elementary-school system we were able to study how they affected teachers' job satisfaction. We found that the class origins of black teachers assigned to ghetto schools of varying SES did affect their job satisfaction slightly, so that in this instance problems of school functioning seemed not to be linked with the culture clash in the schools.

Teachers' functioning problems in ghetto schools are of various orders. Some are linked with the specific characteristics of the students in the schools; within the single ghetto system low-, medium-, and high-SES schools present different problems, and teachers' modes of adaptation may in turn be different. Indeed, we have seen that teachers in low-SES schools were not only likely to be less satisfied with their students but also to be less satisfied with relations with peers and principals and to enjoy autonomy and a high level of participation in decisions about running the schools.

Problems may also arise from the various social and educational characteristics of teachers. But in Washington these characteristics introduced only small variations in teachers' job satisfaction and orientation toward students. Only age and teaching experience introduced significant variation. But the data do not permit us to distinguish among the effects of aging, career stage, and occupational socialization.

Functioning problems can also develop from the structural characteristics of the school itself. We have discussed the school as a social organization, as a professional bureaucracy, and as a social system. The absence of significant variation owing to social characteristics of teachers led us to look at factors within the schools to explain the social processes involved in teachers' adjustment and responses to functioning problems.

We have also considered the school as an institution with two coexisting systems of interaction: "the society of teachers," a network of adult interaction, and the classroom, characterized by isolated adults in interaction with children.[2] Teachers are part of both systems. These two levels of school organization have implications for functioning; indeed, they imply both professional isolation in classrooms and a system of peer-group interaction that, given teachers' lack of professional control over education, is not a formal part of the educational process.

Teachers' isolation in the classroom and the resulting strains between teachers and students were very great indeed in Washington, especially in low-SES schools, where obstacles to teaching and learning are greater than in high-SES schools. This point has been made by Janowitz:

> The sheer wear and tear on the teachers and the resulting drain on their energy are powerful pressures. For example, classroom teaching is more of a personal and psychological strain than nursing, but the cohesion and solidarity of the work group in the hospital is much greater than in the public school. In part, nurses serve more as team members. Retreat into indifference and excessive detachment is clearly an understandable response. Thus teachers require professional and colleague support to meet these pressures. But in its current organization teaching is a solo practice.[3]

Our data suggest that interpersonal relations, especially peer relations, are of prime importance in teachers' job satisfaction as a source of support and help. Teachers' orientations toward students were related to their perceptions of the quality of their own peer relations.

That teaching is a solo practice has very important implications for teachers' orientations toward students and job satisfaction. In the classroom, interaction between teachers and students of varying social origins and academic achievement is not visible to "the society of teachers." We are dealing with "off-stage" behavior. Functioning problems in the classroom thus arise mainly from teacher-student relations. Our data show that teachers' own definitions of the classroom situation, independent of students' characteristics, can help to neutralize such problems. Waller noted that teachers' definitions of the classroom situation were rigid and predetermined:

> The teacher's definition of the situation, a definition in terms of a rigid social order and teacher domination of all social life was established at the start. It was a definition that thought to be inclusive, and to leave nothing for improvisation. There was little opportunity for student definition to arise.[4]

Washington teachers were likelier to be very satisfied in high-SES schools, whereas differences among regular, general, and special academic tracts—rough measures of student performance—were small and nonlinear. In addition, students' achievement levels (represented by tracks) did not affect relations between teachers' job satisfaction and their satisfaction with the quality of students' work. Furthermore, teachers assigned to the lowest track were likelier to be satisfied with their jobs, when they were satisfied with the quality of students' work, than were teachers in higher tracks. Teachers in the lowest and highest tracks were equally likely to be satisfied when they perceived their students as liking school very much (and perhaps as liking them). It seems possible that in ghetto schools, students' social and academic characteristics and educational outcome do not affect teachers' occupational satisfaction.[5]

Teachers' definitions of the classroom situation may reflect various mechanisms like lowering of standards and changes in expectations for students' achievements.[6] Teachers working in the lower tracks in Washington may have become less demanding of their students and have reduced or changed their goals and standards of evaluation, which might explain why they were likelier to perceive their students as doing well and thus to be very satisfied. Of course, there is no way for teachers to evaluate their own classroom performances except by means of students' responses. They may thus lower or change their standards of evaluation in order to obtain some gratification from daily interaction in the classroom.

Teachers may also have predetermined sets or norms to which they expect children to conform. Their perceptions that students like school and satisfaction with the quality of students' work may well reflect the degree to which students conform to their expectations. The professional isolation of the teacher in the classroom, the basically antagonistic relations[7] between students and teachers, and teachers' insecurity may lead them to define the classroom situation in a detached, impersonal manner. As one observer in the Washington schools noted,

> In the three grades visited the children were told what to do, how to do it, and were expected to unquestioningly follow the teachers' direction. The children sang when instructed to do so, chorused in responses when given recognized signals, and worked on written assignments, copying exercises from the chalkboard. The children spent much of their day writing at their desks, rarely speaking except in chorus. No one argued, disagreed, or questioned anything.[8]

Demanding conformity is thus a way to control the classroom situation and to minimize teacher-student relations. Under such conditions students' social and academic characteristics and educational outcome are much less important in teachers' job satisfaction.

We have noted that perceptions of students' liking school and teachers' satisfaction with the quality of students' work were strongly related to teachers' occupational satisfaction. As students' academic characteristics, or tracks, played such an unimportant role, we suggest that teachers' job satisfaction does not result from perceptions that the students like school but comes mainly from students' conformity in the classroom to teachers' expectations and norms. To report some additional information from observers of classroom interaction in the Washington school system seems appropriate. In only 7 of the 69 classrooms visited was the emotional climate considered warm: "In most of the classes the emotional climate was neither cold nor warm."[9] Teachers also acted as if warmth and sensitivity to individual feelings somehow conflicted with the intellectual purposes of school instruction.

The teacher can define the classroom situation, free from exposure to the scrutiny of other teachers. That teachers are thus physically isolated is also conducive to their professional isolation. These two types of isolation have important implications for functionin problems in the schools. We have noted the separation between the world of adult interaction and the classroom. Our data show that, although relations with both peers and students affected teachers' occupational satisfaction independently, there was no interaction effect between the two. Whether teachers had good or bad relations with peers did not affect the association between relations with students and job satisfaction. Our research also suggests how important it is for teachers to be able to share in an adult world and to communicate on adult terms. We said earlier that teachers' perception that their students liked school had an impact on teachers' level of occupational satisfaction. We may now be able to suggest that what affects teachers' perception of their students is their own level of job satisfaction. This would support what Wayson reported from participant observation of a school: "It seems that the child was perceived as responsive by those teachers who were satisfied and as unresponsive by those who were not."[10]

The organization of the school on two levels has further implications for peer relations. Janowitz has mentioned that teaching is a solo profession and that there is no working process that formally involves the peer group, as there is among nurses.[11] Relations among teachers in schools are not based upon professional values, are not officially part of the functioning of the school, and are not reflected in the professional definition of the situation. Teachers are peers, but not, strictly speaking, colleagues. Because "the society of teachers" is not based on professional relations and is not organized around solving professional problems or facilitating relations with students, peer relations may become merely a means for teachers to insulate themselves from the students and to protect themselves from a sense of professional failure. We suggest that because peer relations are not part of the working processes within the school and are not rooted in professional considerations, they may not be motivated by concern for students' needs or better educational outcomes. Our data suggest that the professional isolation of teachers in an organization composed of two distinct systems may function, as Waller suggested, at the expense of both teachers and students.

Teachers interact outside the classroom, exchanging information and communicating ideas. They face similar strains and pressures. We recognize here the two conditions necessary for the creation of a subculture: effective interaction among members of a group experiencing similar functioning problems.[12] Teachers encounter problems based partly on the structural characteristics of the school as a social organization and partly on the type of school to which they are assigned; they try to cope collectively with problems that affect them all. In order to do so, they must have a set of shared meanings, a common frame of reference.

As Cohen has suggested, the emergence of a subculture is sometimes a response to status threats that affect the members of a group.[13] It seems that teachers' professional role and status in schools are in some ways threatened by both students and administration. This very insecurity, to which their professional, social, and psychological isolation contributes, leads to creation of a defensive subculture by means of which they insulate themselves from failure. In ghetto schools teachers may tend to feel even more insecure and inadequate in performing their professional role. The working conditions and inability to attain the most basic educational goals—teaching reading and writing—may lead to the creation of an occupational subculture with significant effects on their professional behavior.

Our data reveal the importance of peer relations in defining professional standards within the schools. Whereas the social and academic characteristics of the student body did not introduce variation in teachers' perceptions that the curriculum met the needs of deprived students, the perceived quality of peer relations did introduce strong variations. This finding suggests that variation among ghetto schools is not reflected in teachers' perceptions of the educational situation and of the students. Perceptions that the needs of the deprived were being met were also strongly related to job satisfaction; this association was not affected by school SES but was strongly affected by the perceived quality of peer relations.

Peer relations were more important in defining the situation when the gap between professional standards and school functioning was widest. Teachers' need to create a shared frame of reference, through which they could achieve recognition of professional competence in the eyes of their peers, was most important when it became exceedingly difficult to meet professional requirements. Teachers in low-SES schools faced articulated community demands that they fulfill the needs of deprived students. Teachers in most slum schools are, however, ill prepared to teach or to cope with the problems of deprived children. One way to avoid a resulting sense of failure is to shift the blame onto others (in psychological language), to redefine or to change the collective frame of reference (in sociological language). As one teacher expressed it, "If the students don't want to learn, it is not our fault!" Teachers are able to share a set of criteria by which their behavior and attitudes will be evaluated. The role of peer relations in creating and maintaining such criteria has been demonstrated; in the example of teachers' perceptions that the needs of deprived children were being met, that role was greater in low-SES schools, where attainment of professional goals is most difficult.

Collective responses to functioning problems appear in any context in which there is a gap between institutional goals and functioning. We have shown how the problem of maintaining standards for the able in high-SES schools also gave rise to a collective response. The impact of peer relations on teachers' beliefs that high academic standards were being kept up for the able was much stronger than in lower-SES schools. In both high- and low-SES schools teachers avoided a sense of failure through collective beliefs that the needs of the deprived were being met and standards for the able were being upheld.

Peer relations are not part of the formal working process within the school, but teachers rely on them to preserve their own professional role and authority. Adherence to collective values in turn reinforces peer relations. In such a context "on-stage behavior" is crucial in maintenance of the norm of strictness, which at the same time ensures support from the group and enhances teachers' collective response in low-SES schools. As a consequence of such mutual reinforcement, peer relations and support may operate as a source of reward or punishment, representing pressures toward conformity. According to Cohen, "Not only is consensus rewarded by acceptance, recognition and respect; it is probably the most important criterion of the validity of the frame of reference which motivates and justifies our conduct."[14]

That peer relations in the school are neither linked with the working process nor organized specifically to provide better services to students leads to their use mainly to preserve teachers' own security. Indeed, support from peers is essential to teachers' coping with problems in the schools. It is because of the structure of the school that peer relations become more than a means to avoid a sense of professional failure or to enhance teachers' authority; they become a source of gratification in themselves, opening the world of adults to teachers. As Janowitz has written, "Teachers (especially in slum schools) must gain their gratifications from the interaction with other adults, for the responses that youngsters can offer are both consciously or unconsciously incomplete for adult psychic needs."[15] Peer relations also provide gratification in another way, offering a sense of control over and belonging to the institution. In low-SES schools participation in operating decisions was a most important factor in teachers' desires to remain teachers in the system—despite the "undesirable" aspects of low-SES schools as perceived by the teachers themselves. Apparently in low-SES schools peer relations become at the same time more important in preserving teachers' professional authority and a greater source of gratification in themselves. When teachers were asked to compare their schools with other public schools in the nation in terms of professional functioning, students' social and educational characteristics were a less important correlate of satisfaction than was the quality of peer relations, especially among teachers dealing with poor, lower-class children. The basis for evaluating the educational achievement in ghetto elementary schools may have shifted from students' performance to teachers' job satisfaction, which itself may have been rooted no longer in the educational outcome of teacher-student relations but rather in the ability to secure through interpersonal relations a sense of professional competence, authority, and social gratification.

Such gratification, we suggest, can even be achieved at the expense of not fulfilling students' specific needs. For example, in slum schools adherence to a norm of strictness, to a student-control ideology, may well preserve teachers' authority, but at the same time the visibility of this adherence (on-stage behavior) permits teachers to arouse support from peers, thus reinforcing the norm itself; this result widens the gap between teachers and students and reinforces teachers' defensive subculture still further at the expense of students needs.

We suggest that peer relations under ghetto conditions, but chiefly in slum schools, simultaneously encourage creation and maint nance of a teachers' subculture and serve as a source of gratification in themselves. Even though peer relations are less likely to be good in low- than in high-SES schools, their influence on adaptations in the schools is greater in low- than in high-SES schools. We may ask whether or not in the slum school the interplay of peer relations and school structure, which affect educational outcome jointly, has given way to behaviors that undermine the optimal interplays of formal and informal resources in the schools. One consequence of the importance taken on by peer relations in slum schools may be to insulat further the group of teachers from the group of students and to undermine further the professional basis of peer relations.

Our research suggests that black teachers in a ghetto school system have various modes of adaptation and various ways of coping with functioning problems, at both the classroom and the over-all school level: They are thus able to minimize or redefine the impact of students' social and academic characteristics. At the classroom level teachers' own definition of the teaching situation makes it possible for them to "enjoy" interaction with students as long as the latter conform to their expectations. At the broader level school SES is much less important than are relations among peers in affecting teachers' job satisfaction. Teachers' modes of adaptation and coping arise from structural characteristics of the school and from the types of students with whom they are in contact, a collective response that can be summarized under the term teachers' subculture.

The effects of the teachers' subculture are stronger in low-SES schools, where threats to professional status are greater. Peer relations seem to have mostly defensive and adaptive functions (preserving teachers' role and authority), geared toward fulfillment of teachers' needs rather than of those of students.

Our findings suggest one reason among many others outside the scope of this research why improvement in working conditions and increases in expenditures seem to affect only the school climate and not the educational achievements of students in ghetto or segregated schools.[16] They may also help to explain why various characteristics of teachers—perhaps including race—are less important in affecting educational achievement than is the social composition of schools and classes.[17]

Improvements in school climate and changes in teachers' characteristics may lead only to better interpersonal relations within "the society of teachers" and increase teachers' occupational satisfaction. They do not necessarily benefit students educationally because, under prevailing forms of school organization, especially in low-SES schools within the ghetto system, teachers' morale is not conducive to higher professional achievement. The teachers' subculture has primarily defensive and adaptive functions, which help teachers to redefine the educational situation to compensate for professionally difficult circumstances. The very marked racial segregation of the Washington school system may thus mask another, less discernible form of "segregation"—that between teachers and students, even when almost all members of both groups are black. The structure of American schools in general, and perhaps of ghetto schools in particular, thus imposes on the working relations between teachers and students a pattern by which teachers may experience satisfaction and gratification only at the expense of their students. Indeed, this pattern has been widely noted in American schools, and ghetto schools—regardless of teachers' race—may be exhibiting only one form of the problem. Nonetheless, it is one that amplifies the already massive difficulties and failures of American schools faced with the challenge of black children.

NOTES

1. Ellis Knox, Democracy in the District of Columbia Public Schools (Washington, D.C.: Judd and Detweiller, 1957), p. 8
2. Talcott Parsons, "The School Class as a Social System: Some of Its Functions in American Society," in A. H. Halsey, Jean Floud, and Arnold C. Anderson, eds., Education, Economy and Society (New York: The Free Press, 1961), pp. 434-55.
3. Morris Janowitz, Institution Building in Urban Education (New York: The Russell Sage Foundation, 1959), p. 30.
4. William Waller, The Sociology of Teaching (New York: Wiley, 1932), p. 309.
5. Waller makes a comparable point. Ibid., pp. 292-317.
6. Ibid., p. 312.
7. Ibid., pp. 189-212.

8. A. Harry Passow, ed., *Toward Creating a Model Urban School System: A Study of the Washington, D.C. Public Schools* (New York: Teachers College, Columbia University, 1967), p. 277.

9. *Ibid.*, pp. 277-78.

10. William W. Wayson, "Expressed Motives of Teachers in Slum Schools" (unpublished Ph.D. dissertation, University of Chicago, 1966).

11. Janowitz, *Institution Building in Urban Education*, p. 30.

12. Albert K. Cohen, *Delinquent Boys: The Culture of the Gang* (New York: The Free Press, 1961).

13. *Ibid.*

14. *Ibid.*, p. 56.

15. Janowitz, *Institution Building in Urban Education*, p. 30.

16. David J. Fox, *Expansion of the More Effective School Program: Evaluation of New York City Title I Educational Projects, 1966-1967* (New York: The Center for Urban Education, 1967).

17. James Coleman, *Equality of Educational Opportunity* (Washington, D.C.: Government Printing Office, 1966).

APPENDIX

A

SOURCES OF DATA AND METHODOLOGICAL NOTE

The data analyzed in this research were drawn from a board investigation of the Washington, D.C., school system—including its organization, finances, and curriculum—which included a self-administered questionnaire survey of all district teachers. A general report of this investigation, frequently cited in this research, was issued as A. Harry Passow, Toward Creating a Model Urban School System: A Study of the Washington, D.C. Public Schools (New York: Teachers College, Columbia University, 1967). We have utilized material from its study of District teachers, material based on self-administered questionnaires that were answered by the teachers on a single day—January 16, 1967—after all students had been dismissed early. The Passow report, in its analysis of teacher characteristics, drew upon a sample of elementary and high schools. In this book, we have utilized all available questionnaires from black teachers in all of the District's elementary schools.* With respect to this population, therefore, we have worked not with a sample but with the universe of black elementary-school teachers of Washington, D.C. This explains why when presenting tables we have not used tests of significance. The percentage differences are the only measures we used in interpreting our data.

The research reported in this book is thus in some, but not all, respects a secondary analysis. The data on teachers were originally collected as part of a comprehensive descriptive study with policy aims; so far as we know, the data were not collected to test a formulated set of hypotheses. For these purposes, the teacher questionnaire

---

*The study of the District teachers is described in Appendix A:1 of the Passow report. Completed questionnaires were received by study representatives stationed in the schools and forwarded at once to the Bureau of Applied Social Research or mailed by the study staff within 24 hours. The teachers' phase of the Passow study was conducted by Drs. Anna Lee Hopson and David Wilder of the Bureau of Applied Social Research. A report by the director of the original teachers' study based on a selected sample of the schools is available as Anna Lee Hopson and David E. Wilder, A Study of Teachers in the Public Schools of Washington, D.C. (New York: Bureau of Applied Social Research, Columbia University, 1967).

included a number of items whose intent lay very close, if it was not identical, with the way in which this book has used them. For example, a question worded as follows was employed as a measure of teachers' job satisfaction:

> "All things considered, do you find your present job to be:
> - very satisfying
> - fairly satisfying
> - not very satisfying, or
> - not satisfying?"

In the construction of indices, too, it was possible to draw upon questions originally designed with our end in view (see, for example, the description of the index of intrafaculty, or peer-group, relationships in Appendix C).

In another sense, however, this study has some of the characteristics of a secondary analysis. We began to work with these data in an attempt to describe and, to whatever extent possible, explain aspects of black teachers' functioning in a ghetto system—a system that, because of its community's history and very high proportion of black personnel, represented a suggestive situation. We explored the possibility that variations in some aspects of teachers' functioning could be attributed to variations in teachers' class and regional origins and in demographic characteristics. We found that such characteristics, readily studied by means of survey research data, were not linked with the phenomena being studied.

This set of findings led us to consider the nature of within-school organization and processes as possible sources of variation in the behavior we were studying. We indeed found that aspects of within-school organization and life did help us to understand the teachers' adjustments and behavior. In particular, we found systematic differences associated, in varying school contexts, with the extent of teachers' satisfaction with peer relations.

For measuring the latter, we were able to draw upon the questionnaire to create a four-item index of satisfaction with peer relations that has a high degree of face validity (Appendix C). However, in interpreting this and other aspects of teachers' functioning as conditioned by within-school characteristics, we often found that the pattern of our findings could be made more coherent if we interpreted them in the light of participant observation or field work on the situation of teachers in American elementary schools—including some by the Passow study itself—and in the light of concepts, such as that of the collective-problem-solving subculture, derived from studies of other populations based on field observations.

It is at this point that this research assumes some of the characteristics of a secondary analysis. There are, at least at present, inherent limits to the use of survey research materials in studying such matters as the generation and effects of subcultures, particularly as in this case when we lack panel data and the questionnaire was not designed so as to minimize the weaknesses of survey analysis for such purposes. Participant observations and field work data are, in principle, more efficient.* Thus, we have made few, if any, inferences about processes over time, and we have interpreted static findings in the light of ideas and observations derived from field observations.

While we have, as it were, attempted to clothe the bare bones of the tabular findings by means of such field observations as are available, we recognize the "leap of inference" involved in this procedure. It would be easy enough, and both insufficient and true, to characterize this research as an exploratory study into matters that have not been well documented. Indeed, we have relied heavily on Waller's seminal book, The Sociology of Teaching, published almost 40 years ago, not only because of its high quality but because there are few disciplined field studies since that bear upon our problem.

However, this mode of interpretation was adopted because of the nature of the findings themselves. The consistent patterns we discovered—for example, those linked with variations in school SES, satisfaction with peer relations, and perceptions of students—both suggested and were, in turn, clarified by, the use of ideas derived from available field observations. Furthermore, the survey materials—enhanced in this instance by a fairly large number of cases—enabled us to pursue these inferential possibilities in a rather wide variety of within-school settings, thus lending weight to the interpretations we have made. Field methods alone would have been incapable of demonstrating the effects of variations in peer relations and other aspects of teachers' functioning in so wide a variety of settings and with comparable precision.

It is not, however, the task of this note to draw invidious distinctions among methods, but rather to characterize what we have done, why we were led to do it, and the limits of our procedures. Drawing upon a few, but often rich, earlier field observations, we developed a pattern of tabular findings drawn from survey research that strongly suggest the importance of an occupational subculture for understanding significant features of the behavior of teachers, in this case black

---

*On the relative advantages and drawbacks of field methods and survey research employing standardized questionnaires, see a recent review of literature and analysis by Sam D. Sieber, "The Integration of Field Work and Survey Methods" (mimeo.; New York: Columbia University, Bureau of Applied Social Research, 1969).

ones, in a major ghetto school system. The further investigation of the interpretive possibilities suggested in this research would certainly require field research designed with these objectives in view.

APPENDIX

B

CONSTRUCTION OF THE SOCIOECONOMIC-STATUS INDEX OF SCHOOLS
(Based on U.S. Census data by tract in Washington, D.C., 1960)

	Scoring of Schools in the Socioeconomic-Status Index			
	0	1	2	3
Median family income	Less than $4,000	$4,000-$4,999	$5,000-$5,999	$6,000 and more
Average years' education	8 years and less	9-10 years	11-12 years	13 years and more

Possible range of the index from 0, the lowest SES schools to 6. Distribution of the index for black teachers:

	Percent
Low (0-2)	41
Medium (3-4)	42
High (5-6)	17
Total	100
	(N= 2,419)

APPENDIX

C

CONSTRUCTION OF THE SES INDEX FOR TEACHERS' FAMILIES

	Score		
	0	1	2
Education of father	elementary school	high school	more than high school
Education of mother	elementary school	high school	more than high school
Occupation of father	semiskilled, unskilled, farmer	sales, office worker, skilled worker	professional, businessman
Income of parents	Lowest 25% of your community	2nd and 3rd highest 25% of your community	Highest 25% of your community

Instruction for rejects: If there is one reject in columns 31, 32, and 33, give respondent a score of 1 for the column left unanswered. If there is more than one reject in these columns give the respondent no score, and punch an x in the index column. If column 34 is rejected, give the respondent a score of 1 in column 34.

Possible scores range from 0 (lowest family SES) to 8.

Distribution on the index for black teachers:

	Percent
Low (0-2)	35
Medium (3-4)	33
High (5-8)	32
Total	100
	(N=2,303)

APPENDIX

D

INTRA-FACULTY RELATIONS INDEX

			Weight		
Section I Question:	Strongly Agree	Agree	Don't Know or No Opinion	Disagree	Strongly Disagree
Faculty members at my school share common ideas on educational objectives.*	4	3	2	1	0
I feel free to discuss professional difficulties with teachers in my school.*	4	3	2	1	0
In general, faculty relations at my school are satisfactory.*	4	3	2	1	0
Teachers at my school share ideas and techniques.*	4	3	2	1	0
Teachers at this school have a close and friendly feeling toward one another.*	4	3	2	1	0

*All rejects were given a score of "2." Possible scores range from 0 (least) to 20 (most) satisfactory intrafaculty relations.

Distribution on the index for black teachers:

	Percent
Low (0-11)	36
Medium (12-15)	41
High (16-20)	23
Total	100 (N=2,452)

Source: From Anna Lee Hopson and David E. Wilder, A Study of Teachers in the Public Schools of Washington, D.C. (New York: Bureau of Applied Social Research, Columbia University, 1967).

APPENDIX

E

RELATIONS WITH PRINCIPAL INDEX

	Weight				
Section I Question:	Strongly Agree	Agree	Don't Know or No Opinion	Disagree	Strongly Disagree
The principal and I get along together very well.*	4	3	2	1	0
The principal tries to be fair and impartial.*	4	3	2	1	0
The principal always gives me a fair hearing on any subject I want to bring up.*	4	3	2	1	0
I am entirely satisfied with the amount of appreciation and recognition I get when I do a good job.*	4	3	2	1	0
The principal has a great deal of real interest in me as a person.*	4	3	2	1	0

*All rejects were given a score of "2." Possible scores range from 0 (least satisfactory) to 20 (most satisfactory).

Distribution on the index for black teachers:

	Percent
Low (0-12)	33
Medium (13-15)	32
High (16-20)	35
Total	100
	(N=2,277)

Source: American Telephone and Telegraph, Management and Non-managem Study, Business Research Division, (New York, 1952).

APPENDIX

F

RANK ORDER OF THE FACTORS THAT ARE CONSIDERED AND SHOULD BE CONSIDERED IN ASSIGNING PUPILS TO TRACKS

Factors That Are Considered	Factors That Should Be Considered
1. Reading level	1. Reading level
2. Teachers' judgment	2. Teachers' judgment
3. Present scholastic achievement	3. Present scholastic achievement
4. IQ	4. Potential scholastic achievement
5. Principal's judgment	5. IQ
6. Potential scholastic achievement	6. Pupils' aspirations
7. Pupils' behavior	7. Counselor judgment
8. Counselor judgment	8. Pupils' behavior
9. Pupils' aspiration	9. Principal's judgment
10. Parents' wishes	10. SES background
11. SES background	11. Parents' wishes
12. Race	12. Pupils' wishes
13. Friendship pattern	13. Friendship pattern
14. Pupils' wishes	14. Race

APPENDIX

G

PRESTIGE RATING OF TEACHERS

According to a study of the relative prestige of various occupational groups as seen through the eyes of the American public, teachers rank just below average for all professional and semiprofessional workers. The average rating of various occupational groups on a scale that runs from 96 for Supreme Court Justice to 33 for shoe-shiner is as follows:

Professional and Semiprofessional Workers	81
Public School Teachers	78
Proprietors, Managers, Officials	75
Clericals, Sales, and Kindred Workers	68
Craftsmen, Foremen, and Kindred Workers	68
Farmers, Farm Managers	61
Semiskilled Operatives and Kindred Workers	53
Service Workers	50
Laborers	40

Source: From the Prestige Rating of the National Opinion Research Centers, in "Jobs and Occupations," in Reinhart Bendix and Seymour Martin Lipset, eds., Class, Status and Power (Glencoe, Ill.: The Free Press, 1953), pp. 412-14.

APPENDIX

INDEX OF PARTICIPATION IN RUNNING THE SCHOOLS

Items	Scores 0	Scores 1
"Suggestions that I make for the improvement of my school are given consideration."	Disagree Strongly disagree Don't know	Agree Strongly agree
"Do you feel that you are usually given adequate voice in the decisions regarding the assignment of students to tracks?"	No Don't know	Yes

The index of participation could range from 0, the lowest level, to 2, the highest level, of participation. Teachers who answered neither question were not included in the index.

Distribution on the participation index for black teachers:

	Percent
High	29
Medium	40
Low	31
Total	100
	(N=2,181)

APPENDIX I

SUMMARY TABLES OF THE EFFECT OF SELECTED VARIABLES ON TEACHERS' JOB SATISFACTION

	Percent teachers who are very satisfied with their job (Percent difference between extreme categories)
Social Characteristics	
Social origin (nonskilled, skilled, business, professional)	6.0
Geographical origin (South, Washington)	7.0
Ascribed status (SES of parents) (low, medium, high)	2.0
Basic Subgroups	
Sex (male, female)	3.0
Marital status (single, married)	5.0
Age (30 years and less, 31-40 years, 41-50 years, 51 years and more)	24.0
Professional Attributes	
Years teaching (0-4, 5-9, 10-16, 17 years and more)	15.0
Income from teaching (low, medium, high)	14.0
Level of education (none, BA, MA)	8.0
Interpersonal Relations	
Perception of students liking school (very much, quite a bit, not much)	37.0
Relationship with peers (low, medium, high)	40.0
Relationship with principal (low, medium, high)	42.0
Participation (low, medium, high)	37.0
Autonomy	19.0
School Characteristics	
SES (low, medium, high)	14.0
Tract (special academic, general, regular)	7.0

BIBLIOGRAPHY

Beale, Howard. A History of Freedom of Teaching in American Schools. New York: Octagon Books, 1966.

Becker, Howard S. "The Career of the Chicago Public School Teacher," American Journal of Sociology, Vol. 57, 1952, pp. 470-77.

_______. "Schools and Systems of Stratification," in A. H. Halsey, Jean Floud, and C. Arnold Anderson, eds., Education, Economy and Society: A Reader in the Sociology of Education. New York: The Free Press, 1964, pp. 93-104.

_______. "Social Class Variation in the Teacher-Pupil Relationship," Journal of Educational Sociology, Vol. 25, 1952, pp. 451-65.

Bidwell, Charles E. "The Administrative Role and Satisfaction in Teaching," Journal of Educational Sociology, Vol. 29, 1955, pp. 41-47.

_______. "The School as a Formal Organization," in James March and A. Simon, eds., Handbook of Organizations. Chicago: Rand McNally, 1965, pp. 1003-9.

Billingsley, Andrew. "Family Functioning in the Low Income Black Community," Social Case Work, Vol. 50, No. 10, 1969, pp. 563-72.

Blau, Peter. The Dynamics of Bureaucracy: A Study of Interpersonal Relations in Two Government Agencies. Chicago: University of Chicago Press, 1955.

_______. "Orientation Toward Clients in a Public Welfare Agency," Administrative Science Quarterly, No. 3, 1960, pp. 341-61.

Boesel, David. "Teachers in Urban Public Schools," in Supplemental Studies for the National Advisory Commission on Civil Disorders. Washington, D.C.: Government Printing Office, 1968.

Bryan, Wilhelmus Bogart. A History of the National Capital. 2 vols. New York: Macmillan, 1914-16.

Carey, George. "Demographic Mapping of the District and Its Schools," in A. Harry Passow, ed., Toward Creating a Model Urban School System: A Study of the Washington, D.C. Public Schools. New York: Teachers College, Columbia University, 1967, pp. 583-93.

________. "The District of Columbia: Its People and Characteristics," in A. Harry Passow, ed., Toward Creating a Model Urban School System: A Study of the Washington, D.C. Public Schools. New York: Teachers College, Columbia University, 1967, pp. 43-51.

Carr-Saunders, A. R. Professions: Their Organization and Place in Society. Oxford: The Clarendon Press, 1928.

Charters, W. W., Jr. "The Social Background of Teaching," in N. L. Gage, ed., Handbook of Research on Teaching: A Project of the American Education Research Association, A Department of the National Education Association. Chicago: Rand McNally, 1963, pp. 715-813.

Cloward, Richard A., et al. Theoretical Studies in Social Organization of the Prison. Pamphlet No. 15. New York: Social Science Research Council, March 1960.

Coffman, L. D. The Social Composition of Teaching Population. New York: Teachers College, 1911.

Cohen, Albert K. Delinquent Boys: The Culture of the Gang. New York: The Free Press, 1961.

________. Deviance and Control. Englewood Cliffs, N.J.: Prentice-Hall, 1966.

Coleman, James. Equality of Educational Opportunity. Washington, D.C.: Government Printing Office, 1966.

Cook, L. A., and Elaine F. A. Cook. A Sociological Approach to Education. 2d ed. New York: McGraw-Hill, 1950.

Cremin, Lawrence A. The Transformation of the School: Progressivism in American Education 1876-1957. New York: Vintage, 1961.

Davis, Allison. "Cultural Factors in Remediation," Educational Horizons, Summer 1965, pp. 231-51.

_______. Social Class Influences upon Learning. Cambridge: Harvard Univeristy Press, 1950.

Dentler, Robert A. "Barriers to Northern School Desegregation," Daedalus, Winter 1966, pp. 45-63.

_______. Major American Social Problems. Chicago: Rand McNally, 1967.

Deutsch, Martin. "The Disadvantaged Child and the Learning Process," in A. Harry Passow, ed., Education in Depressed Areas. New York: Teachers College, Columbia University, 1966, pp. 161-79.

Fox, David J. Expansion of the More Effective School Program: Evaluation of New York City Title I Educational Projects, 1966-1967. New York: The Center for Urban Education, 1967.

Frazier, E. Franklin, Black Bourgeoisie: The Rise of a New Middle Class. New York: The Free Press, 1957.

Goffman, Erving. Asylums: Essays on the Social Situation of Mental Patients and Other Inmates. New York: Doubleday, 1961.

Goode, William J. "Community Within a Community: The Professions," American Sociological Review, Vol. 25, 1960, pp. 902-14.

_______. "The Theoretical Limits of Professionalization," in Amitai Etzioni, ed., The Semi-Professions and Their Organization. New York: The Free Press, 1969, pp. 266-313.

Gordon, C. W. "The Role of the Teacher in the Social Structure of the High School," Journal of Educational Sociology, Vol. 29, 1955, pp. 21-29. Reprinted in Gordon, The Social System of the High School. Glencoe, Ill.: The Free Press, 1957.

Gouldner, Alvin W. "The Norm of Reciprocity: A Preliminary Statement," American Sociological Review, Vol. 25, No. 2, 1960, pp. 161-76.

Grant, Joanne. Black Protest: History, Documents and Analyses. Political Perspective Series. New York: Fawcett, 1968.

Green, Constance McLaughlin. The Secret City: A History of Race Relations in the National Capital. Princeton, N.J.: Princeton University Press, 1967.

Greenberg, Jack. Race Relations and American Law. New York: Columbia University Press, 1959.

Greer, Colin. "Immigrants, Negroes, and the Public Schools," The Urban Review, January 1969, pp. 9-12.

Havighurst, Robert. "Urban Development and Education System," in A. Harry Passow, ed., Education in Depressed Areas. New York: Teachers College, Columbia University, 1966, pp. 24-45.

Herriot, Robert E., and Nancy Hoyt St. John. Social Class and the Urban School. New York: John Wiley & Sons, 1966.

Homans, George. The Human Group. New York: Harcourt, Brace & World, 1950.

Hopson, Anna Lee, and David E. Wilder. A Study of Teachers in the Public Schools of Washington, D.C. New York: Bureau of Applied Social Research, Columbia University, 1967.

Hughes, Everett C. "Profession," Daedalus, Vol. 92, Fall 1953, pp. 655-68.

Janowitz, Morris. Institution Building in Urban Education. New York: The Russell Sage Foundation, 1959.

Katz, Fred. "The School as a Complex Social Organization," Harvard Educational Review, Vol. 34, Summer 1964, pp. 428-55.

Kleinman, Paula. "Role Dissensus and Its Correlates in an Educationa Setting." Unpublished Ph.D. dissertation, Department of Sociology, Columbia University, 1970.

Knox, Ellis. Democracy in the District of Columbia Public Schools. Washington, D.C.: Judd and Detweiller, 1957.

Kob, J. "Definition of the Teacher's Role," in A. H. Halsey, J. Floud, and C. Anderson, eds., Education, Economy and Society. New York: The Free Press, 1967, pp. 558-76.

Kornberg, Leonard. "Meaningful Teachers for Alienated Children," in A. Harry Passow, ed., Education in Depressed Areas. New York: Teachers College, Columbia University, 1963, pp. 262-78.

Lieberman, Myron. Education as a Profession. Englewood Cliffs, N.J.: Prentice-Hall, 1956.

Liebow, Elliot. Tally's Corner: A Study of Negro Streetcorner Men. Boston: Little, Brown and Company, 1967.

Lipset, Seymour M.; Martin Trow; and James Coleman. Union Democracy. Glencoe, Ill.: The Free Press, 1956.

Litwak, Eugene, and H. J. Meyer. "Bureaucratic and Primary Groups," Administrative Science Quarterly, Vol. 2, June 1966), pp. 31-58.

Lortie, Dan C. "The Balance of Control and Autonomy in Elementary School Teaching," in Amitai Etzioni, ed., The Semi-Professions and Their Organization. New York: The Free Press, 1969, pp. 1-53.

McGuire, Garson, and George White. "Social Origins of Teachers in Texas," in L. S. Stiles, ed., The Teacher's Role in American Society. New York: Harper, 1957, pp. 25-41.

Mackler, Bernard. "Up from Poverty: The Price for 'Making It' in a Ghetto School." Unpublished manuscript given at the Seventh Annual Conference of Urban Education. Teachers College, Columbia University, New York, 1969.

McPherson, Gertrude. "The Role Set of Elementary School Teachers." Unpublished Ph.D. dissertation, Columbia University, 1966.

Mason, W. S.; R. J. Dressel; and R. K. Bain. The Beginning Teacher. U.S. Department of Health, Education, and Welfare. Office of Education Circular No. 510. Washington, D.C.: Government Printing Office, 1958.

Meier, August. Negro Thought in America, 1880-1915: Racial Ideologies in the Age of Booker T. Washington. Ann Arbor: University of Michigan Press, 1964.

Merton, Robert K. Social Theory and Social Structure. Rev. ed. New York: The Free Press, 1957.

Morton, Mary. "The Education of the Negro in the District of Columbia," Journal of Negro Education, Vol. 26, 1947, pp. 325-46.

Myrdal, Gunnar. An American Dilemma: The Negro Problem and Modern Democracy. 20th anniversary ed. New York: Harper & Row, 1962.

National Advisory Commission on Civil Disorders. Report of the National Advisory Commission on Civil Disorders. New York: Bantam, 1968. Referred to as the Kerner Commission report.

National Opinion Research Center. "Jobs and Occupations," Opinion News, Vol. 9, September 1, 1947, pp. 3-13. Reprinted in Reinhart Bendix and Seymour Martin Lipset, eds., Class, Status and Power Glencoe, Ill.: The Free Press, 1953. Based on the work of Paul K. Hatt and C. C. North.

Niederhoffer, Arthur. Behind the Shield: The Police in an Urban City. New York: Doubleday, 1967.

Noble, Jeanne Lareta. The Negro Women's College Education. New York: Teachers College, Columbia University, 1956.

Parsons, Talcott. "Full Citizenship for the Negro American? A Sociological Problem," Daedalus, Fall 1965, pp. 1009-54.

________. "The School Class as a Social System: Some of Its Functions in American Society," Harvard Educational Review, Vol. 29, 1959, pp. 297-318. Reprinted in A. H. Halsey, Jean Floud, and Arnold C. Anderson, eds., Education, Economy and Society. New York: The Free Press, 1961.

Passow, A. Harry, ed. Education in Depressed Areas. New York: Teachers College, Columbia University, 1966.

________, ed. Toward Creating a Model Urban School System: A Study of the Washington, D.C. Public Schools. New York: Teachers College, Columbia University, 1967.

Perrow, Charles. "Hospitals: Technology, Structure and Goals," in James March and A. Simon, eds., Handbook of Organizations. Chicago: Rand McNally, 1965, pp. 910-66.

Peterson, Warren. "Teachers Amid Changing Expectations," Harvard Educational Review, Vol. 25, 1954, pp. 106-17.

Pucinski report. Cf. U.S. Congress.

Redefer, Fredrick L. "Factors That Affect Teacher Morale," Nation's Schools, Vol. 63, February 1969, pp. 59-62.

Riesman, David. The Lonely Crowd. New Haven, Conn.: Yale University Press, 1961.

Roethlisberger, F. S., and William J. Dickson. Management and the Worker. Cambridge: Harvard University Press, 1939.

Rossi, Peter S., et al. "Between White and Black: The Faces of American Institutions in the Ghetto." Supplemental Studies for the National Advisory Commission on Civil Disorders. Washington, D.C.: Government Printing Office, 1968, pp. 69-216.

Scott, W. Richard. "Professional Employees in a Bureaucratic Structure," in Amitai Etzioni, ed., The Semi-Professions and Their Organization: Teachers, Nurses, Social Workers. New York: The Free Press, 1969, pp. 82-140.

Sieber, Sam D. "The Integration of Field Methods and Survey Research." New York: Columbia University, 1969. Mimeographed.

________. Memorandum on Educational Research. New York: Bureau of Applied Social Sciences, Columbia University, 1966.

Stouffer, Samuel A., et al. The American Soldier. Princeton, N.J.: Princeton University Press, 1949.

Strayer, George D. Report for the Congressional Subcommittee on Appropriations. Washington, D.C.: Government Printing Office, 1949.

U.S. Commission on Civil Rights. Racial Isolation in the Public Schools. Washington, D.C.: Government Printing Office, 1967.

U.S. Congress, House of Representatives, Committee on Education and Labor. A Task Force Study of the Public School System in the District of Columbia as It Relates to the War on Poverty. Washington, D.C.: Government Printing Office, June 1966. Referred to as the Pucinski report.

Waller, William. The Sociology of Teaching. New York: Wiley, 1932.

Warner, Lloyd. American Life: Dream and Reality. Chicago: University of Chicago Press, 1953.

________; Robert J. Havighurst; and Martin Loeb. Who Shall be Educated? The Challenge of Opportunities. New York: Harper, 1944.

Wattenberg, W. "Social Origin of Teachers: A Northern Industrial City," in L. S. Stiles, ed., Teachers' Role in American Society. New York: Harper, 1957, pp. 13-22.

Wayland, R. Sloan. "The Context of Innovation: Some Organizational Characteristics of Schools." Unpublished manuscript.

________. "Structural Features of American Education as Basic Factors in Innovation," in Matthew Miles, ed., Innovation in Education. New York: Teachers College, Columbia University, 1964.

Wayson, W. William. "Expressed Motives of Teachers in Slum Schools." Unpublished Ph.D. dissertation, University of Chicago, 1966.

________. "Source of Teacher Satisfaction in Slum Schools," Administrator Notebook, Vol. 24, No. 9, 1966, pp. 1-4.

Wheeler, Stanton. "The Structure of Formally Organized Socialization Settings," in Orville Brim and Stanton Wheeler, eds., Socialization After Childhood: Two Essays. New York: John Wiley & Sons, 1967, pp. 51-116.

Willover, Donald. "The School and Pupil Control Ideology." Pennsylvania State Studies, No. 24.

________. "Teachers' Subculture and Curriculum Change." ERIC file ED 020588. New York: Teachers College Library, Columbia University, Faculty seminar, Temple University, 1968.

Zaleznik, Abraham. "Interpersonal Relations in Organizations," in James March and A. Simon, eds., Handbook of Organizations. Chicago: Rand McNally, 1965, pp. 574-614.

________; C. R. Christensen; and F. J. Roethlisberger. The Motivation Productivity and Satisfaction of Workers: A Prediction Study. Boston: Harvard University, Graduate School of Business Administration, Division of Research, 1958.

ABOUT THE AUTHOR

CATHERINE BODARD SILVER is Assistant Professor of Sociology at Brooklyn College, The City University of New York.

Dr. Bodard Silver is the author of "Salon, Foyer, Bureau: Women and the Professions in France," published in the American Journal of Sociology, Vol. 78, No. 4, January 1973. She is presently completing an interpretation, for the University of Chicago Press, of the work of Fréderic Le Play, the 19th-century pioneer of empirical sociology and family analysis. Her current interests are in the sociology of work and leisure and the historical sociology of the family.

Dr. Bodard Silver is "Bachelière Es-Sciences Economiques" from the Faculté des Sciences Economiques in Paris. She holds a "License" in Sociology from the Sorbonne, an MA and a PH.d from Columbia University.

RELATED TITLES
Published by Praeger Special Studies